KU-266-480

PETROGRADSKAYA
See pp64–73
Street Finder maps 1, 2

PALACE EMBANKMENT
See pp74–95
Street Finder maps 2, 5, 6

GOSTINY DVOR
See pp96–113
Street Finder maps 2, 6

Petrogradskaya

Palace Embankment

Gostinyy Dvor

Bol Nevka Бол Невка

Neva Нева

0 metres   600
0 yards   600

EYEWITNESS *TRAVEL GUIDES*

ST PETERSBURG

EYEWITNESS *TRAVEL GUIDES*

St Petersburg

Main contributors:
Catherine Phillips
Christopher and Melanie Rice

DORLING KINDERSLEY
LONDON • NEW YORK • SYDNEY • MOSCOW

A DORLING KINDERSLEY BOOK

PROJECT EDITOR Anna Streiffert
ART EDITOR Marisa Renzullo
EDITOR Ella Milroy
DESIGNERS Gillian Andrews, Carolyn Hewitson,
Paul Jackson, Elly King, Nicola Rodway
VISUALIZER Joy Fitzsimmons
MAP CO-ORDINATORS Emily Green, David Pugh

MANAGING EDITORS Fay Franklin, Georgina Matthews
MANAGING ART EDITOR Annette Jacobs
SENIOR MANAGING EDITOR Vivien Crump
DEPUTY ART DIRECTOR Gillian Allan

PRODUCTION Jo Blackmore, Anna Pauletti, David Proffit
PICTURE RESEARCH Brigitte Arora
DTP DESIGNER Sarah Martin, Pamela Shiels

MAIN CONTRIBUTORS
Catherine Phillips,
Christopher and Melanie Rice

MAPS
Rob Clynes, Maria Donnelly, Ewan Watson
(Colourmap Scanning Ltd)

PHOTOGRAPHERS
Demetrio Carrasco, John Heseltine

ILLUSTRATORS
Stephen Conlin, Maltings Partnership, Chris Orr & Associates,
Paul Weston

•

Text film output by Graphical Innovations, London
Reproduced by Colourscan, Singapore
Printed and bound in Italy by G. Canale

First published in Great Britain in 1998
by Dorling Kindersley Limited
9 Henrietta Street, London WC2E 8PS

Copyright 1998 © Dorling Kindersley Limited, London

Visit us on the World Wide Web at http://www.dk.com

•

Every effort has been made to ensure that the information in
this book is as up-to-date as possible at the time of going to press.
However, details such as telephone numbers, opening hours,
prices, gallery hanging arrangements and travel information are
liable to change. The publishers cannot accept responsibility
for any consequences arising from the use of this book.

We would be delighted to receive any corrections and
suggestions for incorporation in the next edition. Please write to:
Senior Managing Editor, Eyewitness Travel Guides,
Dorling Kindersley, 9 Henrietta Street, London WC2E 8PS.

CONTENTS

Bronze model of ship, a symbol
of St Petersburg

INTRODUCING
ST PETERSBURG

Petersburgers enjoying the snow
outside the Hermitage

ST PETERSBURG
AREA BY AREA

Little Stable Bridge crossing the Moyka river

Pelmeny, a meat or fish dumpling
dish originally from Siberia

15th-century icon of St George
and the Dragon, Russian Museum

SURVIVAL GUIDE

Golden statues of the Grand
Cascade at Peterhof

TRAVELLERS' NEEDS

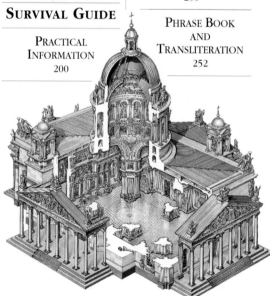
St Isaac's Cathedral, lavishly decorated inside with more than
40 different stones and minerals

How to Use this Guide

This guide will help you to get the most from your visit to St Petersburg, providing expert recommendations as well as detailed practical information. *Introducing St Petersburg* maps the city and sets it in its geographical, historical and cultural context, with a quick-reference timeline on the history pages giving the dates of Russia's rulers and significant events. *St Petersburg at a Glance* is an overview of the city's main attractions. *St Petersburg Area by Area* starts on page 54 and describes all the important sights, using maps, photographs and illustrations. The sights are arranged in two groups: those in St Petersburg's central districts and those a little further afield. The guided walks reveals two characteristics of the city – its canals and its islands. *Beyond St Petersburg* describes sights requiring one- or two-day excursions. Hotel, restaurant, shopping and entertainment recommendations can be found in *Travellers' Needs*, while the *Survival Guide* includes tips on everything from transport and telephones to personal safety.

Finding Your Way around the Sightseeing Section

Each of the seven sightseeing areas is colour-coded for easy reference. Every chapter opens with an introduction to the area it covers, describing its history and character. For central districts, this is followed by a Street-by-Street map illustrating a particularly interesting part of the area; for sights beyond the city limits, by a regional map. A simple numbering system relates sights to the maps. Important sights are covered by several pages.

1 Introduction to the area
For easy reference, the sights are numbered and plotted on an area map, with metro stations shown where helpful. The key sights (great buildings, museums and open-air sights) are listed by category.

A locator map shows where you are in relation to other areas of the city centre.

Each area has colour-coded thumb tabs.

Locator map

The area shaded in pink is shown in greater detail on the Street-by-Street map.

2 Street-by-Street map
This gives a bird's eye view of interesting and important parts of each sightseeing area, with accurate drawings of all the buildings within them. The numbering of the sights ties in with the preceding area map and with the fuller descriptions on the pages that follow.

A suggested route for a walk is shown in red.

ST PETERSBURG AREA MAP
The coloured areas shown on this map *(see pp14–15)* are the five main sightseeing areas into which central St Petersburg has been divided for this guide. Each is covered in a full chapter in the *St Petersburg Area by Area* section *(pp54–131)*. They are also shown on other maps throughout the book. In *St Petersburg at a Glance (pp32–49)*, for example, they help you locate the most interesting museums and palaces or where to see the city's many delightfully designed bridges. The maps' coloured borders match the coloured thumb tabs on each page of the section.

Numbers refer to each sight's position on the area map and its place in the chapter.

Practical information lists all the information you need to visit every sight, including a map reference to the *Street Finder* maps *(pp230–37)*.

3 Detailed information on each sight
All the important sights are described individually. They are listed to follow the numbering on the area map at the start of the section. The key to the symbols summarizing practical information is on the back flap.

A Visitors' Checklist provides the practical information you will need to plan your visit.

Story boxes highlight unique aspects or historical connections of a particular sight.

4 St Petersburg's major sights
These are given two or more full pages in the sightseeing area in which they are found. Buildings of interesting architecture are dissected to reveal their interiors; museums and galleries have colour-coded floorplans to help you find important exhibits.

Stars indicate the best features or works of art.

INTRODUCING
ST PETERSBURG

Putting St Petersburg on the Map

T HE RUSSIAN FEDERATION, or Russia as it is usually known, is the world's largest country, covering an area of 17.4 million sq km (6.7 million sq miles). Situated in its north-west corner, St Petersburg is Russia's second city, with a population of just under five million. Once Russia's capital and known as its "Window on the West" *(see pp20–21)*, the city was built on the marshy lands where the Neva joins the Gulf of Finland. Of the 13 countries bordering Russia, Estonia and Finland are St Petersburg's closest neighbours.

KEY

✈	Airport
⛴	Ferry port
—	Motorway
—	Major road
—	Minor road
—	Railway
—	Country boundary

0 kilometres 180

0 miles 180

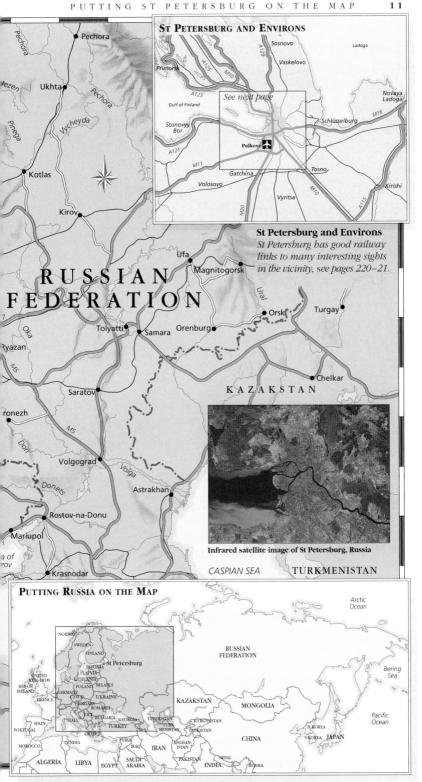

Pechora

Pechora

Ukhta

Vycheyda

Pinega

Mezen

Kotlas

Kirov

RUSSIAN
FEDERATION

Ufa

Magnitogorsk

Oka

Ryazan

Tolyatti   Samara   Orenburg   Orsk   Turgay

Saratov   KAZAKSTAN   Chelkar

Voronezh

Volgograd   Volga

Astrakhan

Don

Donets

Rostov-na-Donu

Mariupol

ea of
zov

Krasnodar   CASPIAN SEA   TURKMENISTAN

St Petersburg and Environs
*St Petersburg has good railway
links to many interesting sights
in the vicinity, see pages 220–21.*

Infrared satellite image of St Petersburg, Russia

ST PETERSBURG AND ENVIRONS

Sosnovo   Ladoga

Vaskelovo

Primorsk   A125   A129   M10

A123   Novaya
Ladoga

Gulf of Finland   *See next page*   Schlüsselburg   M18

Sosnovyy
Bor   A121   Pulkovo ✈

M11   Gatchina   Tosno   M10   Kirishi

Volosovo   Vyritsa   A115

N20

PUTTING RUSSIA ON THE MAP

Arctic
Ocean

NORWAY   RUSSIAN
FEDERATION

SWEDEN

FINLAND   St Petersburg   Bering
Sea

ESTONIA
LATVIA
LITHUANIA

UNITED
KINGDOM
REP. OF
IRELAND   POLAND   BELARUS

GERMANY   UKRAINE   KAZAKSTAN   MONGOLIA   Pacific
Ocean

FRANCE   CZECH
HUNGARY   N KOREA

ROMANIA   S KOREA JAPAN

ITALY   BULGARIA   GEORGIA

SPAIN   GREECE   TURKEY   UZBEKISTAN   KYRGYZSTAN   CHINA

PORTUGAL   TURK-
MENISTAN   TAJIKISTAN

SYRIA   IRAQ   AFGHAN-
ISTAN

MOROCCO   TUNISIA   IRAN   PAKISTAN   NEPAL

ALGERIA   LIBYA   EGYPT   SAUDI
ARABIA   INDIA   BURMA

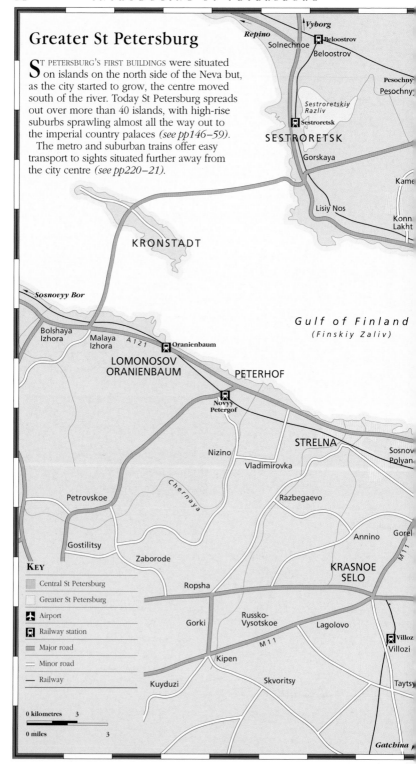

Greater St Petersburg

S T PETERSBURG'S FIRST BUILDINGS were situated on islands on the north side of the Neva but, as the city started to grow, the centre moved south of the river. Today St Petersburg spreads out over more than 40 islands, with high-rise suburbs sprawling almost all the way out to the imperial country palaces *(see pp146–59).*

The metro and suburban trains offer easy transport to sights situated further away from the city centre *(see pp220–21).*

KEY

	Central St Petersburg
	Greater St Petersburg
✈	Airport
🚇	Railway station
▬	Major road
═	Minor road
▬	Railway

0 kilometres   3

0 miles   3

Vyborg

Repino
Solnechnoe

Beloostrov
Beloostrov

Pesochny
Pesochny

Sestroretskiy Razliv

Sestroretsk

SESTRORETSK

Gorskaya

Kame

Lisiy Nos

Konn
Lakht

KRONSTADT

Sosnovyy Bor

Bolshaya
Izhora

Malaya
Izhora   A 1 2 1   Oranienbaum

LOMONOSOV
ORANIENBAUM

PETERHOF

Novyy
Petergof

STRELNA

Sosnov
Polyan

Nizino

Vladimirovka

Chernaya

Razbegaevo

Petrovskoe

Annino   Gorel

Gostilitsy

Zaborode

KRASNOE
SELO

M 1 1

Ropsha

Gorki

Russko-
Vysotskoe

Lagolovo

Villoz
Villozi

M 1 1

Kipen

Kuyduzi

Skvoritsy

Tayts

Gulf of Finland
(Finskiy Zaliv)

Gatchina

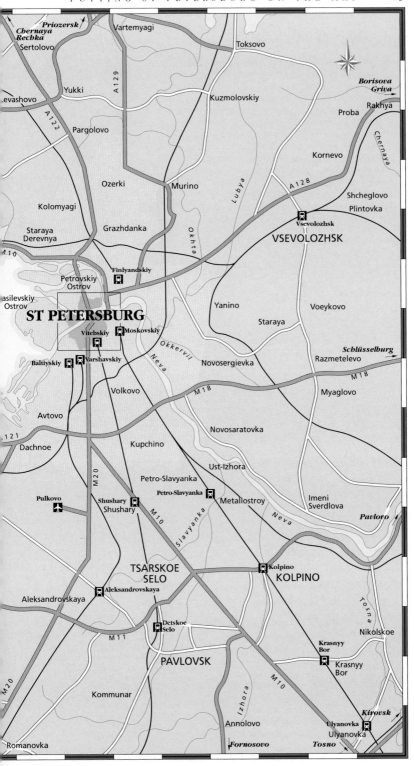

Central St Petersburg

S T PETERSBURG'S five central areas described in this book each have their own character, reflecting different sides of the city's past. The southern bank of the Neva, Palace Embankment, is lined with glorious, stately palaces. Gostinyy Dvor, to the east, has always been the commercial hub of the city with shops, bars and restaurants lining Nevskiy prospekt. To the west lies Sennaya Ploshchad, a mixture of romantic, tree-lined canals and reminders of the 19th-century low life of Dostoevsky's novels. Vasilevskiy Island, the largest in the city, combines a naval heritage with scholarly institutions. Petrogradskaya, to the north, is dominated by the Peter and Paul Fortress.

Vasilevskiy Island

Adorned with figures representing four great Russian rivers, the Rostral Columns (see p60) stand on the eastern tip of the island. From here there are sweeping views of the Neva and its embankments.

Petrogradskaya

*Burial place of the Roma-
nov tsars, the SS Peter and
Paul Cathedral (see p68)
stands within the fortress
where Peter the Great
began building the city in
1703. Its tall gilded spire
dominates the skyline of
Petrogradskaya, an area
otherwise characterized
by many splendid Style-
Moderne buildings.*

Gostinyy Dvor

*Nevskiy prospekt, the city's
main artery, is crossed by
waterways such as Moyka
river (see p36), shown
here. These intersections
are bustling in the summer,
with cafés on river boats
and by the water's edge.*

Palace Embankment

*Part of the Hermitage, the
former imperial Winter
Palace (see pp92–3),
dominates this grand
waterfront with a burst
of Baroque splendour.
The embankment is
lined with monuments
from the famous Bronze
Horseman (p78) to Peter
the Great's modest
Summer Palace (p95).*

Sennaya Ploshchad

*St Petersburg's most famous theatre, the
Mariinskiy (see p119), is best known for its
classical ballet. The surrounding area, with
quiet streets lining its canals, is perfect for
walks during the atmospheric White Nights.*

0 metres   600

0 yards   600

KEY

Major sight

Main sight

M Metro station

Ferry/boat service

Police station

Orthodox church

THE HISTORY OF ST PETERSBURG

OUNDED IN 1703, *within ten years St Petersburg had become capital of the vast Russian empire and quickly gained a reputation as one of Europe's most beautiful cities. In the 20th century it underwent three name changes, three revolutions and a 900-day siege. For a city less than 300 years old, it has an amazing history.*

Some 850 years before St Petersburg became capital of Russia, local Slavic tribes invited the Viking chieftain Rurik to rule them. His successor founded Kiev, which grew into a great princedom. In 988 Grand Prince Vladimir adopted Orthodox Christianity with profound consequences; Orthodoxy was to become a cornerstone of Russian identity. Paradoxically, Russia only emerged as a united entity during the 250-year domination of the Muslim Mongols. In 1237 these fierce tribes conquered all the principalities except Novgorod. In the 14th century the Mongols chose Moscow's power-hungry grand prince, Ivan I (1325–40), to collect tribute from other subjugated principalities. This sealed the fate of the Mongols for, as Moscow thrived under their benevolence, she also became a real threat.

Ivan IV "the Terrible"

Mongol warriors in a 14th-century manuscript illustration

Within 50 years, an army led by Moscow's Grand Prince Dmitriy Donskoy won a first victory over the Mongols, and the idea of a Russian nation was born.

During the long reign of Ivan III (1462–1505) the Mongols were finally vanquished and Moscow's prestige increased. Ivan the Terrible (1533–84) was the first to be called "Tsar of All the Russias". Yet his reign, which began in glory, ended in disaster. Ivan killed his only heir, and the so-called Time of Troubles followed as Russia came under a succession of weak rulers and Polish usurpers invaded Moscow.

THE FIRST ROMANOVS

To end this strife, in 1613 the leading citizens chose Mikhail Romanov to be tsar, thus initiating the 300-year Romanov rule. Under Mikhail, Russia recovered from her upheavals, but his greatest legacy was his son Alexis. Intelligent and pious, Alexis modernized the state, encouraging an influx of foreign architects, codifying laws and asserting the power of the state over the church.

TIMELINE

862 Rurik establishes Viking stronghold at Novgorod	**1147** Moscow is founded	**1480** Ivan III stops paying tribute to Mongols	
863 Cyril and Methodius create early version of Cyrillic	**1462–1505** Reign of Ivan III	**1605–13** Time of Troubles	*Boris Godunov*

800	1000	1200	1400	1600

988 Prince Vladimir converts to Orthodox Christianity	**1108** Town of Vladimir is founded	**1223** First Mongol raid	**1242** Alexander Nevsky defeats the Teutonic Knights	**1533–84** Reign of Ivan IV the Terrible	**1613** Mikhail Romanov becomes first tsar of the Romanov dynasty
		1240 Mongol rule established in Rus	**1598** Boris Godunov claims title of tsar after 12 years as regent	

◁ **Peter the Great instructing his workers during the building of St Petersburg (Alexander von Kotzebue, 1862)**

PETER THE GREAT

In the atmosphere of transition from a medieval to a more modern state, the future Peter the Great, founder of St Petersburg, was born. After his father Alexis' death, Peter's childhood was overshadowed by severe rivalry between his mother's family, the Naryshkins, and that of his father's first wife, the Miloslavskiys. At the age of ten Peter ascended the throne, but the Streltsy Guards, influenced by the Miloslavskiys, started a bloody revolt. As a result his sickly half-brother Ivan became his co-tsar, and Ivan's sister Sophia their regent. The memory of seeing his family brutally killed caused his hatred of Moscow and distrust of its conservative, scheming society.

Peter the Great (1682–1725)

When Ivan died in 1696, the 24-year-old Peter had grown to a giant of a man with a tempestuous combination of willpower and energy. Long hours spent drilling toy soldiers as a child developed into a full-scale reform of the Russian army. But Peter's dream was of a Russian navy. In 1697, he went on a European tour to study shipbuilding and other wondrous achievements. To everyone's dismay the young tsar spent more hours working at the docks than socializing at court. On his return to Russia he lost no time in enforcing westernizing reforms.

A NEW CAPITAL

It was Peter's determination to found a northern port with an unrestricted passage to the Baltic that led to war with Sweden, at the time one of the strongest countries in Europe. By May 1703 Peter had secured the Neva river and began to build the Peter and Paul Fortress and a shipyard opposite *(see pp20–21)*. Only an autocrat with Peter's drive could have succeeded in building a

View of St Petersburg in the early 17th century, with the Admiralty shipyard to the left

TIMELINE

Sophia, regent 1682–9

1672 Birth of Peter the Great at Kolomenskoe Palace, Moscow	**1689** Peter banishes Sophia to Novodevichy Monastery, Moscow	**1697–8** Peter tours western Europe	**1698** Peter destroys the Streltsy Guards *(see p20).*	**1703** St Petersburg is founded **1712** Seat of government moves to St Petersburg
1680	**1690**	**1700**	**1710**
1682 The Streltsy rebellion. Peter becomes co-tsar with half-brother Ivan V, under regency of his half-sister Sophia	**1696** Ivan V dies; Peter becomes sole ruler.	**1700** Start of Northern War against Sweden **1709** Victory over Charles XII of Sweden at Battle of Poltava	**1714** Peter forbids the use of stone in buildings, except in St Petersburg

LIFE AT ELIZABETH'S COURT

When Elizabeth was not busy looking over architectural plans, she would lie around on her bed, gossiping with a group of ladies whose chief task it was to tickle her feet. Her restless nature meant that her courtiers had to endure endless hunts and skating parties, and were required to keep her company at all hours. Her riotous cross-dressing masquerades were notorious, as was her vast wardrobe, allegedly containing over 15,000 dresses.

Tsarina Elizabeth going for a stroll at Tsarskoe Selo, surrounded by eager courtiers

city on this fetid bogland, where daylight and building materials were in short supply and disastrous floodings regular. More than 40,000 Swedish prisoners-of-war and peasants laboured and perished here, their bones contributing to the city's foundations.

Whether or not it was always Peter's intention to make this his new capital, it only became possible after his decisive victory at Poltava in 1709 put an end to the Swedish threat. St Petersburg was named capital of Russia in 1712 and, by Peter's death in 1725, there were 40,000 inhabitants in the city and many more in the surrounding labour encampments.

THE PETTICOAT PERIOD

For most of the rest of the 18th century Russia was ruled by women, whose taste did much to set the celebrated architectural tone of St Petersburg.

During the brief reigns of Peter's wife Catherine I (1725–27) and his grandson Peter II (1727–30), the court abandoned this frontier city for the more comfortable life in Moscow. But when the throne passed to Anna, daughter of Peter's co-tsar Ivan, she decided to create a recognizably European court in St Petersburg. Anna was 37 at the time, and had spent most of her life in Germany. This was obvious in her choice of ministers and favourites, of whom many were German. Fashion and style, however, were imported from France and opera from Italy. Though she herself was serious, plain and somewhat cruel, Anna did much to put the court on a footing with the most frivolous in Europe, as well as encouraging a flowering of civilization.

Tsarina Elizabeth, daughter of Peter the Great, was the ideal successor to this twittering court. Elizabeth was

Elizabeth (1741–61)

attractive, energetic and cheerful, a combination that endeared her to almost everyone, especially the Guards who helped secure her place on the throne. She left the affairs of state to a series of well chosen advisers. The only element of seriousness lay in Elizabeth's perhaps surprising piety, which at times led her to retire temporarily into a convent. Her main legacy is the splendid Baroque architecture she commissioned, mainly designed by her favourite architect Rastrelli (see p93).

1721 Peace of Nystad ends war with Sweden

1733 Cathedral of SS Peter and Paul is finished after 12 years' work

1738 Russia's first ballet school is founded in St Petersburg

1745 Tsarevich Peter marries the future Catherine the Great

1757 St Petersburg Academy of Arts is founded

| **1720** | **1730** | **1740** | **1750** |

1717 Peter travels to Holland and France

1725 Catherine I is empress after death of Peter the Great

1727–30 Reign of Peter II

1730–40 Reign of Anna

Anna Ivanovna, daughter of Ivan V

1741 Ivan VI is deposed and Elizabeth comes to power supported by Guards' officers

1754 Rastrelli's Winter Palace is begun

A Window on the West

DETERMINED TO drag his country out of the medieval period, and inspired by the few westerners he met in Moscow, Peter the Great was the first tsar to travel to Europe. He returned with many ideas for reforms and architectural novelties which he put into practice in his new city. In 1710, when the Swedish threat was over, the reluctant imperial family and government were moved to this chilly, damp outland. But Peter was adamant and soon a rational street plan, stone buildings and academies made St Petersburg a thriving capital in which fashions and discoveries from Europe were tried out before filtering through to the rest of Russia.

EXTENT OF THE CITY

▨ *1712*	☐ *Today*

PLAN OF THE NEW CITY

This map of 1712 shows Peter's original plan for his capital, with Vasilevskiy Island as centre. This was abandoned due to the hazards of crossing the Neva, and the city spread out around the Admiralty instead.

The Carpenter Tsar
During his 1698 tour of Europe, Peter (to the left in this picture) spent months at the Deptford Docks, labouring with his men to learn the basics of ship building.

Based on Amsterdam, the original city grid was meant to follow a strict network of canals but this had to change *(see p57).*

Menshikov palace

New Fashions
Peter's desire to westernize Russia led to a rule forcing his courtiers to have their bushy beards shaved off.

THE STRELTSY REBELLION

As a result of a malicious rumour that Peter's relatives planned the murder of his half-brother Ivan, in 1682 the Streltsy Guard regiments invaded the Kremlin. A horrifying massacre took place in front of the 10-year old Peter who saw his adviser and members of his family murdered. This traumatic event is probably what caused Peter's facial tic and certainly his wish to build another capital city. In 1698 he took a terrible revenge by torturing over a thousand Streltsy Guards to death.

Brutal murders in the Kremlin, 1682

The Battle of Poltava
The struggle with Sweden for control over the Baltic led to the Great Northern War. Nine years after the embarassing defeat at Narva, Peter the Great's army reforms bore fruit. In 1709 he won a decisive battle over Charles XII at Poltava, and thereby Russia's first victory over a major European power.

WHERE TO SEE PETER THE GREAT'S CITY

Some of the buildings from the early St Petersburg still exist in the city centre, including the rustic Peter the Great's Cabin *(p73)*, the Summer Palace *(p95)* and the Baroque Menshikov Palace *(p62)*. Much of Peter and Paul Fortress *(pp66–7)* also dates from this time. It is also well worth visiting Monplaisir, Peter's first home at Peterhof *(pp146–7)*.

Peter the Great's workshop, the Summer Palace

Kronwerk (outer defense walls)

Peter and Paul Fortress

The port was here until the 1880s.

Admiralty

Summer Palace

Wine Goblet
The tsar, who could hold his drink, enjoyed pressing alcohol on his guests until they passed out. This elegant crystal goblet belonged to his close friend Aleksandr Menshikov and is engraved with his coat of arms.

Marshy soil and a lack of local stone made construction difficult. Thousands of labourers died during the first stages.

Catherine I
After an unsuccessful first marriage, Peter was drawn to a Lithuanian girl who had followed the army back from the wars in 1704. Her healthy good looks were brought to the tsar's attention by Aleksandr Menshikov (see p62). Although only two daughters survived, their marriage was happy and Catherine succeeded Peter as the first woman on Russia's throne.

Mice Bury the Cat
Coloured woodcuts, lubki, *served as political cartoons in Peter's day. The tsar was always portrayed as a cat on account of his moustache.*

CATHERINE THE GREAT

Catherine, a German princess, was chosen by Elizabeth as wife for her successor, the petty-minded Peter III. When Peter ascended the throne in 1761 Catherine had resided in Russia for 18 years and was fully fluent in Russian. She had made it her duty to steep herself in the Russian culture which she later came to adore. Six months into Peter's reign, Catherine and her allies in the Imperial Guard deposed the tsar. He was assassinated within days and she was crowned Catherine II.

Catherine the Great in 1762

By Catherine's death at the age of 67, her reputation as an enlightened leader *(see p24)* had been overshadowed by her illiberal reaction to the news of the French Revolution in 1789 and by scandalous rumours concerning her later love-affairs. However, she left a country vastly enlarged after successful campaigns against Turkey and Poland.

WAR AND PEACE

During the Napoleonic Wars, under Catherine's grandson Alexander I, Russia finally took her place alongside the other great European powers.

Despite his part in the murder of his father Paul, much was expected of the handsome new tsar who was infected by the ideals of enlightened government. Russia was by now desperately in need of reform. Of particular concern was the plight of the peasantry, who were tied to the land in serfdom.

However, the necessities of war subsumed everything, and no inroads were made against the Russian autocracy during Alexander I's reign.

Determined to harness the wave of Russian patriotism, Alexander joined Britain and marched against Napoleon in Austria in 1805. After the crushing defeat at the battle of Austerlitz, however, the inexperienced tsar retreated, his army having lost 11,000 men.

At the Peace of Tilsit, signed in 1807, Napoleon divided Europe into French and Russian spheres, lulling Alexander into a false sense of security. In 1812 the French emperor invaded Russia, but was defeated by its size and climate. The Russian army followed his forces to Paris, taking part in the allied campaign which led Napoleon to abdicate in 1814. In celebration, Alexander commissioned a series of imposing public edifices in a fitting Empire style.

Murder of Paul I, 1801. Despite all his precautions, Catherine's unstable, paranoid son was murdered in a coup in his own fortified palace *(see p101)*

TIMELINE

1762 Death of Elizabeth. Peter III becomes emperor but is murdered after six months. His wife takes the throne as Catherine II	**1783** Annexation of the Crimea		**1787–92** 2nd Russo-Turkish War	**1801** Paul I murdered. Alexander I becomes tsar	**1805–1807** War with France ends with Treaty of Tilsit
1760		**1780**			**1800**
1763 Catherine II begins correspondence with Voltaire	**1767** Catherine II publishes her *Bolshoy Nakaz*	**1773–5** Pugachev Rebellion **1768–74** 1st Russo-Turkish War	**1782** Falconet's statue, the Bronze Horseman, is completed	**1796** Death of Catherine II; Paul I accedes *Alexander I (1801–25)*	**1812** Napoleon invades Russia **1816** Alexander I clamps down on reforms

Decembrist rebels defeated by tsarist troops, 1825

THE DECEMBRIST REBELLION

Officers of the Russian army who had witnessed the freedoms of democratic Europe were frustrated by Alexander's failure to consider constitutional reform. When his stern brother Nicholas was declared tsar in 1825, these liberals rallied their soldiers to support the older brother Constantine, who had given up his rights to the throne, in the hope that he would be more open-minded. They made a stand on 14th December on what is now Decembrists' Square *(see p 78)*. Troops loyal to the tsar were instructed to fire on the rebels, killing hundreds before the leaders surrendered. The new tsar, Nicholas I, treated them with the severity which was to become the hallmark of his reign. Five leading figures were hanged, and over a hundred exiled to Siberia.

A CITY OF RICH AND POOR

For much of the 19th century, a walk along Nevskiy prospekt offered a microcosm of an increasingly divided society. Striding past drunks, beggars and prostitutes, the city's courtiers, cocky young officers and leading citizens headed for shops selling imported fashionable accessories, or to the distinguished delicatessen Yeliseev's to buy caviar and champagne. They often lived above their means, mortgaging their serfs and lands to keep up with the astronomical costs of their luxurious lives. This was also a city in which the salary of a low ranking government clerk was never sufficient to feed a family. In the countryside, tension was growing among the serfs tied to the large estates of the aristocracy. With such blatant inequality, growing pressure for political reform was inevitable.

After the unrelenting autocracy of Nicholas I, the "Iron Tsar", liberals welcomed the reign of his fair-minded son Alexander II. In 1861, the tsar passed the Edict of Emancipation, abolishing serfdom, but requiring peasants to buy their land at far from advantageous terms. Thus industrialization finally took off as peasants flocked to the big cities to work in factories, only to be met by even worse living conditions.

THE NAPOLEONIC INVASION

Napoleon's Grand Army of 600,000 men reached Moscow in September 1812, after the victory at Borodino, but was defeated by the tactics of non-engagement devised by the great Russian hero General Kutuzov. Finding himself in a city abandoned by its rulers and set on fire by its people, and with the Russian winter ahead, Napoleon was forced into a retreat over the frozen countryside. He eventually reached the border, with only 30,000 men left alive.

French army retreating from Moscow 1812

1822 Abolition of Masonic and secret societies

1833 Pushkin publishes *The Bronze Horseman*

1855 Death of Nicholas I; Alexander II succeeds him

1853–6 Crimean War

Leo Tolstoy

1865–9 Tolstoy writes *War and Peace*

1820

1840

1860

1825 The Decembrist Rebellion. Nicholas I becomes tsar

1851 The "Nicholas Railway" opens between Moscow and St Petersburg

1818 Construction of St Isaac's Cathedral starts

1861 Emancipation of serfs

1864 Reforms in local government, law and education

1874 3,000 Narodniki (Populists) take their ideals "to the people" in the countryside

The Enlightened Empress

BORN A MINOR GERMAN PRINCESS, Catherine II was a learned and energetic woman. She recognized the importance of the great Enlightenment philosophers Voltaire and Diderot, with whom she corresponded. She bought impressive collections of European art for the Hermitage *(see pp84–93)*, libraries for Russia's scholars and talked much about reducing the burden on Russia's serfs. However, a peasant uprising in the 1770s and news of the French Revolution in 1789 put paid to her liberal notions and, when she died, the majority of Russians were just as badly off as before.

EXTENT OF THE CITY

▨ *1790*   ☐ *Today*

The Temple alludes to Catherine's passion for Neo-Classical architecture.

The medal is presented to Count Orlov for his victory over the Turks at Chesma in 1770.

Royal Guards Swear Allegiance
On 28 June 1762, Catherine usurped the throne of her unpopular husband Peter III in a palace coup. The guards regiments flocked to support her and the tsar was assassinated on 6 July.

CATHERINE THE GREAT

Catherine II "the Great" (1762–96) pursued an expansionist foreign policy. Russia's first naval victory, leading to the annexation of the Crimea, is commemorated allegorically on this fabric.

Count Alexey Orlov, brother of Catherine's one-time lover Grigoriy, played an important role in her takeover of the throne.

Catherine's Instructions
In 1767 the 36-year-old Catherine published her 22-chapter Great Instruction *(Bolshoy Nakaz). The book is a collection of ideas on which a reform of Russia's legal system was to be based.*

Pretender Pugachev
The greatest threat to Catherine's reign was caused by the Cossack Pugachev who claimed to be Peter III. He was arrested, but escaped to lead a widespread peasant uprising which broke out in 1773 and only ended with his execution in 1775.

The New Academy of Sciences
Catherine, who founded over 25 major academic institutions in Russia, also commissioned new buildings for those already existing. Quarenghi built the Neo-Classical Academy of Sciences in 1783–5.

WHERE TO SEE THE NEO-CLASSICAL CITY

Catherine had the Marble Palace *(see p94)* and the Tauride Palace *(p128)* erected for two of her lovers, and added the Small and Large Hermitage and the theatre *(p84)* to the Winter Palace. Her architect Cameron designed the Cameron Gallery and the Agate Pavilion at Tsarskoe Selo *(p150)* and Pavlovsk Palace *(pp156–9)*.

Grecian Hall at Pavlovsk, created by Charles Cameron in 1782–6

Catherine is portrayed as Pallas Athena, goddess of wisdom and warfare, with her attributes of a shield and helmet.

Empire-Style Vase (1790)
Porcelain was much prized at court. In 1744 the first Russian producer, the Imperial Porcelain Factory, opened in St Petersburg.

The fabric, used for a screen, was made by the Pernons factory, Lyons, in 1770.

Mikhail Lomonosov
A philosopher, historian, linguist and scientist, Lomonosov (1711–65) personified the intellectual enlightenment of 18th-century Russia (see p45). This sculpture of him as a boy by the seashore refers to his fisherman origins.

Grigoriy Potemkin (1739–91)
Of all her lovers, Catherine respected and admired Prince Potemkin the most. He was a successful general and an influential counsellor. They remained friends until his death.

Alexander II was murdered by a revolutionary group in 1881. Tragically, he is said to have had the plans for a Russian parliament in his pocket

THE DEATH OF TSARIST RUSSIA

Pressure for reform had built up such a head of steam that in 1881, when still no radical changes had taken place, a revolutionary group murdered Alexander II. The reign of Alexander III was one of rabid reaction. The press was under strict censorship and the secret police more active than ever. But workers began to get organized and opposition was growing. Nicholas II took over a country on the verge of breakdown, in spite of the rapid industrialization of the 1890's. The unsuccessful war with Japan (1904–5) was followed by "Bloody Sunday". On 9th January 1905 a peaceful demonstration carried a petition to the tsar only to be met by bullets. News of the massacre spread like wildfire and the 1905 Revolution broke out with strikes all over Russia. To avert further disaster, Nicholas II promised basic civil rights and an elected Duma (parliament) with the right to veto legislation. However, the tsar simply dissolved the parliament whenever it displeased him. This high-handed behaviour, along with the royal family's unpopular intimate friendship with Rasputin *(see p121)*, further damaged the Romanovs' reputation.

The outbreak of World War I brought a surge of patriotism which the tsar sought to ride. But, by late 1916, Russia had lost three and a half million men, morale at the front was low and food supplies at home scarce.

Red Army badge

REVOLUTION AND CIVIL WAR

In February 1917 strikes broke out in the capital, now renamed Petrograd. The tsar was forced to abdicate, his family put under arrest and a Provisional Government set up. But revolutionaries returning from exile organized themselves and, in October, an armed revolution overthrew the government *(see pp28–9)*.

WORLD OF ART MOVEMENT

Costume design by Leon Bakst, 1911

The oppressive political climate at the turn of the century did not prevent art from flourishing. A small group of St Petersburg artists, including Bakst and Benois, grew into an influential creative movement under the inspired leadership of Sergey Diaghilev. Western art was introduced in their stylish *World of Art* magazine, while their stage designs and costumes for the Ballets Russes *(see p118)* brought Russian culture to the west.

TIMELINE

The Romanov family in 1913

1881 Alexander II is assassinated by the "People's Will" group. Alexander III becomes tsar.	**1902** Lenin publishes *What is to be Done?*	
	1898 Social-Democratic Workers' party is founded. Russian museum opens	**1913** 300th anniversary of Romanov rule

1880   **1900**

1881–2 Anti-semitic pogroms	**1903** Pro-violence Bolsheviks (under Lenin) secede from Social-Democratic Workers' party	**1905** The 1905 Revolution is followed by the inauguration of the first Duma in 1906
1887 Lenin's brother is hanged for attempt on the tsar's life	**1894** Alexander III dies, Nicholas II accedes	
	1904–5 Russo-Japanese War	**1914** Outbreak of WWI; St Petersburg changes name to Petrograd

The leading Bolshevik party proved to be as careless of democracy as the tsar but, in March 1918, they kept their promise to take Russia out of the war. The army was desperately needed at home to fight the developing civil war.

The Bolsheviks (Reds) found themselves threatened by a diverse coalition of anti-revolutionary groups which came to be known as the "Whites", initially supported by foreign intervention. It was the threat of the Whites rallying opposition around the royal family that led to their execution in July 1918. But the Whites were a disparate force and, by November 1920, the last troops had abandoned the struggle, leaving a devastated Soviet Russia to face two years of appalling famine. To manage, Lenin had to revise his aggressive "War Communism" nationalization project. His slightly milder New Economic Policy allowed for private enterprise.

The imperial palaces around St Petersburg were totally destroyed by the Germans in World War II. This photo shows Pavlovsk *(see pp156–9)* in 1944

THE STALIN YEARS

In the five years after Lenin's death in 1924, Joseph Stalin used his position as General Secretary of the Communist Party to eliminate all rivals. He then established his long dictatorship.

The terror began in earnest with the collectivization of agriculture which forced the peasants to give up all livestock, machinery and land to collective farms. During this time, and in the ensuing famine of 1931–2, up to 10 million people are thought to have died.

Joseph Stalin on a propaganda poster from 1933

A first major purge of intellectuals took place in urban areas in 1928–9. Then, in December 1934, Sergey Kirov, the party leader in Leningrad, was assassinated on the secret orders of Stalin *(see p72)* but it was blamed on an anti-Stalinist cell. This became the catalyst for five years of purges throughout the country. By the time they were over, some 15 million people had been arrested, many sent to the Gulag (labour camps) and over a million executed.

Stalin's purge of the Red Army boded badly for World War II, for he had got rid of three quarters of his officers. When the Germans invaded Russia in 1941 they cut off Leningrad in less than three months, subjecting the city to a horrendous siege of 900 days *(see p131)* during which some 670,000 perished, most of them civilians. Leningrad came to be known as a "Hero City".

The Germans were eventually defeated, but the Russian people, who lost 20 million souls to the war, were subjected to a renewed terror by Stalin, which lasted until his death in March 1953.

The Russian Revolution

ST PETERSBURG IS KNOWN as the cradle of the Russian Revolution, a central event in the history of the 20th century. After the 1917 February Revolution which led to the abdication of Tsar Nicholas II, the Provisional Government declared a political amnesty. Exiled revolutionaries such as Lenin and Trotsky flooded into the city. By setting up a network of Workers' and Soldiers' Soviets, representative councils elected by the people, they established an alternative government. In October, when soldiers had deserted from the front in droves, the revolutionary leaders decided on an armed uprising which brought the Communists to power.

EXTENT OF THE CITY

■ *1917*   □ *Today*

The Ex-Tsar
Nicholas II, seen here clearing snow at Tsarskoe Selo during his house arrest in March 1917, was later taken with his family to Yekaterinburg where they were murdered.

Looting was tempting for the mob of sailors and soldiers, especially in the palace's well-stocked wine cellars.

Soldier of the Red Guard

THE WINTER PALACE STORMING

Late on the evening of 25 October 1917 the battleship *Aurora (see p73)* fired some blank shots at the Winter Palace. The Red Guard, trained by Trotsky at the Smolnyy Institute, stormed the palace. Their aim was the arrest of the Provisional Government, unsuccessfully defended by 300 Cossacks.

The Cossacks, who defended the palace with some cadets and members of the Women's Battalion, were too few to offer any serious resistance.

Lenin, Leader of the People
A charismatic speaker, as shown in this painting by Victor Ivanov, Lenin returned from exile in April to lead the Revolution. By 1918, his Bolshevik faction had shown their determination to rule.

Revolutionary Plate
Various ceramics with revolutionary themes, mixed with touches of Russian folklore, were produced to celebrate every occasion, in this case the Third International.

Leon Trotsky
The intellectual Trotsky played a leading military role in the Revolution. In 1927, during the power struggle after Lenin's death, he was exiled by Stalin. In 1940 he was murdered in Mexico by a Stalinist agent.

Propaganda
One hallmark of the Soviet regime was its powerful propaganda. Many a talented artist was employed to design posters spreading its message through striking graphics. War Communism during the Civil War (1918–20) was encouraged by posters such as this one, extolling the "pacifist Army of Workers".

Avant Garde Art
Even before 1917, Russia's artists had been in a state of revolution, producing the world's first truly abstract paintings. A great example of this new movement is Supremus No. 56, *painted in 1916 by Kazimir Malevich.*

Ministers of the Provisional Government tried to keep order but were arrested.

New Values
Traditions were radically altered by the Revolution; instead of church weddings, couples exchanged vows under the red flag. Loudly trumpeted sexual equality meant that women had to work twice as hard – at home and in the factories.

TIMELINE

1917 The February Revolution	**March** The tsar is persuaded to abdicate. Provisional Government is led by Prince Lvov	**October** Bolsheviks storm Winter Palace after signal from *Aurora* and expel Provisional Government	**March** Bolsheviks sign Brest-Litovsk peace treaty with Germany. Capital is moved to Moscow

1917	1918

July Kerensky becomes Prime Minister of Provisional Government	**1918 January** Trotsky becomes Commissar of War	**July** Start of Civil War. Tsar and family are murdered in prison at Yekaterinburg
Cruiser Aurora	**December** Lenin forms the CHEKA (secret police)	

The Washington Dove of Peace, a Russian caricature (1953) from the days of the Cold War

THAW AND STAGNATION

Three years after Stalin's death his successor Nikita Khrushchev denounced Stalin's crimes at the Twentieth Party Congress and the period known as "The Thaw" began. Political prisoners were released, and Solzhenitsyn's *One Day In the Life of Ivan Denisovich,* about life in the Gulag, was published.

In foreign affairs, things were not so liberal. Soviet tanks invaded Hungary in 1956 to prevent the country seceding from the Warsaw Pact and, in 1962,

Khrushchev's decision to put nuclear missiles on Cuba brought the world to the brink of nuclear war.

When Leonid Brezhnev took over in 1964, the intellectual climate froze once more and the persecution of political dissidents was stepped up. The first ten years of his regime were a time of relative plenty. But beneath the surface a vast black market and network of corruption was growing. The party apparatchiks, who benefited most from the corruption, had no interest in rocking the boat. When Brezhnev died in 1982, the politburo was determined to prevent the accession of a younger generation. He was followed by 68-year-old Yuriy Andropov and, when he died, 72-year-old Chernenko.

GLASNOST AND PERESTROIKA

Someone had to admit the bankruptcy of the antiquated system. But when 53-year-old Mikhail Gorbachev announced his policies of *glasnost* (openness) and *perestroika* (restructuring), when he took over in 1985, he had no idea what would follow. By the end of 1991 he was out of a job and the Soviet Union and its empire were no more.

For the first time since 1917 the elections to the Congress of People's Deputies in 1989 contained an element of genuine choice, with rebels such as Boris Yeltsin and humanrights campaigner Andrey Sakharov winning seats. By the autumn

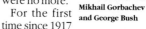

Mikhail Gorbachev and George Bush

FIRST IN SPACE

It was under Krushchev that the Soviet Union achieved her greatest coup against the West, launching the first Sputnik into space in 1957. That same year the dog Laika was the first living creature in space, aboard Sputnik II. She never came down again, but four years later Yuriy Gagarin made spectacular history as the first man in space, returning to a hero's welcome. The Soviets lost the race to put a man on the moon, but their space programme worked as powerful propaganda, backing up the claims of politicians that Russia would soon catch up with and overtake the prosperity of the West.

Spuknik II and the space dog Laika, 1957

TIMELINE

1955 Krushchev comes to power. Warsaw Pact is established

1953 Stalin dies

1964 Brezhnev becomes General Secretary

1962 Cuban missile crisis

1968 Soviet troops enter Czechoslovakia to suppress "Prague Spring"

1969 Strategic Arms Limitation Talks (SALT) with USA

1950	1960	1970

1950–54 Korean War

1956 Stalin denounced by Krushchev at 20th Party Congress. Hungarian uprising is crushed

1957 Sputnik I is launched

1961 Stalin's body removed from its place alongside Lenin in Red Square. Yuriy Gagarin is first man in space

1970 Solzhenitsyn wins Nobel Prize for Literature

Leonid Brezhnev (1906–82)

Demonstrations on Palace Square during the 1991 coup

ST PETERSBURG TODAY

The economic reforms which Russia has undergone since 1991 have widened the gap between rich and poor and, while some revel in the new opportunities for work and travel, others cry out for a return to Communism and the albeit limited social protection it offered. For many, freedom of speech outweighs the economic difficulties, although it too has brought problems, as highly dubious material including pornography and extreme right-wing propaganda is spreading.

The social problems are still being resolved, but increasing economic stability, including the monetary reform of 1998, has brought a flood of investment to the city, in everything from manufacturing to tourism. Meanwhile there has been a major religious revival, with churches used during the Soviet era as warehouses now being returned to their original purpose.

the winds of change had blown through the Eastern bloc, country by country the people rising up against their pro-Soviet governments. In 1991, local elections bought nationalist candidates to power in the republics, and democrats in the major Russian local councils. Russia and the Baltic Republics seceded from the Soviet Union, while the people of Leningrad, always in the vanguard of progressive movement and now led by the reformist lecturer in law, Anatoly Sobchak, voted to restore the city's original name, St Petersburg.

The new Russian State Emblem

With his great victory in the election for President of the Russian Republic, Yeltsin was able to deal the death blow to the Soviet Union. It came after the military coup against Gorbachev in August 1991, when Yeltsin's stand against the tanks in Moscow made him a hero. In St Petersburg no tanks were on the street, but nonetheless Sobchak rallied supporters of democracy. When Gorbachev returned from house arrest, Yeltsin forced him to outlaw the Communist Party and, by the end of the year, the Soviet Union no longer existed.

A church wedding, popular again since religion has gained new importance among the young

1980 Olympic Games in Moscow are boycotted by the West	**1982** Death of Brezhnev; replaced by Andropov	**1991** Yeltsin becomes President of Russia. Dissolution of the USSR on 25 December	*Boris Yeltsin with Russian flag in 1991*	**1998** The rouble is revalued and stabilizes
1980		**1990**		**2000**
1979 USSR invades Afghanistan	**1984** Andropov is replaced by Chernenko	**1985** Gorbachev is elected General Secretary of Communist Party	**1998** The last Romanov tsar, Nicholas II, is reburied with his family in SS Peter and Paul Cathedral on 17 July **1990** Independence of Latvia, Lithuania, Estonia. Gorbachev is elected President of the USSR and awarded the Nobel Peace Prize	

ST PETERSBURG AT A GLANCE

A CITY BUILT ON WATER, St Petersburg offers beautiful scenery and a wide range of sights. The Peter and Paul Fortress (see pp66–7), one of the city's first buildings, contrasts with Baroque monasteries and Neo-Classical palaces. The city's short but stormy history is reflected in many of its museums, which display everything from Catherine the Great's fine art collection in the Hermitage to memorabilia of the Revolution in the Kshesinskaya Mansion (see p72).

To help you make the most of your stay, the following 12 pages are a time-saving guide to the best museums and palaces and the most interesting of the many bridges and waterways. The cultural figures that made St Petersburg a city of importance are also featured. Below is a selection of sights that should not be missed by any visitor.

ST PETERSBURG'S TOP TEN ATTRACTIONS

Russian Museum
See pp104–7

Mariinskiy Theatre
See p119

Nevskiy Prospekt
See pp46–9

Church on Spilled Blood
See p100

The Hermitage
See pp84–93

Stieglitz Museum
See p127

Kazan Cathedral
See p111

St Isaac's Cathedral
See pp80–81

SS Peter and Paul Cathedral
See p68

Alexander Nevsky Monastery
See pp130–31

◁ The Neo-Classical Kazan Cathedral with its impressive semi-circle of granite columns

St Petersburg's Best: Bridges and Waterways

L IKE ITS WATERBOUND SISTERS, Amsterdam and Venice, St Petersburg is built around a network of canals and rivers which are still the life-blood of the city. They contribute to its unique atmosphere by creating eerie mists which rise from the ice-laden waters in winter and, in summer, a glittering mirror of façades during the glowing sunsets and bright White Nights.

Bridges, necessary for communication between the islands, were also an excellent means to adorn the city with decorative sculptures, elaborate lampposts and wrought-iron work.

A walk or a boat trip *(see p134–5 and 218–19)* is the best way to enjoy them.

Winter Canal
Laid out in 1718–20, this narrow canal is crossed by three bridges and Yuriy Velten's Hermitage Theatre foyer (1783–7).

Lieutenant Shmidt Bridge
Rebuilt in 1936–8, this bridge still retains its original cast-iron seahorse railings, designed by Bryullov.

Lion Bridge
One of the earliest of its kind, this pedestrian suspension bridge dates from 1825–6. Its cables are anchored inside four cast-iron lions, by sculptor Pavel Sokolov.

Egyptian Bridge
This bridge spanning the Fontanka was decorated in the Egyptian style fashionable at the time of its construction, in 1826.

Malaya Neva

Vasilevskiy Island

Bolshaya Neva   *Palace Embankment*

Moyka

Sennaya Ploshchad

Kanal Griboedova   *Fontanka*

| 0 metres | 500 |
| 0 yards | 500 |

Trinity Bridge
The ten-arched Trinity Bridge (1897–1903) is famous for its Style-Moderne lampposts and railing decorations, the work of the skilful French engineers Vincent Chabrol and René Patouillard.

Swan Canal
This tree-lined canal (1711–19) leading out to the Neva is named after the swans which were once drawn to its peaceful waters.

Bridge Passage
Cleverly designed to span the confluence of the Moyka and the Griboedov, the Theatre and Small Stable bridges were constructed by Traitteur and Adam in 1829–31.

Anichkov Bridge
This three-span bridge, carrying Nevskiy prospekt across the Fontanka, was built in 1839–41. At each corner are Pyotr Klodt's impressive sculptures of men taming wild horses.

Lomonosov Bridge
The distinctive domed granite towers, built in 1785–7, originally contained the bridge's opening mechanism. The bridge was rebuilt in 1912, but the towers were kept.

Bank Bridge
Dating from the same time as the Lion Bridge, and designed by the same team, this bridge is adorned by four magnificent cast-iron griffons. Its name derives from the nearby former Assignment Bank.

Petrogradskaya

Neva

Gostinyy Dvor

Exploring St Petersburg's Bridges and Waterways

A BOAT TRIP on St Petersburg's canals and waterways is one of the highlights of any visit to the city. From the Anichkov Bridge the river boats *(see p218)* do a loop along the Neva, Fontanka and Moyka rivers, taking in many impressive bridges and landmarks. Alternatively, you can choose your own route to explore the city's rich architectural heritage by taking a water taxi *(see p219)*. A pleasant wander along the embankments of the Griboedov Canal leads past imposing 19th-century apartment houses and fancifully decorated bridges. In the winter months, one can walk on the frozen Neva.

The ice-laden Neva river in front of the Peter and Paul Fortress

THE NEVA AND ITS BRANCHES

G REATEST OF St Petersburg's numerous waterways, the Neva flows from Lake Ladoga in the east through the city to the Gulf of Finland, a distance of only 74 km (46 miles) in total. Vasilevskiy Island, one of more than 100 islands in the Neva Delta, divides the river into two seperate branches, Bolshaya (Great) Neva and Malaya (Small) Neva.

Icebound for at least four months of the year, the Neva usually shows the first signs of cracking in March. The official Opening of Navigation is announced by the port authority in mid-April. Until the Revolution the event was marked with great ceremony. The Commander of the Peter and Paul Fortress *(see pp66–7)*, at the head of a naval flotilla, would scoop some icy water into a silver goblet which he presented to the tsar in the Winter Palace *(see pp92–3)*.

RIVERS AND CANALS

I NSPIRED BY AMSTERDAM, Peter the Great kept the many streams of the delta as canals, which also helped to drain the swampy ground. As the city grew new ones were dug to improve the canal network.

The **Moyka** originally flowed from a swamp near the Field of Mars *(see p94)*. In the 19th century the aristocracy lined its quays with impressive Neo-Classical mansions which are still their main attraction. Canal boats and barges ply the 7-km (4-mile) long **Fontanka**, widest and busiest of the waterways, which was once the border of the city. These two rivers are linked by the **Kryukov Canal**, dug in the 18th century.

The **Griboedov Canal**, first known as the Catherine Canal in honour of Catherine the Great, was designed to move cargo from Sennaya Ploshchad. Today the atmosphere here is more tranquil. The stretch of water running south from the Lion Bridge is particularly picturesque. The narrowest waterway is the **Winter Canal**, just to the east of the Winter Palace. Nearby is the delightful **Swan Canal** which runs along the Summer Gardens *(p95)*.

Steady industrial growth in the 19th century prompted the construction of a new canal, the **Obvodnyy**, in 1834, to take the increasing number of heavy cargo barges and supply water to the city outskirts.

NEVA BRIDGES

T HE MOST CENTRAL of the Neva bridges is the **Palace Bridge** (Dvortsovyy most). The present structure, built early in the 20th century, replaced a seasonal pontoon bridge which linked the mainland to Vasilevskiy Island.

View of the Moyka and its south bank with a water taxi in foreground

Peter the Great Bridge, crossing the Neva near Smolnyy Institute

The other bridge to this island, **Lieutenant Shmidt Bridge** (Most Leytenanta Shmidta, *see p63)*, is named after a naval officer who led a rebellion of sailors of the Black Sea Fleet in 1905. The **Trinity Bridge** (Troitskiy most, *see p73)* was built in 1897–1903, in time for the city's bicentenary, by the French Batignolles company. At 582 m (1,910 ft), the Trinity Bridge was the Neva's longest, until the construction of the **Alexander Nevsky Bridge** (Most Aleksandra Nevskovo) in the 1960s, which is some 900 m (2,950 ft). Between these two is the **Liteynyy Bridge** (Liteynyy most) built in 1874–9. In 1917, the city authorities tried to prevent rebel workers crossing the Neva from the Vyborg Side by raising the central bridge span. The tactic failed since the re-volutionaries decided to cross on foot over the frozen ice.

Near the Smolnyy Institute is the **Peter the Great Bridge** (Most Petra Velikovo), also known by its Soviet name Bolshoy Okhtinskiy most. It has a central drawbridge and distinctive steel twin arches, erected in 1909–11.

From April to November all Neva bridges are raised at night to allow ships to pass to and from the Volga *(see p201)*.

DECORATIVE BRIDGES

In the beginning, wooden bridges spanned the canals and rivers of St Petersburg. They were usually known by their colour – red, blue, green, and so on. The **Red Bridge** (Krasnyy most) which carries Gorokhovaya ulitsa over the Moyka, has pre-served its original name. Built in 1808–14, this iron bridge is decorated with picturesque lamps on four granite obelisks. Lamps are also a feature of the **Lantern Bridge** (Fonarnyy most) which crosses the Moyka river near to the Yusupov Palace *(see p120)*. Here the gilded lampposts are shaped to look like treble clefs. **Singer's Bridge** (Pevcheskiy most) at the other end of the Moyka takes its name from the choir of the nearby Glinka Capella. Its engineer, Yegor Adam, also designed the lace-like patterning of the railings.

At the junction where the Griboedov meets the Moyka is an interesting ensemble, formed by the wide **Theatre Bridge** (Teatralnyy most) and

Small Stable Bridge (Malo-Konyushennyy most). The latter is cunningly designed to look like two bridges.

Among the more attractive bridges is Georg von Traitteur's pedestrian **Bank Bridge** (Bankovskiy most), crossing the Griboedov. Its cables are held up by two pairs of gold-winged griffons. The **Lion Bridge** (Lvinyy most), also by Traitteur, uses a similar device; in this case the suspension cables emerge from the open jaws of four proud lions.

St Panteleymon's Bridge (Panteleymonovskiy most, *see p99)* spans the Fontanka near the Summer Gardens. It was Russia's first chain bridge (1823–4). The Empire-style decoration has survived and includes gilded fasces and double-headed eagles perched on laurel wreaths. Next to the Nevskiy prospekt, the **Anichkov Bridge** (Anich-kovskiy most) is famous for its four vibrant bronze sculptures of wild horses and their powerful tamers, all of them in different positions. Further down the Fontanka, framed by a handsome Neo-Classical square by Carlo Rossi, is the **Lomonosov Bridge** (Most Lomonosova) with its unusual stone turrets.

The **Egyptian Bridge** (Egipetskiy most) spans the Fontanka close to the Kryukov Canal. It

Lamppost, St Panteleymon's Bridge

is ornamented with bronze sphinxes and bridgeheads resembling the entrance to an Egyptian temple. Originally constructed in 1826, the bridge collapsed under the weight of a passing cavalry squadron but was rebuilt in 1955.

A CITY UNDER WATER

Peter the Great should have known it was a bad idea to found a city here. The first flood, just three months after he started the fortress in 1703, swept away his building mater-ials. The water rises dangerously high on average once a year, but four floods, in 1777, 1824, 1924 and 1955, wrought massive damage. In 1824 the whole city went under water and 462 buildings were totally destroyed. This inspired Pushkin's poem *The Bronze Horseman (see p78)*. Markers showing record waterheights can be found by the Winter Canal and the Peter and Paul Fortress. In 1989 construction of a dam was begun to prevent future destruction.

A 19th-century illustration of one of the many floods in St Petersburg

St Petersburg's Best: Palaces and Museums

ST PETERSBURG BOASTS more than 90 museums, many of them housed in palaces or other buildings of historical importance. Some are well known throughout the world, such as the Hermitage which began as Catherine the Great's private collection of European art. Others, including the Russian Museum and the Summer Palace, highlight local art, history and culture. Some of the most evocative museums are those commemorating the lives and work of famous artists, writers and musicians. This selection represents the most interesting in each category.

The Hermitage
Now incorporating the breathtaking state rooms of the Winter Palace, the world-famous Hermitage holds nearly three million exhibits which range from Fine Arts to archaeological finds.

Menshikov Palace
This grandiose Baroque palace on Vasilevskiy Island is testimony to the power of Peter the Great's friend and advisor, Prince Menshikov.

Petrogradskay

Malaya Neva

Vasilevskiy Island

Bolshaya Neva

Palace Embankment

Sennaya Ploshchad

IMPERIAL COUNTRY PALACES

To escape the pressures of the capital, successive Russian rulers built sumptuous retreats in the rural hinterland of St Petersburg. These offer a fascinating insight into the lifestyle of the Romanov dynasty.

Tsarskoe Selo's Catherine Palace was built by Rastrelli in a flamboyant Baroque style.

Peterhof's palace and pavilions are enhanced by the splendid cascades and fountains adorning the attractive grounds.

| 0 km | 15 |
| 0 miles | 15 |

Pavlovsk's Great Palace is set in an extensive naturalistic landscaped park, embellished with ponds, pavilions and monuments.

Kshesinskaya Mansion
Built for a prima ballerina of the Mariinskiy Theatre, this attractive Style-Moderne mansion now houses the Museum of Russian Political History containing souvenirs from the Revolution.

Summer Palace
Interiors and furniture, such as Peter the Great's original four-poster bed, give an idea of the tsar's relatively modest lifestyle.

Neva

Stieglitz Museum
A rich collection of applied art is displayed in Mesmacher's magnificent building which was inspired by palaces of the Italian Renaissance.

Gostinyy Dvor

Russian Museum
Carlo Rossi's Mikhaylovskiy Palace is the splendid setting for an outstanding collection of Russian art, ranging from medieval icons to contemporary paintings and sculptures. This semi-abstract work Blue Crest *by Vasily Kandinsky dates from 1917.*

Pushkin House-Museum
Period furnishings and personal belongings such as this inkstand recreate the atmosphere of Alexander Pushkin's last home.

0 metres	500
0 yards	500

Exploring St Petersburg's Palaces and Museums

THE CITY'S PALACES range from imperial excess to the tasteful homes of the nobility, while art museums cover the fine and applied arts and folk crafts. The history of St Petersburg, from its foundation as Peter the Great's "window on the west" to its role as the "cradle of the Revolution", is covered by a variety of museums while its culture is documented in the apartments of writers, composers and artists. More specialist interests, from railway engines and military paraphernalia to insects and whales, also find reflection in the wealth of museums.

Bedroom in the Chinese Palace (1760s), Oranienbaum

Peter the Great's Summer Palace overlooking the Fontanka

PALACES

THE FABULOUS WEALTH of imperial St Petersburg is reflected in the magnificence of its palaces. No trip to the city would be complete without a visit to at least one of the spectacular out-of-town imperial summer residences, **Peterhof** *(see pp146–9)*, **Pavlovsk** *(see pp156–9)* or the Catherine Palace *(see pp150–151)* at **Tsarskoe Selo**. These luxuriant residences, built and added to in the last 200 years of Romanov rule, illustrate the extravagance of the imperial court and the wealth of the empire's natural resources. An abundance of gold, lapis lazuli, malachite, marble and other precious minerals decorates many of the rich palace interiors. The palace parks and grounds are landscaped and filled with follies and monuments.

At the centre of the city, the **Winter Palace** *(see pp92–93)* in the Hermitage epitomizes the opulence of the court, while Peter the Great's more

intimate **Summer Palace** *(see p95)* makes a pleasing contrast. Peter's friend and counsellor, Prince Alexander Menshikov, also built two sumptuous residences, the **Menshikov Palace** *(see p62)* on Vasilevskiy Island, and his summer country palace at **Oranienbaum** *(see p144)*.

Overlooking the Moyka river is the **Yusupov Palace** *(see p120)* which is famed as the murder scene of Rasputin, the extraordinary peasant who exerted his malign influence over the Russian court.

For those in search of a tranquil setting, a pleasant day can be spent exploring the **Yelagin Palace** *(see p126)* and the island of the same name.

ART MUSEUMS

ONE OF THE WORLD'S greatest collections of Western art is housed in the **Hermitage** *(see pp84–93)* which owns an astounding 2.8 million pieces of art. With collections ranging from Egyptian mummies to Scythian gold, Greek vases,

Colombian emeralds and a vast and dazzling array of Old Master, Impressionist and Post-Impressionist paintings, it is essential to be selective.

The **Russian Museum** *(see pp104–107)* is a showcase for Russian art, including the 20th-century avant-garde and the folk crafts which influenced it. Temporary exhibitions from its holdings are shown in the **Engineers' Castle** *(see p101)*, **Marble Palace** *(see p110)* and **Stroganov Palace** *(see p112)*.

The **Academy of Arts** *(see p63)* exhibits work by past students as well as models of the city's notable buildings.

There are fascinating displays of applied arts from around the world in the **Stieglitz Museum** *(see p127)* which includes ceramics, wood carving, ironwork and embroidery. Its interiors and the glass-roofed exhibition hall are equally impressive.

The Cyclist (1913) by Natalya Goncharova, Russian Museum

HISTORY MUSEUMS

ST PETERSBURG'S dramatic 300-year history is proudly recorded in a number of the city's museums. The **Cabin of Peter the Great** (see p73) was the earliest building to be constructed in the city and it offers an intriguing insight into the surprisingly humble lifestyle of this tsar.

A group of historic sights lies within the Peter and Paul Fortress. The **Cathedral of SS Peter and Paul** (see p68) houses the tombs of all but three of Russia's tsars since Peter the Great. The preserved cells of the grim **Trubetskoy Bastion** (see p69) act as a reminder of the hundreds of political prisoners to be confined within the fortress walls. In the **Commandant's House** (see p69), the courthouse where prisoners were once interrogated, an exhibition looks at medieval settlements in the area, while the **Engineer's House** (see p68) focuses on daily life in St Petersburg before the Revolution.

A wealth of revolutionary memorabilia, including Stalin era posters and a huge propaganda stained-glass panel, can be found in the **Museum of Russian Political History**. The museum is located within the Kshesinskaya Mansion (see p72) which, in 1917, housed the Bolshevik headquarters. The **Cruiser Aurora** (see p73) also played a part in the Revolution, having fired a warning shot before the storming of the Winter Palace in October 1917.

For an impression of the prestigious pre-revolutionary school where poet Alexander Pushkin was a student, some of the class rooms of the **Lycée** at Tsarskoe Selo (see p153) have been restored to their 19th-century appearance.

On the southern outskirts of the city, in Victory Square (see p131), the **Monument to the Heroic Defenders of Leningrad** poignantly evokes the Siege of Leningrad (1941–4) and acts as an important reminder of the great hardships endured by St Petersburgers during World War II.

Office of Leningrad party secretary Sergey Kirov, Kirov Museum

SPECIAL INTEREST MUSEUMS

REMNANTS of Peter the Great's legendary "cabinet of curiosities" can be found in the city's oldest museum, the **Kunstkammer** (see p60). Housed under the same roof is a **Museum of Anthropology and Ethnography**, displaying a large collection of artifacts from all over the world. For natural history, the **Zoological Museum** (see p60) encompasses most known life forms, including a unique collection of molluscs and blue corals.

The **Naval Museum** (see p60) fascinates all ages with its model ships, small boats, figureheads and flags, while the **Artillery Museum** (see p82) covers military hardware, from pikes to ballistic missiles. Train enthusiasts will find plenty to enjoy in the **Railway Museum** (see p123), including an 1835 engine built for the Tsarskoe Selo railway.

The **Museum of Musical Life** in the Sheremetev Palace (see p129) displays period instruments and explains the role of the Sheremetev family as leading music patrons in 19th-century St Petersburg. Stage costumes, including the ones worn by the opera singer Fyodor Shalyapin, are on display alongside photos, set designs and other ephemera in the **Theatre Museum** on Ostrovskiy Square (see p110).

HOUSE-MUSEUMS

A HANDFUL of evocative museums commemorates some of the city's most famous residents. Two lovingly-preserved museums, the **Pushkin House-Museum** (see p113) and the **Dostoevsky House-Museum** (see p130), recapture something of the life and character of their former residents.

The **Anna Akhmatova Museum** in the former service quarters of the Sheremetev Palace (see p129) traces the dramatic life of the poetess who lived here for many years.

For an insight into the life of a powerful Communist official of the 1930s, visit the **Kirov Museum** (see p72). The museum is devoted to the popular leader whose assassination on Stalin's orders initiated the Great Terror (see p27).

Outside the city in **Repino** (see p144), the house of the painter Ilya Repin is set in beautiful woodland on the Gulf of Finland.

18th-century violin and score in Museum of Musical Life, Sheremetev Palace

Celebrated St Petersburgers

AS THE RESIDENCE of the Russian imperial family and court from the early 18th century, St Petersburg was the focus of patronage and an almost boundless source of wealth. It was the perfect seed bed for creativity and the flowering of ideas. Institutions such as the Academy of Arts, the University, the Kunstkammer and the Imperial School of Ballet trained generations of cultural figures and scientists to the highest standards. So successful were they that, by the dawn of the 20th century, St Petersburg had become one of the most important cultural centres in Europe.

Nikolai Gogol
A merciless satirist of St Petersburg society, Gogol lived on Malaya Morskaya ulitsa (see p82) for three years.

Grigoriy Kozintsev
Director Kozintsev confirmed his reputation in the West with his interpretation of Shakespeare's Hamlet (1964), made at Lenfilm (see p70).

Petrogradska

Malaya Neva

Vasilevskiy Island

Ilya Repin
This outstanding realist painter is seen here teaching life drawing at the Academy of Arts (see p63) where he was a professor.

Bolshaya Neva

Sennaya Ploshchad

Pyotr Tchaikovsky
Tchaikovsky graduated from the Conservatory (see p118) in 1865 and went on to compose his world-famous operas and ballets.

Anna Pavlova
A prima ballerina at the Mariinskiy Theatre (see p121), Pavlova took Paris by storm in 1909 when she toured in Les Sylphides with the Ballets Russes.

Alexander Pushkin

The great poet, who sketched this self-portrait on a manuscript, died in the flat which is now a house-museum (see p113).

Sergey Diaghilev

Driving force behind the Ballets Russes, Diaghilev also produced the influential World of Art *magazine in his flat on 45 Liteynyy prospekt. He is shown here with Jean Cocteau (left).*

Neva

Palace Embankment

Anna Akhmatova

The poetess' most famous poem, Requiem, *is a powerful and moving indictment of the Stalinist regime. Akhmatova, seen here in a portrait by Nathan Altman, lived in the service quarters of the Sheremetev Palace (see p129).*

Gostinyy Dvor

Dmitriy Shostakovich

Shostakovich's Seventh Symphony *was broadcast live on the radio from the Great Hall of the Philharmonia (see p98) in August 1942, while the city was under siege. Many testified to its role in boosting the morale of the besieged citizens.*

Fyodor Dostoevsky

The novelist Dostoevsky lived for many years among the slums of Sennaya Ploshchad (see p122) which provided the setting for his greatest work, Crime and Punishment.

0 metres	500
0 yards	500

Remarkable St Petersburgers

THE STREETS of St Petersburg are redolent with literary and artistic associations. Fascinating art collections, house-museums, theatres and concert halls evoke the memory of famous St Petersburgers. The world of the 18th-century genius Lomonosov and 19th-century writers Pushkin and Dostoevsky can be imagined. So too, can the spirit of Russian ballet when dancers such as Anna Pavlova and Vaslaw Nijinsky thrilled the Mariinskiy audiences. During these early years of the 20th century, writers, musicians, dancers and painters flocked to St Petersburg, bringing with them a wealth of creativity.

**Symbolist "Silver Age" poet,
Andrei Bely (1880–1934)**

WRITERS

CONSIDERED THE FATHER of modern Russian literature, **Alexander Pushkin** (1799–1837) was simultaneously intoxicated by St Petersburg's beauty and sensitive to the underlying climate of political suspicion and intolerance which constrained writers in the wake of the Decembrist rebellion of 1825 (see p22). **Nikolai Gogol** (1809–52) responded to these constraints by satirising the status quo. In *The Nose*, he targeted the city's bureaucrats with their inflated sense of self worth and mind-numbing conformity.

Another aspect of the city altogether is revealed by **Fyodor Dostoevsky** (1821–81). His novel *Crime and Punishment*, one of more than 30 works set in the city, takes place against a backdrop of squalor in the notorious slums of Sennaya Ploshchad (see p122). The story of the murder of an old moneylender was based on a real crime and the novel's publication in 1866 was blamed for a series of subsequent copy-cat killings.

Poetry, which flourished in the "Golden Age" of Pushkin, only regained its ascendancy over the novel in the "Silver Age" during the first decade of the 20th century. Some of the most exciting poets of the period, including **Aleksandr Blok** (1880–1921), **Andrei Bely** and **Anna Akhmatova** (1889–1966), gathered at The Tower, a flat overlooking the Tauride Gardens (see p128). Bely later wrote *Petersburg*, one of the earliest stream-of-consciousness novels.

Akhmatova is honoured by a museum in the Sheremetev Palace (see p129) while one of her protégés, **Joseph Brodsky** (1940–96) went on to receive the Nobel Prize for literature in 1987. Brodsky became the bête-noire of the Leningrad literary establishment in the 1960s. The stubborn refusal of the authorities to publish his poetry, which they condemned as pessimistic and decadent, finally forced him to emigrate in 1972.

MUSICIANS

THE FIRST important composer to emerge from the nationalist movement was **Mikhail Glinka** (1804–57), the earliest composer of Russian opera. In 1862, the Conservatory (see p120) was founded by **Anton Rubinstein** (1829–94) and this became the focus of musical life in St Petersburg. **Nikolai Rimsky-Korsakov** (1844–1908) taught here for 37 years and together with composers such as **Modest Mussorgsky** (1839–81), and **Aleksandr Borodin** (1834–87), he formed "the mighty handful". They were a largely self-taught group aiming to develop a musical language based on Russian folk music and Slav traditions. Many of them wrote operas premiered at the Mariinskiy (see p119).

One of the musical geniuses of the 20th century was **Igor Stravinsky** (1882–1971). He spent much time abroad but, as works like *The Rite of Spring* testify, his cultural roots were firmly in his homeland.

The city's most important concert venue is the Great Hall of the Philharmonia (see p194) where **Pyotr Tchaikovsky**'s (1840–93) *Sixth Symphony* was premiered in 1893 and **Dmitriy Shostakovich**'s (1906–75) *Seventh Symphony*, his most famous work, was performed in 1942.

Portrait of composer Mikhail Glinka painted by Ilya Repin in 1887

The Circus (1919) by avant-garde artist Marc Chagall

ARTISTS

FROM THE 18th century, the Academy of Arts *(see p63)* was the centre of artistic life in St Petersburg. **Dmitriy Levitskiy** (1735–1822), **Orest Kiprenskiy** (1782–1836), **Silvestr Shchedrin** (1791–1830), and Russia's first internationally recognised artist, **Karl Bryullov** (1799–1852), were all trained here.

In 1863, a group of students rebelled against the Academy and went on to establish the Wanderers movement *(see p106)*. To some extent the Academy and the Wanderers became reconciled when the most versatile of these artists, **Ilya Repin** (1844–1930), was appointed professor of painting at the Academy in 1893.

Five years later **Sergey Diaghilev** (1872–1929) and painter **Alexandre Benois** (1870–1960) launched the *World of Art* magazine *(see p107)*, proclaiming "Art for art's sake". Another collaborator, **Leon Bakst** (1866–1924), designed the most famous of the Ballets Russes costumes. Bakst also taught **Marc Chagall** (1889–1985) who later settled in France and had a profound impact on art in the West as well as in Russia. Other members of the Russian avant-garde include **Kazimir Malevich** (1878–1935) and **Pavel Filonov** (1883–1941).

Works by all of these artists can be seen at the Russian Museum *(see pp104–107)*.

DANCERS AND CHOREOGRAPHERS

THE SKILLS of Russian dancers are legendary and the performances of the Mariinskiy (Kirov) Ballet Company continue to enthral audiences all over the world. Since 1836 the dancers have been trained at the former Imperial Ballet School *(see p112)*. In 1869–1903 the outstanding choreographer at the Mariinskiy was **Marius Petipa**. He inspired a generation of dancers including **Matilda Kshesinskaya** *(see p72)*, **Vaslaw Nijinsky** (1890–1950) and the legendary **Anna Pavlova** (1885–1931).

Petipa's successor, **Michel Fokine** (1880–1942), is famous as the principal choreographer of the Ballets Russes *(see p119)*. The Mariinskiy tradition was revived after the Revolution by another graduate of the Ballet School, **Agrippina Vaganova** (1879–1951). Her groundwork paved the way for the modern generation of dancers including **Rudolf Nureyev** (1938–93) and most recently, **Galina Mezentseva** and **Emil Faskhoutdinov**.

FILM DIRECTORS

THE LENFILM STUDIOS *(see p70)* were founded in 1918 on the site where the first Russian cine film had been shown in 1896. In its heyday Lenfilm produced 15 movies a year. Its two most remarkable

Poster for *The Youth of Maxim* **(1935) directed by Kozintsev**

directors, **Grigoriy Kozintsev** (1905–73) and **Leonid Trauberg** (1902–90), first joined forces in 1922 and began making short experimental films. The pair then went on to direct *The New Babylon* (1929), remarkable for its montage and lighting effects, and *The Maxim Trilogy* (1935–39). Kozintsev's versions of *Hamlet* (1964) and *King Lear* (1970), with music composed by Shostakovich for both films, mark the height of his success in the West.

SCIENTISTS

The great polymath Mikhail Lomonosov

THE FOUNDATIONS OF modern Russian science were laid in the 18th century by **Mikhail Lomonosov** (1711–65) *(see p61)* who worked for over 20 years in the Kunstkammer *(see p60)*. His treatise, *Elementa Chymiae Mathematica*, published in 1741, anticipates Dalton's theory of the atomic structure of matter.

In 1869, **Dmitriy Mendeleev** (1834–1907), a professor of chemistry, compiled the Periodic Table of Elements.

Many people believe that the world's first radio signal was sent by **Aleksandr Popov** (1859–1906) from the laboratories of St Petersburg University on 24 March 1896.

In 1904, the world-famous physiologist **Ivan Pavlov** (1849–1936) won the Nobel Prize for medicine for his theory of conditioned reflexes which he demonstrated by experimenting on dogs and their hearing responses.

Nevskiy Prospekt
From the Admiralty to the Griboedov Canal

APLEASANT STROLL ALONG this first stretch of St Petersburg's main artery reveals a wealth of attractive buildings. A profusion of architectural styles ranges from the Baroque Stroganov Palace to the magnificent Neo-Classical Kazan Cathedral and the striking Style-Moderne House of Books. The stately avenue was once known as the "Street of Tolerance", referring to the clutch of churches of different denominations which were established here in the late 18th and early 19th centuries. *(See also p108.)*

Literary Café
Once called the Wolf and Beranger, this café was known for its fashionable clientele. Pushkin left from here for his fatal duel in 1837 (see p83).

Admiralty *(p78)*

Palace Square *(p83)* and the **Hermitage** *(pp84–93)*

The 1760s' apartment blocks at Nos. 8 and 10 are an example of early St Petersburg Neo-Classicism.

ADMIRALTEYSKIY PROSPEKT

NEVSKIY PROSPEKT

BOLSHAYA MORSKAYA ULITSA

The Admiralty Gardens were laid out in 1872–4. Near the fountain are busts of composer Mikhail Glinka, writer Nikolai Gogol and poet Mikhail Lermontov.

MALAYA MORSKAYA ULITSA

BOLSHAYA MORSKAYA ULITSA

St Isaac's Cathedral *(pp80–81)* and **Astoria Hotel** *(p79)*

Aeroflot Building
Marian Peretyatkovich's severe granite building (1912) is uncharacteristic of the city's architecture. The upper storeys were inspired by the Palazzo Medici in Florence, the arcades by the Doge's Palace, Venice.

Sign at School No. 210
This school carries a sign, dating from the Blockade, warning "Citizens! This side of the street is more dangerous during artillery bombardment".

ГРАЖДАНЕ!
ПРИ АРТОБСТРЕЛЕ
ЭТА СТОРОНА УЛИЦЫ
НАИБОЛЕЕ ОПАСНА

Barrikada Cinema
Now a cinema, this handsome building was erected in 1768–71, for the city's police chief Nikolay Chicherin.

| 0 metres | 100 |
| 0 yards | 100 |

STAR SIGHT
★ **Kazan Cathedral**

Dutch Church Building
The Dutch church was housed behind the central Neo-Classical portico of Paul Jacot's seemingly secular building (1831–7). The elongated wings are still occupied by offices, flats and shops.

Stroganov Palace
The façade of this splendid Baroque palace, one of the oldest buildings on the street (1753), is embellished with sculptural ornaments and the Stroganov coat of arms (see p112).

The Fashion House
Marian Lyalevich designed this building for Mertens Furriers in 1911–12. The impact of the Neo-Classical arches is heightened by the blue-tinged plate glass.

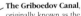

The House of Books
(Dom Knigi) was built for the Singer Sewing Machine Company in 1902–4 by Pavel Syuzor. The building, now a bookshop, is distinguished by a glass globe on a conical tower.

➤ **Continued** *(pp48–9)*

The Lutheran Church
(1833) was an important centre for the evangelical community. Converted into a swimming pool during the Soviet era, it is once again open as a church *(see p112).*

The Griboedov Canal,
originally known as the Catherine Canal, was renamed in 1923 after the 19th-century Russian playwright Aleksandr Griboedov.

★ Kazan Cathedral
Ninety-six Corinthian columns, arranged in four rows, form an extended arc facing Nevskiy prospekt. Andrey Voronikhin's design was inspired by Bernini's colonnade for St Peter's in Rome. (See p111.)

NAB REKI MOYKI
BOLSHAYA KONYUSHENNAYA UL
MALAYA KONYUSHENNAYA ULITSA
NEVSKIY PROSPEKT
ULITSA PLEKHANOVA
KAZANSKIY MOST
KANAL GRIBOEDOVA

Nevskiy Prospekt
From the Griboedov Canal to the Fontanka

NEVSKIY PROSPEKT has been the main focus for St Petersburg's shopping and entertainment since the mid-18th century. As the prospekt continues towards the handsome Anichkov Bridge on the Fontanka river, there are growing numbers of cafés, bars and restaurants as well as three historic shopping arcades, the Silver Rows, Gostinyy Dvor and Passazh. Bustling with life, this stretch of the avenue also has many sights of historic and architectural interest, including the Anichkov Palace.

Passazh Arcade
This popular shopping mall is covered by a glass canopy stretching 180 m (590 ft). The arcade opened in 1848 and was reconstructed in 1900.

Church on Spilled Blood *(p100)*

The Small Hall of the Philharmonia was the city's main concert hall in the early 19th century.

The Church of Saint Catherine (1762–82), by Vallin de la Mothe, is a mixture of Baroque and Neo-Classical styles. It was once the hub of the Catholic community.

Grand Hotel Europe *(p101)*

Russian Museum *(pp104–107)*

The Armenian Church (1771–80) is a fine example of Yuriy Velten's decorative Neo-Classical style *(see p108).*

Gostinyy Dvor

KANAL GRIBOEDOVA

MIKHAYLOVSKAYA ULITSA

NEVSKIY PROSPEKT

Nevskiy Prospekt M

DUMSKAYA ULITSA

Gostinyy Dvor M

SADOVAYA ULITSA

Silver Rows Arcade (1784–7)

The Duma Tower was built in 1804 as a watchtower for fires. The Duma building was the centre of local government from 1786–1918.

The Russian National Library houses over 30 million items, including the earliest surviving handwritten Russian book (1057).

Portik Rusca
Now standing alone, the six-columned portico by Luigi Rusca was originally the entrance to a long arcade of shops. The portico was dismantled during the construction of the metro and rebuilt in 1972.

★ ***Gostinyy Dvor***
This striking arcade has been St Petersburg's main bazaar since the mid-18th century (see p108). It houses more than 300 outlets which sell everything from clothes and cosmetics to souvenirs and chocolates.

| 0 metres | 100 |
| 0 yards | 100 |

★ Yeliseev's
Famous for its beautiful Style-Moderne decor, this building houses Yeliseev's delicatessen on the ground floor (see p109).

LOCATOR MAP

Beloselskiy-Belozerskiy Palace
Now an exhibition and business centre, this sumptuous palace was designed in Neo-Baroque style by Andrey Stakenschneider in 1847–8. The faded red façade is decorated with Corinthian pilasters and atlantes upholding balconies.

STAR SIGHTS

★ Yeliseev's

★ Gostinyy Dvor

Quarenghi's Stalls were built in 1803–6 as trading rows. They were then handed over to the imperial chancellor and became known as the Cabinet.

Number 66 was occupied by the music publishers Bessel and Co in the 19th century. Tchaikovsky was one of many composers who frequented their offices.

The Central District Tax Office has a Neo-Classical appearance, but was not built until the 1940s.

NEVSKIY PROSPEKT

OSTROVSKOVO

FONTANKA

ANICHKOV MOST

Aleksandrinskiy Theatre

A statue of Catherine the Great stands in Ostrovskiy Square *(see p110).*

The Anichkov Palace was first built as a present from Tsarina Elizabeth to her lover, Aleksey Razumovskiy. It later became the winter residence of the heir to the throne *(see p109).*

Moskovskiy railway station

Anichkov Bridge
Four dynamic bronze statues of rearing horses and their tamers adorn this well-known landmark. They were designed in the 1840s by Pyotr Klodt (see p35).

St Petersburg Through the Year

WHATEVER THE weather, Russians are always ready to celebrate and consequently take their public holidays very seriously. Flowers have great symbolic significance, from mimosa for International Women's Day, to lilac to mark the beginning of summer. Every official holiday, as well as some local festivals such as City Day, are celebrated both in the centre of town and in the many

Lilac, a symbol of summer

different districts, with regattas, balloon rides and fireworks at night, when the torches on the Rostral Columns *(see p60)* are lit. Classical music is the central theme of a large number of festivals each year, attracting talented performers from all over the world. But even without an official holiday, Russian people love to get out and about, whether to ski or ice-skate in the winter months or gather mushrooms in late summer and autumn.

SPRING

SPRING HAS SET IN for good when the first sunbathers gather on the beaches outside the Peter and Paul Fortress *(see pp66–7)* and when, in early April after the waterways have thawed, the city's bridges open to allow ships through.

To warm themselves up after the months of cold, locals celebrate "maslennitsa", the making of pancakes (*blini*) prior to Lent. They then gather bunches of willow as a symbol of the approaching Palm Sunday. On the eve of Lent, "Forgiveness Sunday", it is common practice to ask forgiveness of those you might have offended during the year.

Once the snows have gone, the first trips to the *dacha*, or country house, are made to put the gardens in order.

Early sunbathers on the banks of the Peter and Paul Fortress

MARCH

International Women's Day (*Mezhdunarodnyy den zhenshchin*), 8 Mar. Men rush around the city buying flowers for their womenfolk. It is a

Candles lighting up Russian Orthodox church during Easter service

tradition to say *s prazdnikom* (congratulations, on the holiday) to everyone. Theatres put on special performances and concerts and, however sexist it may seem to non-Russians, it is a very popular day.

From the Avant Garde to the Present (*Ot avangarda do segodnya*), mid-Mar. A celebration of 20th-century art and music in a city-wide festival.

Virtuosi 2000, late Mar/early Apr. Aspiring young musicians from all over the world come together to perform and compete on St Petersburg's stages.

Easter Sunday (*Paskha*). The dates on which Lent and Easter fall change every year. On Easter Sunday, St Petersburg churches are filled with worshippers, the evocative sound of ethereal music and chanting and the smell of incense. Russians traditionally greet each other with *Khristos voskres* (Christ is risen), to which the reply is *Voistine voskres* (He is truly risen).

APRIL

Musical Spring in St Petersburg (*Muzikalnaya Vesna v Sankt-Peterburge*), mid-Apr. As fur clothing and heavy boots are laid aside after the cold winter months, the public flock to concert halls throughout the city to hear St Petersburg's talented classical musicians celebrate the disappearance of the last snows.

Cosmonauts' Day (*Den Kosmonavtiki*), 12 Apr. Space exploration was one of the glories of the Soviet Union and this occasion is celebrated with fireworks at 10pm.

MAY

Victory Day (*Den Pobedy*), 9 May. After a rather sombre ceremony at Piskarevskoe Cemetery *(see p126)*, smartly-dressed veterans, festooned with medals and awards, fill Nevskiy prospekt *(see pp46–9)* and Palace Square *(see p83)* in commemoration of the Nazi surrender in 1945.

City Day (*Den goroda*), last week of May. To celebrate the day the city was founded, 27 May 1703, the City Day festival is packed full of events, from Peter the Great *(see p18)* look-alike contests to one of the most impressive fireworks displays to be held in the city all year. The manifold festivities all take place in and around the Peter and Paul Fortress *(see pp66–7)*.

Proud war veteran on Victory Day

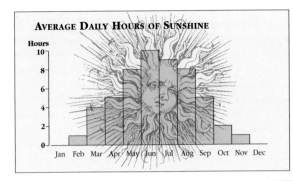

AVERAGE DAILY HOURS OF SUNSHINE

Hours

10 — 8 — 6 — 4 — 2 — 0

Jan Feb Mar Apr May Jun Jul Aug Sep Oct Nov Dec

Sunshine Hours
St Petersburg's climate can vary dramatically from hot, sunny days and occasional heavy downpours during the summer months, to winters with sub-zero temperatures and snow. From mid-June to mid-July, it never gets dark. During the winter months the days are extremely short, but there can be days of bright sunshine.

SUMMER

A LILAC IN FLOWER is the real symbol that warm weather has set in and there is an air of excitement once the Field of Mars *(see p94)* comes into bloom. Throughout the warm months, the city is deserted at weekends when people go off to their *dacha* usually situated around the pine forests in the area northwest of the city.

St Petersburg's main festive season is during the acclaimed White Nights in June, when the sun hardly sets and it never quite gets dark. Concerts, ballets and other performances take place all over the city, which fills with thousands of visitors *(see p193)*. The most favoured place to be at night-time is on the embankments of the Neva which are crowded with revellers watching the bridges being raised at 2am.

JUNE

Independence Day *(Den nezavisimosti)*, 12 Jun. The day Russia became "independent"

of the Soviet Union is marked with fireworks at 10pm.

Trinity Sunday *(Troytsa)*, 50 days after Easter. Believers and atheists alike go to tidy the graves of their loved ones and raise a glass of vodka for their souls. Hundreds of special buses are laid on to get to cemeteries further afield.

The White Nights Swing, Jazz Festival, mid-June. A large jam session supported by local and visiting musicians for anyone with an interest in jazz.

Stars of the White Nights, Classical Music Festival *(Zvezdy Belykh nochey)*, late Jun. This is the original White Nights festival, with first-class opera, classical music and ballet concerts performed at all major venues.

White Nights, Rock Music Festival *(Belye nochi)*, late Jun. Numerous outdoor rock concerts are held at the Peter and Paul Fortress *(see pp66–7)* featuring a jamboree of both local bands and internationally known groups.

Festival of Festivals *(Festival-festivaley)*, last week in Jun. This is an international

Russian battleships moored on the Neva, Navy Day

non-competitive film festival showing the best international films released over the past year. The festival attracts film stars from all over the world.

JULY

Handball on the Square *(Gandbol na Ploschadi)*, date variable. Palace Square *(see p83)* is transformed into a vast handball pitch for a day.

Volleyball by the Fortress *(Voleybol u Kreposti)*, date variable. Volleyball champion-ships take place on the beach by the Peter and Paul Fortress *(see pp66–7)*.

Navy Day *(Den Voenno-Morskovo Flota)*, first Sun after 22 July. The Neva resembles an enormous shipyard, with submarines and torpedo boats adorned with flags and bunting.

AUGUST

With schools on holiday and temperatures at their highest, most families escape to their *dacha* in the pine forests around the city. The majority of theatre groups also go on tour and many of the main theatres are closed.

Bridge opening in front of the Peter and Paul Fortress on a White Night

AVERAGE MONTHLY RAIN AND SNOWFALL

MM		Inches
100		4
80		3
60		2
40		1
20		
0		0

Jan Feb Mar Apr May Jun Jul Aug Sep Oct Nov Dec

Rain and Snow-fall Chart
St Petersburg summers are humid and wet, but the downpours are a welcome relief from the summer heat. In winter frequent snowfalls build up to create metre-high drifts, usually not thawing until late March.

■ Rainfall (from axis)

■ Snowfall (from axis)

AUTUMN

CITY LIFE begins to gain pace as people return from their *dacha* and children begin to prepare for the start of school. In the last weeks of August, St Petersburg is filled with posters heralding the advent of a new academic year and shops are packed with parents frantically buying school clothes and stationery.

In September, when theatres re-open after the summer break, the city's cultural life resumes. The Mariinskiy (Kirov) returns from touring, and new plays and operas are premiered. October marks the start of the festival season, with guest musicians and theatre groups from all over the world taking part.

The crisp autumn weather is ideal for gathering mushrooms. Popular hunting spots can be found to the northwest of the city around Zelenogorsk and Repino *(see p144)*. Enthusiastic mushroom-gatherers rise early to hunt for chanterelles, oyster mushrooms, *podberyozoviki* (brown mushrooms) and *podosinoviki* (orange-cap bolens). The locals are skilled in identifying edible mushrooms while amateur pickers should be aware of the dangers of poisonous ones.

Chanterelle mushrooms

An activity with fewer potential side-effects might be a trip on the hydrofoil to Peterhof

Children dressed up for Teachers' Day, the first day of school

(see pp146–9) to see the playful fountains before they are switched off for the winter.

SEPTEMBER

Teachers' Day
(Den uchiteley), 1 Sep. The city is full of children heading for their first day back at school, laden with flowers and gifts for their teachers.

OCTOBER

Theatre Festival of the Baltic Countries *(Teatralnyy festival Baltiyskikh stran)*, Oct. Actors, clowns and pantomime artists gather from the Baltic countries to perform in a few of the city's theatres with two weeks of mayhem.
Autumn in Tsarskoe Selo *(Osen v Tsarskom Sele)*, mid-Oct. A two-week festival of arts in the town of Tsarskoe Selo *(see pp150–53)*. Exhibitions, performance art and concerts are held. Frequent buses are laid on to and from the city.

NOVEMBER

Sound Ways, Modern Music Festival *(Zvukovyye puti)*, mid-Nov. Catch up with the most avant-garde trends in Russian and European jazz and modern classical music.

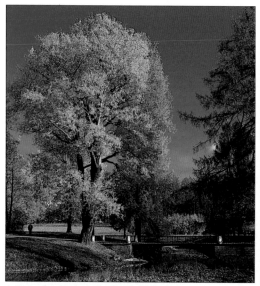

Autumn colours in the park at Tsarskoe Selo

Temperature Chart
St Petersburg's climate is maritime and milder than might be expected. Summers are warm and often punctuated with hot days as early as May, though during the winter months temperatures often fall below freezing. St Petersburg's average minimum and maximum temperatures throughout the year are shown in this chart.

WINTER

As the ice thickens on the waters and the snow deepens, people head for the outdoors once more. Children's sledges are not expensive to buy, and all other equipment can be hired. Cross-country skiing needs no lessons to make it fun. Tsarskoe Selo *(see pp150–53)* and Pavlovsk *(see pp156–9)* parks both provide ski and sledge hire at the ski bases *(lyzhnaya baza)*. Skates can be hired for use in the rink at Moskovskiy Park Pobedy, by Moskovskaya metro in the southern suburbs.

The truly hardened members of the local "walruses" swimming club break the ice by the Peter and Paul Fortress *(see pp66–7)* every day to take an early morning dip. The less courageous are welcome to stand by and watch.

In the midst of winter activities come New Year and Christmas. New Year is the big holiday, while Christmas itself is celebrated according to the Orthodox calendar, on 7 January. Many people also still celebrate Old New Year, which

Sledging on the frozen Neva outside the Hermitage *(see pp84–93)*

Drilling a hole through the ice for winter-time fishing

falls on 14 January. A seasonal delight is the traditional staging of the enchanting Christmas ballet, *The Nutcracker*, at the Mariinskiy Theatre *(see p119)*.

DECEMBER

Constitution Day *(Den konstitutsii)*, 12 Dec. When Yeltsin's new constitution replaced the Brezhnev version, a new constitution day replaced the old one. Fireworks are set off all over town at 10pm.

Musical Encounters in the Northern Palmyra *(Muzykalnyye vstrechi v Severnoy Palmire)*, Dec–Jan. This classical music festival is the last one of the year and is made even more magical by the outside backdrop of snowy streets and frozen waterways.

New Year's Eve *(Novyy god)*, 31 Dec. Still the biggest holiday of the year, New Year's Eve is best celebrated with the local "champagne", Shampanskoye *(see p179)*. This is considered to be a family celebration, with people dressed as Grandfather Frost (the Russian equivalent of Father Christmas) and the Snow Maiden, the traditional bearers of gifts.

JANUARY

Russian Orthodox Christmas *(Rozhdestvo)*, 7 Jan. Christmas is celebrated in a quieter fashion than Easter, with a traditional visit to an evening service on Christmas Eve (6th), when the church bells ring out all over the city.

FEBRUARY

Defenders of the Motherland Day *(Den zashchitnikov rodiny)*, 23 Feb. The male equivalent of Women's Day. Men are congratulated and given flowers and presents.

PUBLIC HOLIDAYS

New Year's Day (1 Jan)
Russian Orthodox Christmas (7 Jan)
International Women's Day (8 Mar)
Russian Orthodox Easter (Mar/Apr)
Labour Day (1 May)
Victory Day (9 May)
Independence Day (12 Jun)
Constitution Day (12 Dec)

St Petersburg
Area by Area

VASILEVSKIY ISLAND

I T WAS PETER THE GREAT'S intention that Vasilevskiy Island (*Vasilevskiy ostrov*), the largest island in the Neva delta, was to be the administrative heart of his new capital. However, lack of access (the first permanent bridge was not built until 1850) and the hazards of floods and stormy crossings led to the abandonment of Peter's project, and the centre grew up

Allegorical sculpture of Neptune on the façade of the National Museum

across the river around the Admiralty (*see p60*) instead. The island's original street plan, based on canals that were never dug (*see p20*), survives in the numbered streets known as lines

(*linii*), which run from north to south. The focal point of the island is at the east end with the fine ensemble of public buildings around the spit or Strelka. The rest of the island developed with the spread of industrialization in the 19th century and it became a middle-class haven. There was also a thriving German community here which is reflected in the several Lutheran churches. Today much of the island has a sedate air, with broad tree-lined avenues, a clutch of museums and some attractive 19th-century architecture.

SIGHTS AT A GLANCE

Museums
Kunstkammer ❹
Menshikov Palace ❻
Naval Museum ❷
Zoological Museum ❸

Historic Buildings and Monuments
Academy of Arts ❾
Rostral Columns ❶
Twelve Colleges ❺

Churches
St Andrew's Cathedral ❽

Streets and Bridges
Bolshoy Prospekt ❼
Lieutenant Shmidt Bridge ❿

KEY

▨	Street-by-Street map *See p58–9*
Ⓜ	Metro
🚊	Tram stop

0 metres 400

0 yards 400

◁ **One of the two imposing 14th-century BC sphinxes situated in front of the Academy of Arts**

Street-by-Street: the Strelka

THE EASTERN END of Vasilevskiy Island is known as the Strelka, or "spit". Once St Petersburg's main centre of commerce, it has become an area of learning. The Academy of Sciences and St Petersburg University are situated here, as are various museums, institutes and libraries, housed in the former warehouses and customs buildings. The nautical theme is preserved in the Naval Museum and the two Rostral Columns. In front of these lighthouses is a lawn, a popular spot for newly married couples to have their picture taken. From here there are views across the Neva towards the Peter and Paul Fortress *(see pp66–7)* and the Hermitage *(see pp84–93).*

The Naval Museum and Rostral Columns from across the Neva

The Lomonosov Monument honours Mikhail Lomonosov (1711–65), who taught at the Academy of Sciences.

Twelve Colleges
Originally erected to house the 12 ministries of Peter the Great's government, they now form the main building of St Petersburg University ❺

The Academy of Sciences was founded in 1724. The present building was constructed by Giacomo Quarenghi in 1783–5.

★ **Kunstkammer**
The Kunstkammer houses Peter the Great's collection of biological curiosities. Its tower, crowned by a sundial, is a St Petersburg landmark ❹

MENDELEEVSKAYA LINIYA

BIRZHEVOY PROEZD

UNIVERSITETSKAYA NABEREZHNAYA

Palace Embankment

DVORTSOVYY MOST

Zoological Museum
With over 100,000 specimens the museum is one of the finest of its kind in the world. The exhibits include a set of stuffed animals that belonged to Peter the Great and a world-famous collection of mammoths ❸

STAR SIGHTS
★ **Naval Museum**
★ **Kunstkammer**

Academy of Sciences Library
was founded in 1714 with Peter the Great's personal book collection. It now has over 17 million volumes.

PETROGRADSKAYA

Malaya Neva

VASILEVSKIY ISLAND

Bolshaya Neva

LOCATOR MAP
See Street Finder, map 1

The New Exchange Bazaar
was designed by Quarenghi in the early 19th century. At the time a busy market filled its Neo-Classical loggias. Today students have replaced the shoppers, as the building houses departments of the university.

NABEREZHNAYA MAKAROVA

ZHEVOY PROEZD

The Institute of Russian Literature
was built in 1832 as the Customs House. It now includes a literary museum.

BIRZHEVOY MOST

→ Peter and Paul Fortress

★ **Naval Museum**
Among the museum's many fine model boats is the botik, *also known as the "Grandfather of the Russian Navy", on which Peter the Great learnt to sail* ❷

RZHEVAYA PLOSHCHAD

Rostral Columns
Originally lighthouses guiding ships through the busy port of St Petersburg, these imposing 32-m (105-ft) high columns are a distinctive feature of St Petersburg's skyline. They are still lit for Navy Day (see p51) and other water festivals ❶

KEY

— — — Suggested route

0 metres   400
0 yards   400

Rostral Columns **❶**
Ростральные колонны
Rostralnye kolonny

Birzhevaya ploshchad. **Map** 1 C5.
Э1, 7, 10, Э47, T128, 492.
1, 7, 10.

Sɪᴛᴜᴀᴛᴇᴅ ᴏɴ the Strelka before the Naval Museum, the impressive twin russet-coloured Rostral Columns were designed as lighthouses by Thomas de Thomon in 1810. During the 19th century the oil lamps were replaced by gas torches which are still lit on ceremonial occasions such as Navy Day *(see p51)*. Following a Roman custom, the columns are decorated with protruding ships' prows in celebration of naval victories. The monumental figures around the base represent four of Russia's great rivers, the Neva, Volga, Dnieper and Volkhov.

Rostral Column on the Strelka

Naval Museum **❷**
Центральный
Военно-Морской музей
Tsentralnyy Voenno-Morskoy muzey

Birzhevaya ploshchad 4. **Map** 1 C5.
218 2502. Э1, 7, 10, 47, Э47, T128, 492. 1, 7, 10.
10:30am–5:30pm Wed–Sun.
English.

Tʜᴇ ꜰᴏʀᴍᴇʀ Stock Exchange *(birzha)* was built in 1805–10 as the focal point of the Strelka. The building was designed by the Swiss architect Thomas de Thomon and was modelled on one of the famous Greek temples at Paestum in Italy. Above the columned east façade is an allegorical sculpture featuring the sea-god Neptune in a chariot drawn by sea horses; a reminder that maritime

commerce was traditionally the lifeblood of this sea-oriented city.

The exchange became redundant after the Revolution and in 1940 it was turned into a museum. Beneath the magnificent coffered ceiling of the spacious trading hall is an exhibition on the history of the Russian and Soviet navy from its origins under Peter the Great to the present day. Pride of place belongs to the *botik*, the small masted wooden vessel on which Peter learned to sail. There is plenty of interest besides, from model ships and carved prow figureheads to uniforms, flags and guided missile submarines. There is also a superb diorama of the storming of the Winter Palace *(see pp28–9)* on the second-floor landing.

The photographic displays around the hall concentrate on the revolutionary period. These were redesigned only in 1995 to present a more balanced view of events, such as the involvement of Western powers in World War II.

Neo-Classical façade of the Naval Museum, overlooking the Strelka

Zoological Museum **❸**
Зоологический музей
Zoologicheskiy muzey

Universitetskaya naberezhnaya 1/3.
Map 1 C5. 218 0112. Э1, 7, 10, Э47, T128, 492. 1, 7, 10.
11am–5pm Sat–Thu.
English.

Hᴏᴜsᴇᴅ ɪɴ a former customs warehouse designed by Giovanni Lucchini in 1826, this museum has one of the world's largest natural history collections containing more than 100,000 specimens. Some of the stuffed animals belonged to Peter the Great's *Kunstkammer* collection, including the horse he rode at the Battle of Poltava *(see p18)*.

Dioramas atmospherically recreate natural habitats for giant crabs, weasels, polar bears and blue whales. The museum is renowned for its collection of mammoths. The most prized carcass was exhumed from the frozen wastes of Siberia in 1902 and is almost 44,000 years old.

Weasel in the Zoological Museum

Kunstkammer **❹**
Кунсткамера
Kunstkamera

Universitetskaya naberezhnaya 3.
Map 1 C5. 218 1412. Э1, 7, 10, Э47, T128, 492. 1, 7, 10.
11am–6pm Fri–Wed.
English.

Tʜᴇ ᴅᴇʟɪᴄᴀᴛᴇ, sea green lantern tower of the Baroque Kunstkammer ("art chamber") is visible across this part of Vasilevskiy Island. The building, by Georg Mattarnovyy, was constructed in 1718–34 to exhibit Peter the Great's infamous *Kunstkammer* collection. While touring Holland in 1697 Peter attended the lectures of Frederik Ruysch (1638–1731),

The restrained Baroque façade of the Kunstkammer (1718–34), St Petersburg's first museum

the most celebrated anatomist of his day. He was so impressed with Ruysch's collection of rarities that on a return visit in 1717, he purchased the entire collection of over 2,000 anatomical preparations. He transported it to St Petersburg and exhibited it to a wide-eyed public, who were enticed by free glasses of vodka. At the time, Peter's collection also included bizarre, live exhibits of deformed or unusual people, including an hermaphrodite. This, Russia's first museum, also included a library, an anatomical theatre and an observatory.

Today the Kuntskammer houses the Museum of Anthropology and Ethnography, with the remnants of Peter's bizarre collection on display in the central rotunda. Included are the heart and skeleton of Peter's personal servant, "Bourgeois", a giant at 2.27 m (7.5 ft), and a cabinet of teeth extracted by the tsar who was an enthusiastic amateur dentist. Most gruesome of all is the collection of pickled oddities which include Siamese twins and a two-headed sheep.

The halls surrounding the *Kuntskammer* collection contain exhibitions on the peoples of the world. Unfairly neglected by most foreign visitors, these marvellously old-fashioned displays present a vast and informative range of artifacts, from an Inuit kayak to Javanese shadow puppets.

Twelve Colleges ❺
Двенадцать коллегий
Dvenadtsat kollegiy

Universitetskaya naberezhnaya 7.
Map 1 C5. 🚌 *7, 47, Э47, T128, 492.* 🚊 *10.* ⬤ *to public.*

THIS DISTINGUISHED Baroque building of red-and-white stuccoed brick is almost 400 m (1,300 ft) in length. It was intended for Peter the Great's newly-streamlined administration of 12 colleges or ministries. The single, uninterrupted façade was designed to symbolize the government's unity of purpose, while the curious alignment, at right angles to the embankment, is explained by Peter's unrealized plan for a large

Mikhail Lomonosov (1711–65)

A section of the west façade of Trezzini's Twelve Colleges

square with an unbroken view across the Strelka. Another popular theory is that Prince Menshikov changed the plan in Peter's absence so that the building would not encroach on his grounds. Domenico Trezzini won the competition for the design in 1723, but subsequent bureaucratic wrangling delayed its completion for 20 years. The building's function gradually changed and in 1819 part of it was acquired by St Petersburg University. A string of revolutionaries, including Lenin in 1891, were educated here. Among the famous Russian lecturers to teach here were the chemist Dmitriy Mendeleev (1834–1907) *(see p45)* and the physiologist Ivan Pavlov (1849–1936) *(see p45)*.

Overlooking the Neva, outside the Twelve Colleges, is the engaging bronze statue of the great 18th-century polymath Mikhail Lomonosov (unveiled in 1986). The son of a fisherman, Lomonosov was the first Russian-born member of the nearby Academy of Sciences. A "universal genius", he wrote poetry, systematized Russian grammar and was a pioneer in mathematics and the physical sciences. Thanks to his scientific discoveries, the art of porcelain, glass and mosaic production began in Russia.

The southern façade of Prince Menshikov's 18th-century palace

Menshikov Palace ➏

Меншиковский дворец

Menshikovskiy dvorets

Universitetskaya naberezhnaya 15.
Map 5 B1. 🄲 213 1112. 🚌 7, 47,
947, T128. 🚃 10. 🕐 10:30am–
4:30pm Tue–Sun. 🎟 11. 🄰
🎦 compulsory (English available).

THE OCHRE-PAINTED Baroque
Menshikov Palace, with
its beautifully carved pilasters,
was one of the earliest stone
buildings in St Petersburg. Designed by Giovanni Fontana
and Gottfried Schädel for the
infamous Prince Menshikov,
the palace was completed in
1720. The palace estate originally extended as far as the
Malaya Neva river to the north.

Prince Menshikov entertained
here on a lavish scale, often
on behalf of Peter the Great,
who adopted the palace as a
pied-à-terre. Guests would

cross the Neva by boat and
arrive to the grand welcome
of a liveried orchestra.

The palace is now a branch
of the Hermitage (*see pp84–
93*), housing a collection on
early 18th-century Russian culture which successfully evokes
the spirit of the age and reveals the extent to which
Peter the Great's court was
influenced by Western tastes.

The conducted tour begins
on the ground floor; besides
the kitchen there are displays
of Peter's cabinet making
tools, period costumes, sturdy
oak chests and ships' com-
passes. Adorning the beautiful
vaulted hallway are marble
statues imported from Italy
which include a Roman Apollo
dating to the 2nd century AD.

Upstairs, the secretary's
rooms are decorated with 17th-
century Dutch engravings of
Leyden, Utrecht and Kraków.
A series of breathtaking rooms
are lined with hand-painted
blue and white 18th-century
Dutch tiles. Tiles were not
only fashionable, but
also a very practical
means of deterring
flies and dust.

In the tiled bed-
room of Varvara
(Menshikov's
sister-in-law and
confidante) is a
German-made
four-poster bed,
with a Turkish coverlet
woven from cotton, silk
and silver thread. Hanging
behind it is an exquisite 17th-
century Flemish tapestry.

Menshikov and Peter often
received guests in the aptly
named Walnut Study which
has Persian walnut panelling
and commanding views of
the Neva. Paintings hang from
coloured ribbons, as was the

fashion, including a late 17th-
century portrait of Peter the
Great by the Dutch painter Jan
Weenix. The mirrors were a
novelty at that time and such
displays of vanity were ana-
thema to the Orthodox Church.

The Great Hall, decorated
in gold and stucco, is where
balls and banquets were held.
On one famous occasion, it
was the setting for a "dwarfs'
wedding" which Menshikov
arranged for the amusement
of his royal master.

**The fine, Style-Moderne *apteka*,
just off Bolshoy prospekt**

Bolshoy Prospekt ➐

Большой проспект

Bolshoy prospekt

Map 1 A5. Ⓜ *Vasileostrovskaya.*

THIS IMPOSING AVENUE was
opened early in the 18th
century to connect Menshikov's
estate to the Gulf of Finland.
It was widened in the 1930s.

The mix of architectural
styles ranges from the elegant
Neo-Classicism of St Catherine's
Lutheran Church (1768–71) at
No. 1 to the simple Troyekurov
House (No. 13, 6-ya liniya) in
17th-century Petrine Baroque.

Other buildings of note include the arcaded St Andrew's
food market (1789–90) and
two Style-Moderne edifices.
One of these is the former
pharmacy or *apteka* (1907–10)
around the corner on 7-ya
liniya, with its fine mosaics
and tiling, and the other,
Adolph Gaveman's Lutheran
orphanage at No. 55 (1908).

PRINCE MENSHIKOV

A leading advisor, com-
rade-in-arms and
friend of Peter the
Great, Aleksandr
Menshikov
(1673–1729)
rose from hum-
ble origins to
his position as
the first governor
of St Petersburg.
After Peter's death
in 1725, Menshikov
engineered the ascension
of Catherine I (Peter's wife,
and Menshikov's former
mistress) to the throne, thus
maintaining his power until
her demise. His notorious
extravagance and venality
eventually caught up with
him. Accused of treason,
he died in exile in 1729.

The Academy of Arts (1764–88) on the Neva embankment, an example of early Russian Neo-Classicism

St Andrew's Cathedral ❽

Андреевский собор
Andreevskiy sobor

6-ya liniya 11. **Map** 5 B1.
Ⓜ *Vasileostrovskaya.* ♿

F IRST BUILT under the initiative of Peter the Great's
second wife, Catherine I *(see
p21)*, who donated 3,000
rubles towards its construction,
the original wooden church on
this site was destroyed by fire.

The present Baroque church
with its distinctive steeple-like
bell tower was constructed by
Aleksandr Vist in 1764–80.
The most stunning feature of
the interior is the elaborately
carved 18th-century iconostasis which incorporates icons
from the original church.

**The treasure of St Andrew's Cathedral, its
beautiful Baroque iconostasis**

Situated next door is Giuseppe
Trezzini's small Church of the
Three Saints (1740–60) which
is dedicated to SS Basil the
Great, John Chrysostom and
Gregory of Nazianzus.

Academy of Arts ❾

Академия Художеств
Akademiya Khudozhestv

Universitetskaya naberezhnaya 17.
Map 5 B1. Ⓒ *213 3578.*
Ⓜ *Vasileostrovskaya.* ◯ *11am–6pm
Wed–Sun.* 🖼 🎫

F OUNDED in 1757 to train
home-grown artists in the
preferred Western styles and
techniques of art, the Academy
spawned a galaxy of talent,
including the great painter
Ilya Repin *(see p42)* and
architects Andrey Zakharov
(1761–1811) and
Andrey Voronikhin
(1759–1814).

The innate con-
servatism of the
Academy tended to
discourage innova-
tion and experiment
and in 1863 a band
of 14 students
walked out of their
graduation exams in
protest. They went
on to found a realist
art movement and
became known as
the Wanderers or
peredvizhniki
(see pp106–7).

The imposing
Academy, built be-
tween 1764–88 by
Aleksandr Kokorinov
and Vallin de la
Mothe, is an exam-
ple of the transition
from Baroque to
Neo-Classicism. Still

an art school, it exhibits the
work of students past and
present, including canvases,
plaster casts of famous sculptures, architectural drawings
and models of many of the
city's notable buildings, such
as the magnificent Smolnyy
Convent *(see p128)*.

The splendid Neo-Classical
halls and galleries, though
faded, retain something of
their original grandeur. Of note
are the Conference Hall on
the first floor, with its ceiling
painting by Vasiliy Shebuev,
and the adjoining Raphael
and Titian galleries, adorned
with copies of Vatican frescoes.

Flanking the river stairs
outside the Academy are two
sphinxes from the 14th century
BC. Discovered among the
ruins of Thebes in ancient
Egypt, they were installed
here in 1832. The faces are
thought to bear a likeness of
the pharaoh Amenhotep III.

Lieutenant Shmidt Bridge ❿

Мост Лейтенанта Шмидта
Most Leytenanta Shmidta

Map 5 B2. 🚎 *1, 5, 11, 31.*

O RIGINALLY KNOWN as the
Nicholas Bridge, this was
the first permanent crossing
of the Neva when it opened
in 1850. The reconstruction of
the bridge which was carried
out in 1936–8 incorporated
Aleksandr Bryullov's original
railings, fancifully decorated
with sea horses and tridents.

The bridge commemorates
Lieutenant Pyotr Shmidt, a
sailor on the cruiser *Ochakov*,
who led an uprising of the
Black Sea fleet in 1905 and was
executed shortly afterwards.

PETROGRADSKAYA

THE CITY was founded on the northern banks of the Neva river in 1703, at the height of the Great Northern War (see p18). Building began with the construction of a wooden fortress and Petrogradskaya, or the Petrograd Side, soon became a marshy suburb of wooden cabins occupied by craftsmen working on Peter the Great's new city.

Nearby, the area around Trinity Square was originally a small merchants' quarter centred around a now demolished church and St Petersburg's first stock exchange.

Detail on bridge to Peter and Paul Fortress

Petrogradskaya was sparsely populated until the late 1890s when the construction of the Trinity Bridge made the area accessible from the city centre. The bridge caused a housing boom at the height of a fashion for Style-Moderne architecture which is still in evidence today. The population quadrupled and the area became very popular with artists and professionals.

The highlight of the area, which is still largely residential, is the Peter and Paul Fortress with its cathedral, museums and grim history.

SIGHTS AT A GLANCE

Museums
Artillery Museum **7**
Cabin of Peter the Great **13**
Commandant's House **4**
Cruiser Aurora **12**
Engineer's House **2**
Kirov Museum **10**
Kshesinskaya Mansion **11**
Trubetskoy Bastion **6**

Gates
Neva Gate **5**
Peter Gate **1**

Cathedrals
Cathedral of SS Peter and Paul **3**

Streets, Squares and Parks
Aleksandrovskiy Park **8**
Kamennoostrovskiy Prospekt **9**
Trinity Square **14**

| 0 metres | 400 |
| 0 yards | 400 |

KEY

	Street-by-Street map See pp66–67
M	Metro
	Tram stop
	River boat stop

◁ **The Baroque Cathedral of SS Peter and Paul in the Peter and Paul Fortress**

Street-by-Street: Peter and Paul Fortress

THE FOUNDING OF the Peter and Paul Fortress in 1703, on the orders of Peter the Great, is considered to mark the founding of the city itself. The fortress was first built in wood and was later replaced, section by section, in stone by Domenico Trezzini. Its history is a gruesome one, since hundreds of forced labourers died while building the fortress and its bastions were later used to guard and torture many political prisoners, including Peter's own son Alexis.

The cells where prisoners were once kept are open to the public, alongside a couple of museums and the magnificent cathedral which houses the tombs of the Romanovs.

Artillery Museum *(see p70)*

Kronverkskiy most

The Archives of the War Ministry occupy the site of the "Secret House", a prison for political criminals in the 18th and 19th centuries.

Zotov Bastion

Trubetskoy Bastion
From 1872–1921 the dark, damp, solitary-confinement cells in the bastion served as a grim prison for enemies of the state. Today, the bastion is open to visitors **6**

The Mint, founded in 1724, still produces ceremonial coins, medals and badges.

The beach is popular in summer and in winter, when members of the "walruses" swimming club break the ice for an invigorating dip.

The Naryshkin Bastion (1725) is where the noon cannon is fired. The tradition began in 1873, stopped after the revolution and was resumed in 1957.

Commandant's House
For 150 years this attractive Baroque house was the scene of interrogations and trials of political prisoners. It now houses a museum of local history **4**

Neva Gate
This riverside entrance, also known as "Death Gateway", leads to the Commandant's pier from which prisoners embarked on their journey to execution or exile. The Neva river's flood levels (see p37) are recorded under the arch **10**

★ SS Peter and Paul Cathedral

Marbled columns, glittering chandeliers and painted decor combine with Ivan Zarudnyy's carved and gilded iconostasis to create a magnificent setting for the tombs of the Romanov monarchs ❸

The Boat House is now a souvenir shop.

Golovkin Bastion

The Grand Ducal burial vault is the last resting place of several Grand Dukes shot by the Bolsheviks in 1919 and of Grand Duke Vladimir who died in exile in 1992.

LOCATOR MAP
See Street Finder, map 2

Peter Gate
The entrance to the fortress, by Domenico Trezzini, completed in 1718, features the Romanov double eagle with an emblem of St George and the dragon ❶

STAR SIGHT

★ SS Peter and Paul Cathedral

| 0 metres | 100 |
| 0 yards | 100 |

Ticket office

Ivan Gate, in the outer wall, was constructed from 1731–40.

Ioannovskiy most

Kamennoostrovskiy prospekt, Gorkovskaya Metro and Trinity Bridge

This statue of Peter the Great is by Mikhail Chemiakin (1991). **Peter I Bastion**

Engineer's House
This building, dating from 1748–9, houses temporary exhibitions of artifacts used in everyday life in St Petersburg before the revolution ❷

KEY

– – – Suggested route

Peter Gate ❶
Петровские ворота
Petrovskie vorota

Petropavlovskaya krepost.
Map 2 E3. Ⓜ *Gorkovskaya.*

THE MAIN ENTRANCE to the
Peter and Paul Fortress is
through two contrasting arches.
The plain Neo-Renaissance
Ivan Gate (1730s) leads to the
more imposing Peter Gate
(1717–18), an ornate Baroque
structure with scrolled wings
and a rounded-gable pediment.
Domenico Trezzini redesigned
the Peter Gate, retaining Karl
Osner's expressively carved
bas-relief which allegorizes
Peter the Great's victory over
Charles XII of Sweden *(see
p18)*. It depicts St Peter
casting down the winged
sorcerer Simon Magus who
attempts to soar above him.

Peter Gate, entrance to fortress

Engineer's House ❷
Инженерный дом
Inzhenernyy dom

Petropavlovskaya krepost. **Map** 2 D3.
📞 *238 4540.* Ⓜ *Gorkovskaya.*
🕐 *11am–6pm Thu–Tue.* 🎫
🇬🇧 *English.*

THE ENGINEER'S HOUSE, built
in 1748–9, has a changing
exhibition which gives a
fascinating glimpse of daily
life in St Petersburg before
the Revolution. Architectural
backdrops and historical paintings give way to an engaging
miscellany of artifacts, ranging
from old shop fronts to model
boats, duelling pistols, court
costumes and ball masks.
In 1915 there were more
than 100 outlets selling musical instruments in the city

**An accordion and organ surrounded by Style-
Moderne furniture, Engineer's House**

and the museum displays
an excellent collection which
includes phonographs, gramo-
phones, symphoniums and
piano accordions of the period.
A section on vintage tech-
nology features Singer sewing
machines, typewriters, Bakelite
telephones and box cameras.

Cathedral of
SS Peter and Paul ❸
Петропавловский собор
Petropavlovskiy sobor

Petropavlovskaya krepost. **Map** 2 D4.
📞 *238 4540.* Ⓜ *Gorkovskaya.*
🕐 *11am–6pm Thu–Tue.* 🎫
🇬🇧 *English.*

DOMENICO TREZZINI designed
this magnificent church
within the fortress in 1712.
Employed by Peter the Great,
who wished to turn his back
on traditional Russian church
architecture, Trezzini produced

a Baroque master-
piece of singular
elegance. The bell
tower was com-
pleted first to test
the foundations and
this served as an
excellent viewpoint
from which Peter
could oversee the
construction work
of his new city. The
cathedral was com-
pleted in 1733, but
was badly damaged
by fire in 1756 when
the soaring 122-m
(400-ft) spire was struck by
lightning. The gilded needle
spire, crowned by a weather-
vane angel, remained the
tallest structure in St Petersburg until the building of the
TV transmitter in the 1960s.
The interior, with its glittering chandeliers, pink and
green Corinthian columns and
overarching vaults, is also a
far cry from the traditional
Russian Orthodox church.
Even the iconostasis, culminating in a triumphal arch, is a
Baroque flight of fancy. This
masterpiece of gilded wood-
carving was designed by Ivan
Zarudniy and executed in the
1720s by Moscow craftsmen.
After Peter's death in 1725,
the cathedral became the last
resting place of the tsars. The
sarcophagi are all of a uniform
white Carrara marble, except
the tombs of Alexander II and
his wife Maria Alexandrovna,
which are carved from Altai

Cathedral of SS Peter and Paul, with Dvortsovyy most in foreground

jasper and Ural rhodonite. Peter the Great's tomb, with a bronze bust often adorned with fresh flowers, lies to the right of the iconostasis.

The only tsars not buried here are Peter II, Ivan VI and, until recently, Nicholas II. In 1998 a controversial decision was taken to rebury the remains of the last Romanov tsar, his wife and children, and the servants that died together with them, in the cathedral.

The Grand Ducal Mausoleum, where relatives of the tsars are buried, was added to the northeast of the cathedral at the end of the 19th century.

Commandant's House ❹

Комендантский дом
Komendantskiy dom

Petropavlovskaya krepost. **Map** 2 D4.
☎ 238 4540. **Ⓜ** *Gorkovskaya.*
⏰ 11am–6pm Thu–Tue. **⏸**
✔ English.

DATING FROM the 1740s, the plain brick, two-storey Commandant's House served both as the residence of the fortress commander and as a courthouse. Over the years, political prisoners, including the Decembrist rebels *(see p23)*, were brought here for interrogation and sentencing.

The house is now a museum, with a ground-floor exhibition on medieval settlements in the St Petersburg region, and temporary exhibitions upstairs.

Neva Gate ❺

Невские ворота
Nevskie vorota

Petropavlovskaya krepost. **Map** 2 E4.
Ⓜ *Gorkovskaya.*

THIS AUSTERE river entrance to the fortress was once known as the "Death Gate". Prisoners to be transported to the even more notorious Schlüsselburg Fortress (to the east of St Petersburg) for capital punishment, or to a "living death" in penal servitude, were led down the granite steps and taken away by boat. The appropriately dour, grey gateway dates from

Neva Gate leading from the river into the Peter and Paul Fortress

1784–7 and is unornamented apart from an anchor in the pediment. In the archway, brass plaques mark record flood levels. The catastrophic inundation of November 1824 is the one commemorated in Pushkin's poem, *The Bronze Horseman (see p78)*.

Trubetskoy Bastion ❻

Трубецкой бастион
Trubetskoy bastion

Petropavlovskaya krepost. **Map** 2 D4.
☎ 238 4540. **Ⓜ** *Gorkovskaya.*
⏰ 11am–6pm Thu–Tue. **⏸**
✔ English.

PETER THE GREAT'S SON, the Tsarevich Alexis, was the first political prisoner to be detained in the grim fortress prison. Unjustly accused of treason in 1718 by his overbearing father, Alexis escaped abroad only to be lured back to Russia with the promise of

a pardon. Instead, he was tortured and beaten to death, almost certainly with Peter's consent and participation.

For the next 100 years prisoners were incarcerated in the much feared Secret House, since demolished. In 1872 a new prison block opened in the Trubetskoy Bastion which has existed as a museum since 1924. On the ground floor there is a small exhibition of period photographs, prison uniforms and a model of the guardroom. Upstairs are 69 isolation cells, restored to their original appearance, while downstairs there are two unheated, unlit punishment cells where the recalcitrant were locked up for 48 hours at a time. Once every two weeks, all detainees were taken to the Bath House in the exercise yard for de-lousing. Here prisoners were also put in irons before being carted off to penal servitude in Siberia.

POLITICAL PRISONERS

The fortress' sinister role as a prison for political activists continued until after the Revolution. Generations of rebels and anarchists were interrogated and imprisoned here, including Leon Trotsky in the wake of the 1905 Revolution. Other prominent detainees were the leading Decembrists in 1825 *(see p23)*, Dostoevsky in 1849 *(see p123)* and, in 1874–6, the anarchist Prince Pyotr Kropotkin. In 1917 it was the turn first of the tsar's ministers, then of members of the Provisional Government. Then, during the Civil War, the Bolsheviks held hostage four Romanov Grand Dukes who were subsequently executed in 1919 *(see p27)*.

Leon Trotsky (1879–1940) in the Trubetskoy Bastion

Rocket launcher in the courtyard of the Artillery Museum

Artillery Museum **❼**
Музей Артиллерии
Muzey Artillerii

Kronverk. **Map** 2 D3. **M** *Gorkovskaya.*
☎ *232 0296.* **◯** *11am–5pm
Wed–Sun.* **📷**

THIS VAST, horseshoe-shaped
building in red brick stands
on the site of the Kronverk,
the outer fortifications of the
Peter and Paul Fortress *(see
pp66–67)*. Designed by Pyotr
Tamanskiy and constructed in
1849–60, the building was
originally used as the arsenal.

The museum boasts more
than 600 pieces of artillery
and military vehicles, including
tanks. There are uniforms,
regimental flags, muskets
and small arms dating back
to medieval times, as well as
several rooms devoted to
World War II. A star exhibit
is the armoured car in which
Lenin rode in triumph from
Finland Station *(see p126)* to
Kshesinskaya Mansion *(see
p72)* on 3 April 1917.

Aleksandrovskiy Park **❽**
Александровский парк
Aleksandrovskiy park

Kronverkskiy prospekt. **Map** 2 D3.
M *Gorkovskaya.* **♿**

THE PARK'S UNIQUE character
as a centre of popular
culture and entertainment was
established in the year 1900
with the inauguration of the
Nicholas II People's House.
This was where pantomime
artists, wild animal trainers,
magicians and circus acts

entertained the crowds, while
the more serious-minded were
drawn to the lecture halls,
reading galleries and tea
rooms. The *pièce de résistance*
was the magnificent domed
Opera House (1911), where
the legendary bass singer,
Fyodor Shalyapin, sometimes
gave performances.

Today the Opera
House offers less
highbrow entertain-
ment, as its change
of name to Music Hall
suggests. The adjoin-
ing buildings, erected
in the late 1930s, in-
clude the innovatory
Baltic House Theatre
and the Planetarium.

The park still draws crowds
on summer weekends and
public holidays, although some
of the attractions, especially
the zoo, are now rather tawdry.

Kamennoostrovskiy Prospekt **❾**
Каменноостровский проспект
Kamennoostrovskiy prospekt

Map 2 D2. **M** *Gorkovskaya.*

DEVELOPED DURING the con-
struction boom of the late
1890s, this eye-catching avenue
is noted for its Style-Moderne
architecture. The first house,
at No. 1–3 (1899–1904) was
designed by one of the leading
proponents of the style, Fyodor
Lidval. The multi-textured
façade, windows of contrasting
shapes and sizes, ornate iron
balconies and fanciful carvings
are the most typical features
of this Russian version of Art
Nouveau. The neighbouring

house (No. 5) was once occupied by Count Sergey Witte,
a leading industrialist who
negotiated the peace treaty
with Japan in 1905 *(see p26)*.

Situated just off the start of
the avenue is the city's only
mosque (1910–14). Designed
by Russian architects, its mina-
rets, majolica tiling and the
rough granite surfaces of the
walls are fully in keeping with
the surrounding Style-Moderne
architecture. The mosque was,
in fact, modelled on the
Mausoleum of Tamerlane in
Samarkand and involved
Central Asian craftsmen.

At No. 10 is the tall portico
of the Leningrad Film Studios
(Lenfilm). It was on this site,
in May 1896, that the Lumière
brothers showed the first moving picture in Russia. Since its
founding in 1918, some of the
most innovative Soviet film
directors such as Leonid Trauberg and Grigoriy
Kozintsev *(see p70)*
have worked there.

At the intersection
with ulitsa Mira, each
house has indivi-
dually designed
turrets, spires, reliefs
and iron balconies
forming a handsome
Style-Moderne

**Griffon, No. 1–3
Kamennoostrovskiy**

ensemble. Other buildings of
interest include No. 24
(1896–1912), with its red
brick majolica and terracotta
façade; No. 26–28 where
Sergey Kirov lived *(see p72)*;
and on the corner of Bolshoy
prospekt, the "Turreted House"
with its Neo-Gothic portal.

**Turreted House (1913–15),
Kamennoostrovskiy prospekt**

Style Moderne in St Petersburg

IN VOGUE throughout Europe from the 1890s to the 1900s, Art Nouveau marked a break with imitation of the past. The movement, known as Style Moderne in Russia, began in the decorative arts and was then reflected in architecture, where it led to an abundance of ornamental elements. Inspired by new industrial techniques, artists and architects made lavish use of natural stone and brick, wrought iron, stucco, coloured glass and ceramic tiles.

Kshesinskaya Mansion railing detail

Dominated by sinuous and undulating lines, with a predominance of floral and vegetal elements, even traditional forms such as doors and windows are broken up, distorted or given unexpected curves.

In fin-de-siècle St Petersburg, the Style Moderne flourished as the city underwent a building boom, particularly on Petrogradskaya. The city became a showcase for the talents of leading architects such as Fyodor Lidval and Aleksandr von Gogen.

Kshesinskaya Mansion reveals von Gogen's relatively severe version of Style Moderne. Asymmetrical in composition, it is enlivened with wrought iron and glazed tiles (see p72).

Yeliseev's is evidence of the skill of Gavriil Baranovskiy, who made excellent use of industrial techniques in the creation of large window spaces. The rich exterior detailing is matched by elegant shop-fittings and chandeliers inside (see p109).

28 Bolshaya Zelenina ulitsa is one of the most outstanding examples of the use of stylized animal and fish motifs and a variety of surface decoration techniques. Fyodor von Postel's 1904–5 apartment block is reminiscent of the work of his contemporary, the Catalan architect Gaudí.

1–3 Kamennoostrovskiy pr is the work of St Petersburg's master of Style Moderne, Fyodor Lidval. Delicate details such as floral and animal reliefs stand out against a background of discreetly elongated proportions and unusual window shapes.

House of Books (1910–14) reveals Pavel Syuzer's use of an unusually eclectic mix of architectural styles. Ornate Style-Moderne wrought-iron balconies and decorative wooden window frames combine with elements of Renaissance and Baroque revivals.

Portrait of Sergey Kirov made of feathers (1933–4), Kirov Museum

Kirov Museum ➓

Музей С. М. Кирова

Muzey S M Kirova

Kamennoostrovskiy prospekt 26–28, 4th floor. **Map** 2 D1. 🄲 *346 1481*. 🅼 *Petrogradskaya.* 🕒 *11am–5.30pm Thu–Tue.* 🖼

FROM 1926–36 this flat was home to one of Stalin's closest political associates, Sergey Kirov. As the charismatic first Secretary of the Leningrad Communist Party, Kirov soon gained national importance. His increasing popularity led Stalin to see in him a potential rival. On 1 December 1934, Kirov was gunned down at his office at the Smolnyy Institute *(see p128)* by Leonid Nikolaev, a party malcontent. Stalin used the assassination as an excuse to launch the Great Purges *(see p27)*, although most historians believe Stalin himself was behind Kirov's murder.

Kirov acquired the status of a martyr after his death, with countless buildings named in his honour. His apartment has been preserved as it was in his lifetime. It is a unique example of the reverent, near cult-like status awarded Party leaders, with not only documents and photographs chronicling Kirov's political career, but a touching array of memorabilia including Kirov's shooting attire and favourite books.

Kshesinskaya Mansion ➓

Особняк М. Кшесинской

Osobnyak M Kshesinskoy

Ulitsa Kuybysheva 4. **Map** 2 E3. 🄲 *233 7052.* 🅼 *Gorkovskaya.* 🕒 *10am–5pm Fri–Wed.* 🖼 🖼

THIS REMARKABLE example of Style-Moderne architecture was commissioned for prima ballerina Matilda Kshesinskaya. Designed in 1904 by the court architect, AI Gogen, the building is almost playfully asymmetric with a single, octagonal tower. Most eye-catching of all are the many contrasting building materials with bands of pink and grey granite, cream-coloured bricks, delicately ornamented iron railings and majolica tiles.

The most impressive interior is the splendid recital hall with its pillared archway and palms. Nearby, the Kshesinskaya memorial room has some of the dancer's possessions, including sketches of Nicholas II.

In March 1917 the mansion was commandeered by the Bolsheviks and became their headquarters and, on Lenin's return to Russia *(see p126)*, he addressed the crowds from the balcony facing the square.

The mansion, previously home to a museum glorifying the October Revolution, now houses a Museum of Russian Political History. On the first floor the Bolshevik Party secretariat and Lenin's office have been faithfully restored. Upstairs is a fascinating collection of memorabilia from the revolutionary era, including Communist posters, Nicholas II coronation mugs and even a police file on Rasputin's murder *(see p121)*.

The final exhibition (ground floor), entitled "Democracy or Dictatorship?", traces Russia's troubled political history via documents, photographs and artifacts, with a section on each of Russia's pre-revolutionary political parties.

MATILDA KSHESINSKAYA

One of the finest prima ballerinas ever to grace the stage of the Mariinskiy Theatre *(see p119)*, Matilda Kshesinskaya (1872–1971) graduated from the Imperial Ballet School *(see p118)* in 1890. She was equally famous for her celebrated affair with the tsarevich, later Tsar Nicholas II, which began soon after she graduated. Kshesinskaya emigrated to Paris in 1920 where she married the Grand Duke Andrey Vladimirovich, another member of the imperial family and the father of her 11-year old son. It was in Paris that she wrote her controversial memoirs, *Dancing in St Petersburg*, which tells the tale of her affair with the last Russian tsar.

AI Gogen's elegant recital hall in the Kshesinskaya Mansion

The historic cruiser Aurora (1900), moored in front of the Neo-Baroque Nakhimov Naval Academy (1912)

Cruiser Aurora ⓬
Крейсер Аврора
Kreyser Avrora

Petrogradskaya naberezhnaya 4.
Map 2 F3. 📞 230 8440. 🚌 6, 30, 54, 63. ⏰ 10:30am–4pm Tue–Thu, Sat & Sun. 📷 for a fee. Phone to book.

ACCORDING to the annals of the Revolution, at 9:40pm on 25 October 1917, the cruiser *Aurora* signalled the storming of the Winter Palace *(see p28)*, by firing a single blank round from its bow gun.

Completed in 1900, the vast cruiser was put into active service in 1903. It was later converted into a training ship and at the start of the Siege of Leningrad *(see p27)* it was sunk to protect it from German forces. The ship was raised in 1944, 950 days later, and has been a museum since 1956. The famous gun, bell and the crew's quarters can be viewed, along with an exhibition on the history of the *Aurora*.

Cabin of Peter the Great ⓭
Музей-домик Петра I
Muzey-domik Petra I

Petrovskaya naberezhnaya 6. **Map** 2 F3. 📞 232 4576. Ⓜ Gorkovskaya. ⏰ 10am–6pm Wed–Mon. 📷 ♿ 📷 English (book in adv).

THIS PINE-LOG cabin was built for Peter the Great by his soldier-carpenters in just three days in 1703. Peter lived here for six years while overseeing the construction of his new

city *(see pp20–21)*. Catherine the Great, ever keen to glorify Peter, had a protective brick shell erected round the cabin.

Marvellously evocative of the stark simplicity of Peter's lifestyle, there are only two rooms, both with period furnishings, and a hallway which doubled as a bedroom. Among Peter's personal possessions are a compass, frock coat and his rowing boat.

Adorning the steps outside are two statues of the mythical Shih Tze frog-lions, brought from Manchuria during the Russo-Japanese War *(see p26)*.

Trinity Square ⓮
Троицкая площадь
Troitskaya ploshchad

Map 2 E3. Ⓜ Gorkovskaya.

THROUGHOUT the early 18th century, the whole of Petrogradskaya was known as Trinity Island. The name was

derived from the Church of the Trinity (built in 1710; demolished 1930s) in Trinity Square, which formed the nucleus of the city's merchant quarter. Despite having no direct links to the mainland until the early 20th century, the area flourished with shops, a printing house and the city's first stock exchange.

In the 1905 Revolution *(see p26)* the square witnessed one of the worst massacres of "Bloody Sunday" when 48 workers were killed by government troops. During the Communist era, the square became known as ploshchad Revolyutsii, commemorating those who had lost their lives.

From the square, across the widest point of the Neva, the Style-Moderne Trinity Bridge *(see p35)* stretches nearly 600 m (1,970 ft). Its construction led to a building boom in Petrogradskaya *(see p65)* and its completion in 1903 coincided with the city's bicentenary.

The ornate Trinity Bridge, crossing the Neva from Trinity Square

PALACE EMBANKMENT

IN TERMS OF SHEER SCALE and grandeur, St Petersburg's magnificent south waterfront has few equals. Its formidable granite quays, stretching over 2 km (1 mile) from the Senate building in the west to Peter the Great's Summer Palace in the east, and the surrounding area of stately aristocratic palaces and ornamental canal bridges are justly famous worldwide.

Every aspect of the city's history is juxtaposed in this rich area. Falconet's statue of Peter the Great, the Bronze Horseman, is an eloquent testimony to imperial ambition while the square in which it stands is named

Alexander Column, Palace Square

in honour of the Decembrist rebels who retaliated against the tsarist regime in 1825. In Palace Square, Rastrelli's Winter Palace (part of the Hermitage) evokes the opulence of Imperial Russia while the Eternal Flame, flickering in the Field of Mars, is a more sombre reminder of revolutionary sacrifice.

Dominating St Petersburg's skyline are the magnificent dome of St Isaac's Cathedral and the gilded spire of the Admiralty. Some of the best views can be appreciated by making a boat trip along the waterways *(see pp218–19)*, or by strolling through the Summer Gardens.

SIGHTS AT A GLANCE

Palaces and Gardens
Marble Palace **14**
Summer Gardens **16**
Summer Palace **17**

Museums
The Hermitage pp84–93 **12**

Historical Buildings and Monuments
The Admiralty **1**
The Bronze Horseman **3**
Horseguards' Manège **4**
House of Fabergé **9**

Churches
St Isaac's Cathedral pp80–81 **5**

Streets and Squares
Decembrists' Square **2**
Field of Mars **15**
Malaya Morskaya Ulitsa **8**
Millionaires' Street **13**
Palace Square **11**
St Isaac's Square **6**

Hotels and Cafés
Astoria Hotel **7**
Literary Café **10**

KEY

| | Street-by-Street map *See pp76–7* |

| | Tram stop |

| | River boat stop |

0 metres 400
0 yards 400

◁ **The golden dome** of St Isaac's Cathedral above elegant façades along the Neva

Street-by-Street: St Isaac's Square

Detail from the frieze on the Admiralty gate tower

T HE HIGHLIGHT OF St Isaac's Square is the imposing cathedral at its centre, which opened in 1858 and is the fourth church to stand on this site. The cathedral, and subsequently the square, were named after St Isaac of Dalmatia, because Peter the Great's birthday fell on this saint's day. The busy square, used as a market place in the first half of the 19th century, is now at the heart of an area teeming with buildings and statues of historical and architectural interest. Among them are the Admiralty, the Mariinskiy Palace and the Bronze Horseman.

Horseguards' Manège
Built in 1804–7 by Giacomo Quarenghi, this building housed the Life Guards' Mounted Regiment ❹

The Bronze Horseman
Etienne Falconet's magnificent statue of Peter the Great, his horse trampling the serpent of treason, captures the spirit of the city's uncompromising and wilful founder ❸

Decembrists' Square
Dominating the western side of the square are Carlo Rossi's monumental Senate and Synod buildings, linked by a triumphal arch ❷

The Glory Columns, topped by bronze angels, were erected in 1845–6.

Myatlev House

★ **St Isaac's Cathedral**
The magnificent golden dome of the cathedral is visible all across the city. 100kg (220lb) of gold leaf were needed to cover the dome's surface ❺

The Former German Embassy was designed by Peter Behrens in 1911–12.

0 metres	100
0 yards	100

The Hermitage and Winter Palace

LOCATOR MAP
See Street Finder maps 2, 5 & 6

The Admiralty

Sculptures and reliefs, celebrating the power of Russia's navy, decorate the Admiralty's façade. The archway of the main entrance is framed by nymphs carrying globes on their shoulders ❶

Former Prince Lobanov-Rostovskiy Mansion is now a design institute. The lions in front of the arcade are by Italian sculptor Paolo Triscorni.

STAR SIGHT

★ **St Isaac's Cathedral**

Nevskiy prospekt

The Former Ministry of State Property, designed by Nikolay Yefimov in 1844, is a fine example of Neo-Renaissance architecture.

Astoria Hotel

The elegant ground floor hallway of the Angleterre wing of the historic Astoria Hotel (see p173) reflects the major refurbishment undertaken in the early 1990s. Now under new management, the hotel enjoys an enviable location in the heart of the city ❼

Siniy most *(see p79)*

The Mariinskiy Palace, named in honour of Maria, daughter of Nicholas I, now houses the St Petersburg city hall.

St Isaac's Square

Overlooking the square is Pyotr Klodt's statue of Tsar Nicholas I. The reliefs on the pedestal depict episodes from his reign. Tellingly, two of them show the suppression of rebellions ❻

KEY

– – – Suggested route

The Admiralty ❶

Адмиралтейство
Admiralteystvo

Admiralteyskaya naberezhnaya 2.
Map 5 C1. ⬤ to public. 🚌 7, 947,
T128. 🚋 1, 5, 7, 10, 17, 22. 🚎 31.

Having founded a city and built a fortress, Peter the Great's next priority was to create a Russian navy to guarantee access to the sea and dominance over Sweden.

The Admiralty began life as a fortified shipyard built on this site between 1704–11. Two years later, some 10,000 men were employed in building the first battleships of the embryonic Russian navy.

One of Russia's most inspired architects, Andrey Zakharov, began to rebuild the Admiralty in 1806. The remarkable façade is 407 m (1,335 ft) in length and is adorned with an abundance of sculptures and reliefs which document the glory of the Russian fleet. Zakharov retained some of the original features, including the central gate tower and spire which he recast in Neo-Classical style with columned porticos and pavilions. The heightened spire was gilded and topped with a model frigate. This has become a symbol of the city, just like the trumpet-blowing pair of angels on the portals of the façade overlooking the Neva.

In the 1840s, shipbuilding was moved downstream and the Admiralty was handed over to the Russian navy. It has been occupied by the Naval Engineering School since 1925.

Tower and spire of the Admiralty (1806–23)

Decembrists' Square ❷

Площадь Декабристов
Ploshchad Dekabristov

Map 5 C1. 🚌 T8, 10. 🚋 5, 22.

The name of this square alludes to the momentous event in Russian history which took place here on 14 December 1825 *(see p23)*. During the inauguration of Nicholas I, liberal-minded Guards officers intent on imposing a constitutional monarchy attempted to stage a coup d'état in the square. After a confused stand-off which lasted several hours, the rebel forces were routed with grapeshot by the new tsar and loyalist troops. Five of the ringleaders were later executed and 121 others exiled to Siberia, thus effectively ending Russia's first revolution.

The imposing Neo-Classical buildings that command the western side of Decembrists' Square were intended to harmonize with the Admiralty. Designed by Carlo Rossi between 1829–34, they were the headquarters of two important institutions which were originally created by Peter the Great: the Supreme Court, or Senate, and the Holy Synod which was responsible for the administration of the Orthodox Church. The two buildings, which now house historical archives, are linked to each other by a triumphal arch supported by Corinthian columns and decorated with a Neo-Classical frieze and a plethora of statuary.

The Bronze Horseman (1766–78)

The Bronze Horseman ❸

Медный Всадник
Mednyy Vsadnik

Ploshchad Dekabristov. **Map** 5 C1.
🚌 T8, 10. 🚋 5, 22.

The magnificent equestrian statue of Peter the Great was unveiled in Decembrists' Square in 1782, as a tribute from Catherine the Great. The statue is known as the Bronze Horseman after Pushkin's famous poem. A French sculptor, Etienne Falconet, spent more than 12 years overseeing this ambitious project. The pedestal alone weighs

---

THE BRONZE HORSEMAN BY PUSHKIN

1956 stamp of Pushkin and the statue that inspired his poem

The famous statue of Peter the Great is brought to life in Alexander Pushkin's epic poem *The Bronze Horseman* (1833). In this haunting vision of the Great Flood of 1824 *(see p37)*, the hero is pursued through the mist-shrouded streets by the terrifying bronze statue. Pushkin's words evoke the domineering and implacable will for which the tsar was renowned: *"How terrible he was in the surrounding gloom! ... what strength was in him! And in that steed, what fire!"*

1,625 tonnes and was hewn from a single block of granite, which was hauled from the Gulf of Finland. It bears the simple inscription "To Peter I from Catherine II" in Latin and Russian. A serpent, symbolizing treason, is crushed beneath the horse's hooves.

Newlyweds often pose for photographs under the statue which is meant to bring luck.

Horseguards' Manège ❹

Конногвардейский манеж
Konnogvardeyskiy manezh

Isaakievskaya ploshchad 1. **Map** 5 C2. 📞 *314 5959*. ⏰ *11am–7pm Fri–Wed*. 🚌 *T8, 10, 22, 39Э, 43*. 🚋 *5, 22*. 📷

THE ENORMOUS INDOOR riding school of the Life Guards' Mounted Regiment was built by Giacomo Quarenghi in 1804–7 to resemble a Roman basilica. Two clues to the building's original function are the dynamic frieze of a horse race beneath the pediment and the statues on either side of the portico. The statues of the un-clad twin sons of Zeus reining in wild horses are copies from the Quirinale Palace in Rome. The Holy Synod, scandalized by this display of nakedness so near to St Isaac's Cathedral, ordered their removal. The statues were re-erected in 1954.

Next to the manège, which is now used for contemporary art exhibitions, are two marble pillars surmounted by bronze angels cast in Berlin, which were sent over as a gift in 1840.

St Isaac's Cathedral ❺

See pp80–81.

St Isaac's Square ❻

Исаакиевская площадь
Issakievskaya ploshchad

Map 5 C2. 🚌 *T8, 10, 22, 39Э, 43*. 🚋 *5, 22*.

DOMINATED BY Auguste de Montferrand's majestic St Isaac's Cathedral, this impressive square was created during the reign of Nicholas I,

St Isaac's Cathedral, statue of St Nicholas I and the Astoria, St Isaac's Square

although a few of its earlier buildings date from the 18th century. The monument to Nicholas I at its centre was also designed by Montferrand. Erected in 1859 and sculpted by Pyotr Klodt, it depicts the tsar in the uniform of one of Russia's most prestigious regiments, the Kavalergardskiy guards. The pedestal is embellished with allegorical sculptures of his daughters and his wife who represent Faith, Wisdom, Justice and Might.

On the western side of the square at No. 9, the Myatlev House is a Neo-Classical mansion, dating from the 1760s, which belonged to one of Russia's most illustrious families. The French encyclopedist, Denis Diderot, stayed here in 1773–4 following an invitation from Catherine the Great. In the 1920s it became the premises of the State Institute of Artistic Culture where some of Russia's most influential avant-garde artists, including Kazimir Malevich and Vladimir Tatlin *(see p107)*, worked.

The forbidding granite-faced building alongside is the former German embassy, designed in 1911–12 by the German architect, Peter Behrens.

Across the 100-m (330-ft) wide Siniy most (Blue Bridge), which was the site of a serf market until 1861, the Mariinskiy Palace *(see p67)* dominates the southern end of the square.

Astoria Hotel ❼

Гостиница Астория
Gostinitsa Astoriya

Bolshaya Morskaya ulitsa 39. **Map** 6 D2. 📞 *210 5757*. 🚌 *T8, 10, 22, 39Э, 43*. 🚋 *5, 22*. *See Where to Stay p173.*

NOW ONE OF St Petersburg's leading hotels, the seven-storey Astoria was designed by Fyodor Lidval in the Style Moderne *(see p71)* in 1910–12.

American writer, John Reed, author of the famous eyewitness account of the Revolution *Ten Days that Shook the World*, was staying here when the Bolsheviks seized power.

In 1925, the poet Sergey Yesenin, husband of Isadora Duncan, hanged himself in the annexe, after daubing the walls of his room with a farewell verse in his blood "To die is not new – but neither is it new to be alive".

The hotel's banqueting hall was to be the venue for Hitler's prematurely planned victory celebration, so sure was he that he would conquer the city.

Restored Style-Moderne foyer in the Astoria Hotel, on the eastern edge of St Isaac's Square

St Isaac's Cathedral ❺

Исаакиевский собор
Isaakievskiy sobor

S<small>T ISAAC'S</small>, one of the world's largest cathedrals, was designed in 1818 by the then unknown architect Auguste de Montferrand. The construction of the colossal building was a major engineering feat. Thousands of wooden piles were sunk into the marshy ground to support its weight of 300,000 tonnes and 48 huge columns were hauled into place. The cathedral opened in 1858 but was designated a museum of atheism during the Soviet era. Officially still a museum today, the church is filled with hundreds of impressive 19th-century works of art.

The Dome
From the dome there are panoramic views over the city which include the Admiralty (see p78) and the Hermitage (see pp84– 93). Adorning the gilded dome are angels sculpted by Josef Hermann.

The mosaic icons on the iconostasis are by Bryullov, Neff and Zhivago.

Angels with Torch
Ivan Vitali created many of the cathedral's sculptures, including the pairs of angels supporting gas torches which crown the four attic corners.

This chapel honours Alexander Nevsky who defeated the Swedes in 1240 *(see p17)*.

The north pediment is ornamented with a bronze relief (1842–4) of the Resurrection designed by François Lemaire.

Exit

★ Iconostasis
Three rows of icons surround the royal doors through which a stained-glass window (1843) is visible. Above the doors is Pyotr Klodt's gilded sculpture, Christ in Majesty (1859).

Malachite and lapis lazuli columns frame the iconostasis. About 16,000 kg (35,280 lbs) of malachite decorate the cathedral.

St Catherine's Chapel has an exquisite white marble iconostasis, crowned by a sculpted Resurrection (1850–6) by Nikolay Pimenov.

The silver dove (1850) hanging in the cupola is a symbol of the Holy Spirit.

VISITORS' CHECKLIST

Isaakievskaya ploshchad.
Map 5 C2. 315 9732.
Nevskiy Prospekt, Sadovaya.
T8, 222, 43. 5, 22.
1, 5, 11, 31. 11am–6pm
Thu–Tue.
Easter and Christmas period.

★ Ceiling Painting
The celestial Virgin in Majesty *by Karl Bryullov* (see p105), *dating to 1847, covers an area of 816 sq m (8,780 sq ft). It is ringed by exuberant gilded stucco mouldings and white marble.*

Portraits of apostles and evangelists

Statue of St Matthew

The entrance is through the side doors on St Isaac's Square.

South Doors
Three great doors of oak and bronze (1841–6), weighing 20 tonnes, are decorated with carved reliefs by Ivan Vitali. The exteriors of the doors show scenes from the life of Christ and saints, including Alexander Nevsky (see p17).

The relief of St Isaac blessing the Emperor Theodosius and his wife Flaccilla is by Ivan Vitali. On the extreme left, Montferrand is depicted clutching a model of his cathedral.

The walls are adorned with 14 coloured marbles and 43 other types of semi-precious stones and minerals.

The vast interior covers 4,000 sq m (43,000 sq ft).

Red granite columns, each weighing 114 tonnes, were transported from Finland by specially constructed ships.

STAR SIGHTS

★ **Iconostasis**

★ **Ceiling Painting**

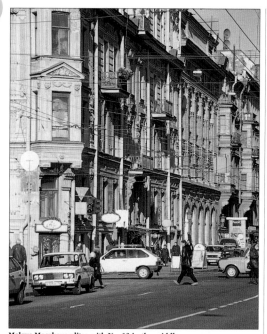

Malaya Morskaya ulitsa with No. 13 in the middle

Malaya Morskaya Ulitsa ❽

Малая Морская улица

Malaya Morskaya ulitsa

Map 6 D1. ▦ *10, Э10, 22, 43.*
🚋 *9, 22, 44.* 🚎 *31.*

MALAYA MORSKAYA ULITSA is sometimes still referred to as ulitsa Gogolya after the great prose-writer, Nikolai Gogol (1809–52) who lived at No. 17 from 1833–6. It was here that Gogol wrote *The Diary of a Madman* and *The Nose*, two biting satires on the archetypal Petersburg bureaucrat "drowned by the trivial, meaningless labours at which he spends his useless life". Gogol's bitingly humorous, fantastical and grotesque tales reveal a nightmarish and deeply pessimistic view of modern urban life.

The composer, Pyotr Tchaikovsky *(see p42)*, died in the top floor apartment of No. 13 shortly after the completion of his *Pathétique* symphony in November 1893. Officially he was supposed to have died of cholera, but it is commonly believed that he

committed suicide, due to pressure from Conservatory colleagues wishing to avoid a scandal after Tchaikovsky's alleged homosexual affair.

The house at No. 23 was occupied by the novelist Fyodor Dostoevsky *(see p44)* from 1848–9. It was here that he was arrested and charged with political conspiracy for his participation in the socialist Petrashevsky circle *(see p123)*. Today, the street manages to exude a 19th-century feel despite the many busy shops and businesses.

House of Fabergé ❾

Дом Фаберже

Dom Faberzhe

Bolshaya Morskaya ulitsa 24.
Map 6 D1. ⬤ *to public.* ▦ *22,*
Э22, 43. 🚋 *9, 22, 44.* 🚎 *31.*

THE WORLD-FAMOUS Fabergé jeweller's was established in Bolshaya Morskaya ulitsa in 1842 by Gustav Fabergé, of French Huguenot origin. It was not until the 1880s that his sons Carl and Agathon abandoned conventional jewellery-making for intricate and exquisitely crafted *objets d'art* of a highly innovative design. Most famous of all their works are the imaginatively designed Easter eggs made for the tsars.

In 1900 Carl moved the business from No. 16–18 into purpose-built premises at No. 24, where it remained until the Revolution. The exterior, designed by his relative, Karl Schmidt, has striking triangular roof gables and multi-textured stonework. The original showroom, with its squat red granite pillars, was on the ground floor. It is still a jeweller's, but with no connection to Fabergé. In the workshops above, boy apprentices were trained by master craftsmen in the arts of enamelling, engraving, stone cutting and jewelling.

In 1996, the 150th anniversary of Carl Fabergé's birth was marked by the unveiling of a memorial plaque at No. 24 and of a monument, designed by the sculptor Leonid Aristov and others, on the corner of Zamnevskiy prospekt and prospekt Energetikov.

FABERGÉ EGGS

In 1885 Alexander III commissioned the Fabergé brothers to create an Easter egg for Tsarina Maria Fyodorovna. Inside the shell of gold and white enamel was a beautifully sculpted golden hen. A tradition was established and, by the Revolution, there were 54 Fabergé Easter eggs, no two of which were alike. The *pièce de résistance* is the Siberian Railway Egg, commissioned by Nicholas II in 1900. It contains a miniature replica of the royal train, complete with ruby headlamps, rock crystal windows and a clockwork engine. The Bonbonnière Egg was commissioned by Kelch, a wealthy industrialist, for his wife Varvara in 1903.

The Kelch Bonbonnière Egg

DEATH OF A POET

In November 1836 Pushkin received an anonymous letter which awarded him the title of "Grand Master of the Most Serene Order of Cuckolds". It had been sent by Georges d'Anthès, a ne'er-do-well cavalry officer who for some time had been making overtures towards Pushkin's wife, the beauty and socialite Natalya Goncharova. Pushkin challenged d'Anthès to a duel and, on the afternoon of 27 January 1837, he met his opponent in snow-bound woodland to the north of the city. D'Anthès fired first and Pushkin was mortally wounded. He died two days later, aged 38. D'Anthès was later reduced to the ranks and banished from Russia.

A Naumov's painting of Pushkin, fatally wounded after his duel

The resplendant square is the work of the inspired architect Carlo Rossi (see p110). Facing the Winter Palace on its southern side is Rossi's magnificent General Staff Building (1819–29), the headquarters for the Russian army. Rossi demolished an entire row of houses to make room for it.

The two graceful, curving wings are connected by a triumphal double arch leading to Bolshaya Morskaya ulitsa. The arch is crowned by a lively sculpture of Victory in her chariot (1829), by Stepan Pimenov and Vasiliy Demut-Malinovskiy. Forming the eastern side of this striking architectural ensemble is the Guards Headquarters, designed by Aleksandr Bryullov in 1837–43. To the west lies the Admiralty (see p78).

The Alexander Column in the centre of the square is dedicated to Tsar Alexander I for his role in the triumph over Napoleon (see pp22–3). On the pedestal are inscribed the words "To Alexander I, from a grateful Russia". The red granite pillar is balanced only by its immense 600-tonne weight, making it the largest free-standing monument in the world. The column was designed by Auguste de Montferrand in 1829 and it took 2,400 soldiers and workmen two years to hew and transport the granite. It was actually erected in 1830–34. The column is surmounted by a bronze angel holding a cross, and together they stand 47 m (154 ft) high.

Sign outside the Literary Café

Literary Café ⑩

Литературное сафе
Literaturnoe kafe

Nevskiy prospekt 18. **Map** 6 E1.
📞 312 6057. ⏰ noon–midnight.
Ⓜ Nevskiy Prospekt. ♿
See also p180.

ALSO KNOWN AS the Café Wulf et Beranger after its original owners, this café is famous for its association with Alexander Pushkin, Russia's greatest poet (see p43). It was here that Pushkin met his second, Konstantin Danzas, before setting out for his ill-fated duel with Baron d'Anthès. The café was a popular haunt for St Petersburg writers from its beginning, frequented by Fyodor Dostoevsky and the poet Mikhail Lermontov (1814–41), among others.

Despite its hallowed literary importance and elegant setting, in Vasiliy Stasov's handsome building of 1815, the café itself does not merit the high prices.

Palace Square ⑪

Дворцовая площадь
Dvortsovaya ploshchad

Map 6 D1. 🚌 7, Э10, Э47.
🚎 1, 7, 10.

PALACE SQUARE has played a unique role in Russian history. Before the Revolution the square was the setting for colourful military parades, often led by the tsar on horse-back. In January 1905, it was the scene of the massacre of "Bloody Sunday" (see p26) when gathered troops fired on thousands of unarmed demonstrators. Then, on 7 November 1917, Lenin's Bolshevik supporters secured the Revolution by attacking the Winter Palace (see pp28–9) from the square, as well as its west side. Today it is still a favourite venue for political meetings and for popular entertainment such as rock concerts (see p51).

The Alexander Column and General Staff Building in Palace Square

The Hermitage 🕛

Эрмитаж
Hermitazh

The New Hermitage (1839–51) was designed by Leo von Klenze to form a coherent part of the Large Hermitage. It is the only purpose-built museum within the whole complex.

O NE OF THE MOST FAMOUS museums in the world, the Hermitage has a vast collection occupying a grand ensemble of buildings. The most impressive is Rastrelli's Baroque Winter Palace *(see pp92–3)*, to which Catherine the Great soon added the more intimate Small Hermitage. In 1771–87, she erected the Large Hermitage to house her rapidly growing collection of art. The theatre was built in 1785–7, and finally the New Hermitage in 1839–51. The New and Large Hermitages were opened by Nicholas I in 1852 as a public museum. Between 1918 and 1939, after the establishment of Soviet power, the Winter Palace was slowly incorporated into the Hermitage museum ensemble.

Court ministries were located here until the 1880s.

Atlantes
Ten 5-m (16-ft) tall granite atlantes hold up what was the public entrance to the Hermitage museum from 1852 until after the Revolution.

A gallery spanning the canal connects the theatre to the Large Hermitage and forms the theatre foyer.

The Winter Canal *(see p36)*

Theatre
During Catherine's reign, there were regular performances held in Quarenghi's theatre. Today it hosts exhibitions and concerts (see p194).

The Large Hermitage was designed by Yuriy Velten to house Catherine's paintings.

★ **Raphael Loggias**
Catherine was so impressed by engravings of Raphael's frescoes in the Vatican that in 1787 she commissioned copies to be made on canvas. Small alterations were made, such as replacing the Pope's coat of arms with the Romanov two-headed eagle.

Hanging Gardens

This unusual raised garden is decorated with statues and fountains. During the Siege of Leningrad (see p27) Hermitage curators grew vegetables here.

VISITOR'S CHECKLIST

Dvortsovaya nab 34–6. **Map** 2 D5.
311 3465. 7,10, Э47,
Т128. 1, 7,10. 10:30am–
6pm Tue–Sat; 10.30am–5pm Sun.
Last adm 1 hour before closing.
in English (213 1112 to
book).

The Small Hermitage

(1764–75), by Vallin de la Mothe and Yuriy Velten, served as Catherine's retreat from the bustle of the court.

Winter Palace Façade

Rastrelli embellished the palace façades with 400 columns and 16 different window designs.

STAR SIGHTS

★ **Winter Palace State Rooms**

★ **Pavilion Hall**

★ **Raphael Loggias**

Palace Square

Main entrance

Neva river

The Winter Palace

(1754–62) was the official residence of the Imperial family until the Revolution.

★ **Pavilion Hall** (1850–8) *Andrey Stakenschneider's striking white marble and gold hall replaced Catherine's original interior. It houses Englishman James Cox's famous Peacock Clock (1772), previously owned by Catherine's lover Prince Potemkin, but now forming part of her collection.*

★ **Winter Palace State Rooms** *The tsars spared no expense in decorating rooms such as the Hall of St George. These rooms were not intended for private life, but to symbolize the power and wealth of imperial Russia.*

The Hermitage Collections

CATHERINE THE GREAT purchased some of Western Europe's best collections between 1764 and 1774, acquiring over 2,500 paintings, 10,000 carved gems, 10,000 drawings and a vast amount of silver and porcelain with which to adorn her palaces. None of her successors matched the quantity of her remarkable purchases. After the Revolution, the nationalization of both royal and private property brought more paintings and works of applied art, making the Hermitage one of the world's leading museums.

The Litta Madonna (c.1491)
One of two works by Leonardo da Vinci in the museum, this masterpiece was admired by his contemporaries and was frequently copied.

The Knights' Hall (1842–51) is used for displays of armour and weapons from the former imperial arsenal.

Stairs to ground floor

Raphael Loggias *(see p84)*

First Floor

The Gallery of Ancient Painting (1842–51) is decorated with scenes from ancient literature. It houses a superb display of 19th-century European sculpture.

Ground Floor

Special Collection

The Hall of Twenty Columns (1842–51) is painted in Etruscan style.

Main entrance from the Neva embankment

Entrance for tours and guided groups

STAR EXHIBITS

- ★ **Abraham's Sacrifice by Rembrandt**

- ★ **Ea Haere Ia Oe by Gauguin**

- ★ **La Danse by Matisse**

GALLERY GUIDE

Individual visitors enter from the Neva embankment, group tours from Palace Square. Start with the interiors of the Winter Palace state rooms on the first floor to get an overview of the museum. Select one or two topics of interest to concentrate on. 19th- and 20th-century European Art is best reached by either of the staircases on the Palace Square side of the Winter Palace.

★ **Abraham's Sacrifice** (1635)
In the 1630s Rembrandt was painting religious scenes in a High Baroque style, using dramatic and striking gestures rather than detail to convey his message.

Second Floor

Stairs to first floor

The Numismatic Collection consists of more than 90,000 coins and medals. Only part of it is on display in temporary exhibitions.

Stairs to first floor

Stairs to second floor

Stairs to second floor, Numismatic Collection only

The Winter Palace state rooms *(see pp92–3)* contain magnificent Russian and European *objets d'art*.

★ Ea Haere Ia Oe (1893)
This is one of the first paintings Paul Gauguin did after he had left France for Tahiti. His desire to escape convention and artificiality found expression in his innovative use of primitive art as inspiration.

★ La Danse (1910)
Henri Matisse used strong tones of three colours – blue, green and red – to heighten the drama and concentration of the figures, totally lost in their dance.

Statue of Voltaire (1781)
Catherine the Great corresponded with Voltaire for over 15 years. She commissioned Jean-Antoine Houdon's marble statue, in which the French writer is dressed in the style of a Greek philosopher.

KEY TO FLOORPLAN

- ☐ **Prehistoric:** Rooms 11–24, 26, 33
- ☐ **Classical:** 102, 107–117, 121, 127–131
- ☐ **Oriental:** 34–47, 55–66, 69, 100, 351–371, 381–397
- ☐ **Russian:** 147–153, 155–189, 190–198, 204, 260, 269–271, 282, 304–307
- ☐ **Italian and Spanish:** 207–223, 226–242
- ☐ **Flemish, Dutch and German:** 243, 245–254, 258–259, 261–268
- ☐ **French and English:** 272–281, 283–287, 290–302
- ☐ **19th- and 20th-century European:** 314–325, 328–350
- ☐ **Temporary exhibition space**
- ☐ **Non-exhibition space**
- ☐ **No access**

Exploring the Hermitage Collections

IT IS IMPOSSIBLE to absorb the Hermitage's vast, encyclopedic collection in one or even two visits. Whether it be Scythian gold, antique vases and cameos, or Iranian silver, every room has something to capture the eye. The furniture, applied art, portraits and rich clothing of the imperial family went to make up the Russian section, which also includes the superb state rooms. The collection of European paintings was put together largely on the personal taste of the imperial family while most of the 19th- and 20th-century European art, notably the Impressionists, Matisse and Picasso, came from private collections after the Revolution. These are now regarded as the most popular exhibits.

Scythian gold stag dating from 7th–6th century BC

PREHISTORIC ART

PREHISTORIC artifacts found all over the former Russian Empire include pots, arrow heads and sculptures from Palaeolithic sites, which date back nearly 24,000 years, and rich gold items from the time of the Scythian nomads living in the 7th–3rd centuries BC.

Peter the Great's famous Siberian collection of delicate gold work includes Scythian animal-style brooches, sword handles and buckles. Objects continued to be discovered in Siberia and, in 1897, a large stylized stag, which once decorated an iron shield, was found at Kostromskaya. This is one of the few gold pieces not held in the Special Collection (for which a separate ticket is required), where most precious metals are concentrated.

Greek masters also worked for the Scythians, and from the Dnepr region came a late 5th-century comb decorated with amazingly naturalistic figures of Scythians fighting, as well as the late 4th-century Chertomlyk Vase with scenes depicting animal taming.

Excavations in the Altai, notably at Pazyryk in 1927–49, uncovered burials nearly 2,500 years old. Many perishable materials were preserved by the frozen land, including textiles, a burial cart and even a man's heavily tatooed skin.

Gonzaga Cameo (285–246 BC), made in Alexandria

CLASSICAL ART

THE LARGE NUMBER of Graeco-Roman marble sculptures range from the famous Tauride Venus of the 3rd century BC, acquired by Peter the Great in 1720, to Roman portrait busts. The smaller objects, however, are the real pride and joy of the Classical department.

The collection of red-figured Attic vases of the 6th–4th centuries BC is unequalled anywhere in the world. Exquisitely proportioned and with a lustrous shine, they are decorated with scenes of libation, episodes from the Trojan War, and in one case a famous image of the sighting of the first swallow (c.510 BC).

In the 4th and 3rd centuries BC, Tanagra was the centre for the production of small, elegant terracotta figurines. They were discovered in the 19th century and became so popular that fakes were produced on a grand scale. The Russian ambassador in Athens, Pyotr Saburov, put his collection together in the 1880s before the copies appeared, making it unusually valuable.

Catherine the Great's true passion was for carved gems, which she bought en masse. In just ten years, she purchased some 10,000 pieces. The largest and most stunning gem in the Classical collection, however, is the Gonzaga Cameo, which was presented by Napoleon's ex-wife Josephine Beauharnais to Tsar Alexander I in 1814.

The Special Collection contains items of 5th-century gold jewellery made by Athenian craftsmen. They used a filigree technique for working gold so finely that the detail can only be seen properly through a magnifying glass.

ORIENTAL ART

THIS SELECTION of artifacts covers a wide range of cultures; from ancient Egypt and Assyria, through Byzantium, India, Iran, China, Japan and the marvels of Uzbekistan and Tajikistan. The most complete sections are those where excavations were conducted by the Hermitage, mainly in China and Mongolia before the Revolution, and in Central Asia during the Soviet period.

Dating back to the 19th century BC, at the time of the Middle Egyptian Kingdom, is a seated porphyry portrait of

8th-century fresco of a wounded warrior from Tajikistan

Excavations and expeditions to Central Asia have produced carpets, bronzes and wonderful glazed tiles. Uzbekistan and Tajikistan revealed marvellous complexes of 8th-century buildings at Varaksha, Adjina-Tepe and Pendzhikent, which have been a source of beautiful frescoes, such as the one depicting the wounded warrior.

RUSSIAN ART

Although major Russian works of art were transferred from the Winter Palace to the Russian Museum (*see pp104–107*) in 1898, everything else that belonged to the imperial family was nationalized after the Revolution. This included anything from official portraits and thrones to looking glasses and petticoats. Over 300 items of apparel belonging to Peter the Great alone survive. Later, the department also began acquiring medieval Russian art, including icons and church utensils.

The tsars from Peter the Great onwards invited foreign craftsmen and artists to train

Pharaoh Amenemhet III. The star of the Egyptian collection is an extremely rare, small, wooden statue of a standing man from the 15th century BC.

From the Far East – Japan, India, Indonesia, China and Mongolia – come an array of objects ranging from Buddhist sculptures and fabrics to a display of tiny netsukes (ivory toggles). Excavations at the cave temple of the Thousand Buddhas near Dun Huan in western China revealed 6th–10th-century icons, wall paintings and plaster sculptures, including the lions that once guarded the cave. During the 13th-century Mongol invasion, the town of Hara-Hoto was destroyed and taken over by the surrounding desert. The sand preserved many usually perishable objects, from 12th-century silks to woodcuts.

From Byzantium come early secular items, such as icons, religious utensils and a 5th-century ivory diptych with scenes from a Roman circus.

Iran produced a large number of silver and bronze vessels, many of which were taken by medieval traders to Siberia and the Urals where they were rediscovered by specialists in the 19th century. There is also a large collection of traditional Persian miniatures and a rich display of 19th-century Persian court portraits, which combine traditional elements with western oil painting, as in the *Portrait of Fatkh-Ali Shah* (1813–14).

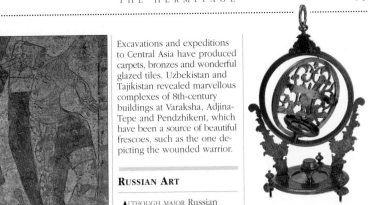

Universal sundial (1714–19) from Peter the Great's collection

locals. Peter studied with them and his fascination for practical things is reflected in his large collection of sundials, instruments and wood-turning lathes which includes the universal sundial by Master John Rowley. A bust by Bartolomeo Carlo Rastrelli (1723–30), however, portrays Peter as the mighty and cruel emperor, rather than the rough workman.

Russian artists were soon combining traditional art forms with European skills to create such intricate marvels as the openwork walrus ivory vase by Nikolay Vereshchagin (1798), and the large silver sarcophagus and memorial to Alexander Nevsky, truly Russian in scale (1747–52).

The gunsmiths of Tula (south of Moscow) perfected their technique to such an extent that they began producing unique furniture in steel inlaid with gilded bronze, such as the decorative, Empire-style dressing table set (1801).

The state interiors (*see pp92–3*) are the pride of the Russian department, revealing the work of Russian and foreign craftsmen from the mid-18th to the early 20th century. The discovery of large deposits of coloured stones in the Urals inspired Russian artists to decorate whole rooms with malachite and to fill every corner of the Winter Palace with marble vases. It was through these rooms that the imperial family paraded on state occasions, greeting courtiers and ambassadors en route in the Field Marshals' Hall.

Steel dressing table set from Tula dating from 1801

ITALIAN AND SPANISH ART

T HE DISPLAY of Italian art is superb. A few early works reveal the rise of the Renaissance in the 14th and 15th centuries and the styles then in vogue. Simone Martini's stiff *Madonna* (1340–44) contrasts with Fra Angelico's more humane fresco of the Virgin and Child (1424–30).

In the late 15th and early 16th century, artists disputed the merits of line, as practised by the Florentine school, and the merits of colour, virtue of the Venetians. The former can be seen in the *Litta Madonna* (c.1491) and the *Madonna Benois* (1478) by Leonardo da Vinci, a marble *Crouching Boy* by Michelangelo (c.1530) and two early portraits of the Virgin by Raphael (1502 and 1506). The Venetian school dominates with *Judith* by Giorgione (1478–1510) and an array of works by Titian, from his *Young Woman* (1530s) through to late, much darker works such as *St Sebastian* (1570). Caravaggio's *A Young Man Playing a Lute* (1598) represents the northern schools.

Applied arts such as majolica and Venetian glass are the best way to appreciate later periods. The works of Antonio Canova, 18th-century sculptor (*Cupid and Psyche, The Three Graces*), also have a place of honour.

The Spanish collection on the other hand is more modest, but Spain's Golden-Age heroes can all be seen, from El Greco with *The Apostles Peter and Paul* (1587–92), through to Ribera, Murillo, and Zurbarán with *St Lawrence* (1636). The portrait of a courtier, *Count Olivares*, painted c.1640 by Velázquez, contrasts with a much earlier genre scene of a peasant's breakfast (1617–18).

Venus and Cupid (1509) by Lucas Cranach the Elder

FLEMISH, DUTCH AND GERMAN ART

T HE SMALL COLLECTION of early paintings from the Netherlands includes a marvellous, jewel-like *Madonna and Child* (1430s) by the Master of Flemalle. He is thought to have been the teacher of Rogier van der Weyden, who is represented by *St Luke Painting the Madonna* (c.1435).

Over 40 works by Rubens include religious subjects (*The Descent from the Cross*, 1617–18) and scenes from Classical mythology (*Perseus and Andromeda*, 1620–21), as well as landscapes and an immensely obese *Bacchus* (1636–40). His portraits, such as the *Infanta's Maid* (1625), reveal his common Flemish heritage with Van Dyck, whose paintings include a series of formal, full-length portraits and a dashing and romantic self-portrait from the late 1620s.

The Dutch section is rich in Rembrandts. Within a short period of time he produced the dramatic *Abraham's Sacrifice* (1635), the gentle *Flora* (1634) and the brilliant effects of *The Descent from the Cross* (1634). One of his last works was the *Return of the Prodigal Son* (1668–9), with an emotional depth unseen before.

Among the many small-genre paintings is Gerard Terborch's *Glass of Lemonade* from the mid-17th century. All the usual elements of a genre scene are imbued with psychological tension and heavy symbolism.

In the German collection, it is the works of Lucas Cranach the Elder which captivate the viewer. His *Venus and Cupid* (1509), the stylish *Portrait of a Woman in a Hat* (1526) and the tender *Virgin and Child Beneath an Apple Tree* reveal the varied aspects of his talent.

FRENCH AND ENGLISH ART

F RENCH ART was *de rigueur* for collectors in the 18th century, and this period is particularly well represented. Some major artists of the 17th century, including Louis Le Nain and the two brilliant and contrasting painters Claude Lorrain and Nicolas Poussin, are also exhibited. Catherine the Great had more sympathy for the naughtiness of later art, such as Antoine Watteau's elegant *Difficult Proposal*

A Young Man Playing a Lute, by Michelangelo Caravaggio (1573–1610)

Still Life with the Attributes of the Arts (1766), by Jean-Baptiste Chardin

(c.1716), *Stolen Kiss* (1780s) by Jean Honoré Fragonard and several of François Boucher's fleshy and certainly far-from-virtuous heroines. At the same time, she bought *Still Life with Attributes of the Arts* (1766) by Chardin and, on the advice of Denis Diderot, Jean-Baptiste Greuze's moralizing *The Fruits of a Good Education* (1763). She also patronized sculptors, purchasing works by Etienne-Maurice Falconet (*Winter*, carved 1771) and Jean-Antoine Houdon (*Voltaire*, 1781).

The Green Frog Service, Wedgwood (1773–4)

Catherine also acquired English works, including a portrait of the philosopher John Locke (1697) by Sir Godfrey Kneller, who was also author of a portrait of Pyotr Potemkin (1682) in Russian 17th-century court dress. From Sir Joshua Reynolds Catherine commissioned *The Infant Hercules Strangling the Serpents* (1788). Her most daring purchase was of works by the still largely unknown Joseph Wright of Derby. *The Iron Forge* (1773) is a masterpiece of artificial lighting, but *Firework Display at the Castel Sant'Angelo* (1774–5) is a truly romantic fiery spectacle. She provided much work for English cabinet-makers and carvers of cameos. She became one of Josiah Wedgwood's most prestigious clients, ordering the famous Green Frog Service for her Chesma Palace (*see p130*).

19TH- & 20TH-CENTURY EUROPEAN ART

Although the royal family did not patronize the new movements in art in the 19th century, there were far-sighted private individuals whose collections were nationalized and entered the Hermitage after the 1917 Revolution. Thanks to them, the Barbizon school is represented by works such as Camille Corot's charming silvery *Landscape with a Lake*, French Romanticism by two richly-coloured Moroccan scenes of the 1850s by Delacroix, and German Romanticism by Caspar David Friedrich's *On the Prow of the Ship* (1818–20).

Two collectors, Ivan Morozov and Sergey Shchukin, brought the Hermitage its superb array of Impressionist and Post-Impressionist paintings. Monet's art can be admired both in his early *Woman in a Garden* (1860s) and in the later, more exploratory *Waterloo Bridge, Effect of Mist* (1903). Renoir and Degas perpetually returned to women as subjects, as in Renoir's charming *Portrait of the Actress Jeanne Samary* (1878) and Degas' pastels of women washing (1880s–90s). Pissarro's *Boulevard Montmartre in Paris* (1897) is typical of his urban scenes, while Alfred Sisley painted weather effects and light in the French countryside.

A change in colour and technique appeared as artists investigated new possibilities. Van Gogh used deeper tones in his *Women of Arles* (1888) and stronger brushstrokes in *Cottages* (1890). Gauguin turned to a different culture for inspiration, and his Tahitian period is represented by enigmatic works, such as *Ea Haere Ia Oe* (1893). In *The Smoker* (c.1890–2) and *Mont Ste-Victoire* (1896–8), Cézanne introduced experiments with plane and surface which were to have a strong influence on the next generation.

Matisse played both with colour and surface, in the carpet-like effect of *The Red Room* (1908–9) and the flatness of the panels *La Musique* and *La Danse* (1909–10). His visit to Morocco introduced new light effects, as in *Arab Coffeehouse* (1913), but it was Picasso who took Cézanne's experiments one stage further. In early works such as *Visit* (1902) from his Blue Period, Picasso concentrates on mood, but the surface destruction of the Cubist period of 1907–12, including *L'Homme aux Bras Croisés*, fills a whole room.

L'Homme aux Bras Croisés, painted by Pablo Picasso in 1909

The Winter Palace

PRECEDED BY three earlier versions on this site, the existing Winter Palace (1754–62) is a superb example of Russian Baroque. Built for Tsarina Elizabeth, this opulent winter residence was the finest achievement of Bartolomeo Rastrelli. Though the exterior has changed little, the interiors were altered by a number of architects and then largely restored after a fire gutted the palace in 1837. After the assassination of Alexander II in 1881, the imperial family rarely lived here. During World War I a field hospital was set up in the Nicholas Hall and other state rooms. Then, in July 1917, the Provisional Government took the palace as its headquarters, which led to its storming by the Bolsheviks *(see pp28–9)*.

The 1812 Gallery (1826) has portraits of Russian military heroes of the Napoleonic War, most by English artist George Dawe.

The Armorial Hall (1839), with its vast gilded columns, covers over 800 sq m (8,600 sq ft). It now houses the European silver collection and a restored imperial carriage.

★ **Small Throne Room**
Dedicated in 1833 to the memory of Peter the Great, this room houses a silver-gilt English throne, made in 1731.

The Field Marshals' Hall (1833) was the reception room where the devastating fire of 1837 broke out.

The Hall of St George (1795) has monolithic columns and wall facings of Italian Carrara marble.

The Nicholas Hall, the largest room in the palace, was always used for the first ball of the season.

North façade overlooking the Neva

★ **Jordan Staircase**
This vast, sweeping staircase (1762) was Rastrelli's masterpiece. It was from here that the imperial family watched the Epiphany ceremony of baptism in the Neva, which celebrated Christ's baptism in the Jordan.

★ **Malachite Room**
Over two tonnes of ornamental stone were used in this sumptuous room (1839) which is decorated with malachite columns and vases, gilded doors and ceiling, and rich parquet flooring.

Alexander Hall
*Architect Aleksandr Bryullov
employed a mixture of Gothic
vaulting and Neo-Classical
stucco bas-reliefs of military
themes in this reception
room of 1837.*

BARTOLOMEO RASTRELLI

The Italian architect Rastrelli (1700–71) came to Russia with his father in 1716 to work for Peter the Great. His rich Baroque style became highly fashionable and he was appointed Chief Court Architect in 1738. During Elizabeth's reign, Rastrelli designed several buildings, including the grandiose Winter Palace and impressive Smolnyy Convent *(see p128)*. Unlike Elizabeth, Catherine the Great preferred Classical simplicity and Rastrelli retired in 1763, after she came to power.

The French Rooms,
designed by Bryullov in
1839, house a collection
of 18th-century French art.

The White Hall was decorated for the wedding of the
future Alexander II in 1841.

**South façade
on Palace
Square**

Dark Corridor
The French and Flemish tapestries here include The Marriage
of Emperor Constantine, *made
in Paris in the 17th
century to designs
by Rubens.*

The Rotunda
(1830) connected
the private apartments in
the west with the state apartments on the palace's north side.

West wing

The Gothic Library and
other rooms in the northwest
part of the palace were adapted
to suit Nicholas II's bourgeois lifestyle. This wood-panelled library
was created by Meltzer in 1894.

The Gold Drawing Room
*Created in the 1850s, this
room was extravagantly decorated in the 1870s with all-over
gilding of walls and ceiling.
It houses a display of Western
European carved gems.*

STAR FEATURES

★ **Small Throne Room**

★ **Malachite Room**

★ **Jordan Staircase**

Millionaires' Street ⓭
Миллионная улица
Millionnaya ulitsa

Map 2 E5. 🚇 *12, 53.*

MILLIONAIRES' STREET takes its name from the aristocrats and members of the imperial family who once inhabited its opulent residences. Since the main façades and entrances overlook the river, some house numbers correspond to the embankment side.

On the eve of the Revolution, No. 26 (on the embankment) was the home of Grand Duke Vladimir Aleksandrovich who was responsible for firing on peaceful demonstrators on Bloody Sunday *(see p26)*. His consort, Maria Pavlovna, was one of Russia's leading society hostesses who gave soirées and balls that eclipsed even those of the imperial court. The building (1867–72), which was designed by Aleksandr Rezanov in the style of the Florentine Renaissance, is now the House of Scholars.

Putyatin's house, at No. 12 Millionaires' Street, witnessed the end of the Romanov dynasty. It was here that Grand Duke Mikhail Aleksandrovich, Nicholas II's brother, signed the decree of abdication in March 1917. Next door, No. 10, was where French novelist Honoré de Balzac stayed in 1843, while courting his future wife, Countess Eveline Hanska. The mid-19th-century house was designed by Andrey Stakenschneider for his own use.

The delicately sculpted façade of No. 10 Millionaires' Street

Gala staircase of the Marble Palace

Marble Palace ⓮
Мраморный дворец
Mramornyy dvorets

Millionnaya ulitsa 5 (entrance from the Field of Mars). **Map** 2 E4. 📞 *314 3448.* 🚇 *12, 53.* ⏰ *10am–5pm Wed–Sun, 10am–4pm Mon.* 🎫 ✔ *English.*

THE MARBLE PALACE was built as a generous present from Catherine the Great to her lover Grigoriy Orlov who had been instrumental in bringing her to power in 1762 *(see p22)*. An early example of Neo-Classical architecture, dating from 1768–85, the building is considered to be Antonio Rinaldi's masterpiece.

The palace takes its name from the many and varied types of marble used in its construction. Most of the interiors were reconstructed in the 1840s by Aleksandr Bryullov, although the gala staircase and the Marble Hall are Rinaldi's original work. The latter has marbled walls of grey, green, white, pink and lapis lazuli, and a ceiling painting of the *Triumph of Venus* (1780s) by Stefano Torelli.

The palace, which housed a Lenin museum for 55 years, is now a branch of the Russian Museum *(see pp104–107)*. On display are works by foreign artists working in Russia and modern art bequeathed by the German collectors Peter and Irene Ludwig. Their collection includes a Picasso, *Large Heads* (1969), and work by post-war artists Jean-Michel Basquiat, Andy Warhol, Ilya Kabakov and Roy Lichtenstein.

In front of the palace stands a curious equestrian statue of Alexander III by Prince Pavel Trubetskoy. Unveiled on ploshchad Vosstaniya in 1911, the ridiculed statue was removed from its original site in 1937 and its vast pedestal was cut up to create statues of new heroes, such as Lenin.

Field of Mars ⓯
Марсово Поле
Marsovo Pole

Map 2 F5. 🚌 *25, 46, 134.* 🚇 *2, 12, 32, 34, 53, 54.*

ONCE A VAST marshy expanse, this area was drained during the 19th century and utilized for military manoeuvres and parades, fairs and other festivities. It was appropriately named after Mars, the Roman god of war. Between 1917 and 1923 the area, by then a sandy expanse, was nicknamed the "Petersburg Sahara". It was landscaped and transformed into a war memorial. The granite *Monument to Revolutionary Fighters* (1917–19), by Lev Rudnev, and the Eternal Flame (1957) commemorate the victims of the Revolutions of 1917 and the Civil War *(see p27)*.

Eternal Flame, Field of Mars

The west of the square is dominated by an imposing Neo-Classical building erected by Vasiliy Stasov in 1817–19. This was formerly the barracks of the Pavlovskiy Guards which were founded by Tsar Paul I in 1796. The military-obsessed tsar is said to have only recruited guardsmen with snub noses like his own. The Pavlovskiy officers were among the first to turn against the tsarist government in the 1917 Revolution *(see pp28–9)*.

Today the huge square is a popular spot for locals in the bright spring evenings, when it is alive with lilac blossom.

Summer Gardens ⑯
Летний сад
Letniy sad

Letniy Sad. **Map** 2 F4. 🚌 *46, 134.*
🚎 *2, 12, 32, 34, 54.* ⏰ *8am–8pm
daily (May–Oct: 8am–10pm).*
⚫ *mid–end-Apr.* ♿

IN 1704 Peter the Great commissioned these beautiful
gardens which were among
the first in the city. Designed
by a Frenchman in the style
of Versailles, the allées were
planted with imported elms
and oaks and adorned with
fountains, pavilions and some
250 Italian statues dating from
the 17th and 18th centuries. A
flood in 1777 destroyed most
of the Summer Gardens and
the English-style garden which
exists today is largely the result
of Catherine the Great's more
sober tastes. A splendid feature
is the fine filigree iron grille
(1771–84) along the Neva
embankment, created by Yuriy
Velten and Pyotr Yegorov.

For a century the Summer
Gardens were an exclusive
preserve of the nobility. When
the gardens were opened to
"respectably dressed members
of the public" by Nicholas I,
two Neo-Classical pavilions,
the Tea House and the Coffee
House, were erected over-
looking the Fontanka. These
are now used for temporary
exhibitions of art by modern
St Petersburg artists.

Nearby, the bronze statue
of Ivan Krylov, Russia's most
famous writer of fables, is a
favourite with Russian children. It was sculpted by Pyotr
Klodt in 1854 with charming
bas-reliefs on the pedestal depicting animals from his fables.

Ivan Krylov's statue amidst autumn foliage in the Summer Gardens

Summer Palace ⑰
Летний дворец
Letniy dvorets

Naberezhnaya Kutuzova. **Map** 2 F4.
📞 *314 0374.* ⏰ *11am–7pm daily.*
⚫ *11 Nov–30 Apr.* 🚌 *46, 134.*
🚎 *2, 12, 32, 34, 54.* 📷 ✔

BUILT FOR Peter the Great,
the modest two-storey
Summer Palace is the oldest
stone building in the city. It
was designed in the Dutch
style by Domenico Trezzini
and was completed in 1714.
The celebrated Prussian sculptor Andreas Schlüter created
the delightful maritime bas-
reliefs (1713) which are an
allegorical commentary on
Russia's naval triumphs under
Peter the Great's stewardship.

Grander than his wooden
cabin *(see p73)*, Peter's second St Petersburg residence is
still by no means comparable
to the magnificent palaces
built by his successors.

On the ground floor, the
reception room is hung with
portraits of the tsar and his
ministers and contains Peter's
oak Admiralty Chair. The
tsar's bedroom has its original four-poster bed with a
coverlet of Chinese silk, and
an 18th-century ceiling painting showing the triumph of
Morpheus, the god of sleep.
Next door is the turnery
which contains some original
Russian lathes as well as
an elaborately carved wooden
meteorological instrument,
designed in Dresden in 1714.

The palace boasted the city's
first plumbing system with
water piped directly into the
kitchen. The original black
marble sink can still be seen,
along with the beautifully
tiled kitchen stove and an
array of early 18th-century
cooking utensils. The kitchen
opens onto the exquisite
dining room, imaginatively
refurbished to convey an
atmosphere of domesticity.
It was used only for small
family gatherings since major
banquets were held at the
Menshikov Palace *(see p62)*.

An original staircase leads up
to the first floor and the more
lavish suite of Peter's second
wife, Catherine. The throne in
the aptly named Throne Room
is ornamented with Nereides
and other sea deities. The glass
cupboards in the Green Room
once displayed Peter's fascinating collection of curiosa
before it was transferred to
the Kunstkammer *(see p60)*.

The remarkable stove in the Summer Palace's tiled kitchen

GOSTINYY DVOR

THE GREAT BAZAAR, Gostinyy Dvor, was the commercial heart of St Petersburg at the beginning of the 18th century and today it still hums with activity. A profusion of smaller retail outlets soon appeared on and around Nevskiy prospekt. Thriving communities of foreign merchants and businessmen also took up residence in the neighbourhood.

Until the mid-19th century, shops in this area catered almost exclusively for the luxury end of the market, fulfilling the limitless demand, created by the royal and aristocratic households, for gold and silverware, jewellery and

Statues on façade of the Russian Museum

haute couture. Increasing commercial and financial activity created a new middle class of business entrepreneurs. By the Revolution, banks proliferated around Nevskiy prospekt, their imposing new offices introducing diverse architectural styles to a largely Neo-Classical setting. Today the wheels of capitalism are turning again and Nevskiy prospekt still attracts a wealthy clientèle. In contrast to the bustling commercial atmosphere of much of the area is the calm oasis of Arts Square, with the Russian Museum and other institutions which act as a reminder of the city's rich cultural life.

SIGHTS AT A GLANCE

Churches
Armenian Church ❼
Church on Spilled Blood p100 ❶
Kazan Cathedral ❶⑤
Lutheran Church ❶⑦

Museums
Engineers' Castle ❷
Pushkin House-Museum ❶⑨
Russian Museum pp104–107 ❸

Streets and Squares
Arts Square ❹
Nevskiy Prospekt ❻
Ostrovskiy Square ❶❶
Ulitsa Zodchevo Rossi ❶❷

Markets and Shops
Apraksin Market ❶❹
Gostinyy Dvor ❽
Yeliseev's ❾

Palaces
Anichkov Palace ❶⓪
Stroganov Palace ❶❻
Vorontsov Palace ❶❸

Hotels
Grand Hotel Europe ❺

Historic Buildings
Glinka Capella ❶⑧
Imperial Stables ❷⓪

KEY

	Street-by-Street map See pp98–9
M	Metro
🚋	Tram

◁ **The busy Nevskiy prospekt, with the Duma tower on the left and the Admiralty in the background**

Street-by-Street: Around Arts Square

Peter the Great statue

THE APTLY NAMED Arts Square, one of Carlo Rossi's finest creations, is surrounded by buildings revealing the city's impressive cultural heritage. The grand palace housing the Russian Museum is flanked by theatres and the Philharmonia concert hall. Behind it are the leafy Mikhaylovskiy Gardens, a haunt of St Petersburg's intellectuals. The gardens stretch down to the beautiful Moyka river which together with two other waterways, the Griboedov and Fontanka, create a shimmering frame for this picturesque area.

★ Church on Spilled Blood
Colourful mosaics an[d] elaborate stone carvin[g] are the main features [of] the church's exterior, which emulates traditional 17th-century Russian style ❶

Mikhaylovskiy Gardens

NABEREZHNAYA REKI MO

MOY

★ Russian Museum
Located in Rossi's Mikhaylovskiy Palace, this famous gallery boasts a fabulous collection of Russian painting, sculpture and applied art. The grand staircase and White Hall are original features ❸

KANAL GRIBOEDOVA

NAB KANALA GRIBOEDOVA

INZHENERNAYA ULITS[A]

Arts Square
The square's present name derives from the number of cultural institutions situated here. On the western side, the Mussorgsky Theatre of Opera and Ballet opened in 1833 ❹

ITALYANSKAYA ULITS[A]

Statue of Pushkin (1957)

Nevskiy prospekt

The Great Hall of the Philharmonia is one of the major concert venues in St Petersburg (see p194).

Grand Hotel Europe
This famous St Petersburg hotel was constructed by Ludwig Fontana in 1873–5. Mighty atlantes adorn its eclectic façade which stretches all the way down to Nevskiy prospekt ❺

The Panteleymon Bridge was rebuilt in 1907–8 to support the new tramway but it retains its original Empire-style decor by Lev Ilyin *(see p37)*.

The bird statue, cast in 1995 by Rezo Gabriadze, refers to a popular rhyme about vodka drinking.

Statue of Peter the Great (1747)

LOCATOR MAP
See Street Finder map 6

GOSTINYY DVOR

SENNAYA PLOSHCHAD

Engineers' Castle
Originally built for Paul I in 1797–1801, this castle was acquired by the Guards Corps of Engineers in 1823. Today it forms part of the Russian Museum and displays historical portraits ❷

STAR SIGHTS

★ **Russian Museum**

★ **Church on Spilled Blood**

KEY

— — — Suggested route

| 0 metres | 100 |
| 0 yards | 100 |

NAB REKI FONTANKA

ZAMKOVAYA ULITSA

FONTANKA

INZHENERNAYA ULITSA

SADOVAYA ULITSA

KLENOVAYA ALLEYA

PLOSHCHAD BELINSKOVO

KARAVANNAYA ULITSA

MANEZHNAYA PLOSHCHAD

Nevskiy prospekt

Museum of Hygiene, with macabre displays of preserved human organs, was established in 1919 to teach the public about health and hygiene.

The Circus or *"tsirk"*, advertised by a colourful neon sign, began performing in the 19th century when it was known as the Ciniselli Circus. It still offers traditional performances *(see p193)* in its original venue by the Fontanka.

Church on Spilled Blood ❶

Храм Спас-на-Крови
Khram Spas-na-Krovi

VISITORS' CHECKLIST

Konyushennaya ploshchad. **Map**
2 E5. 📞 *315 1636.* Ⓜ *Nevskiy
Prospekt, Gostinyy Dvor.* 🚎 *12,
53.* ◯ *11am–6pm Thu–Tue (last
ticket sold 5:30pm).* 📷 🚫 ✓ ✓

THE CHURCH ON SPILLED BLOOD was built on the spot where Tsar Alexander II was murdered on 1 March 1881 *(see p26).* In 1883 his successor, Alexander III, launched a competition for a permanent memorial. The winning design, in the Russian Revival style favoured by the tsar himself, was by Alfred Parland and Ignatiy Malyshev. The foundation stone was laid in October 1883 but the building took almost a quarter of a century to complete.

A riot of colour, the overall effect of the church is created by the imaginative juxtaposition of materials. Inside, more than 20 types of minerals, including jasper, rhodonite, porphyry and Italian marble are lavished on the mosaics of the iconostasis, icon cases, canopy and floor. The interior is temporarily open but might close for more restoration.

Mosaic Tympanum
Mosaic panels showing scenes from the New Testament adorn the exterior. They were based on designs by artists such as Viktor Vasnetsov and Mikhail Nesterov.

The tent-roofed steeple is 81 m (265 ft) high.

Coat of Arms
The 144 mosaic coats of arms on the bell tower represent the regions, towns and provinces of the Russian empire. They were intended to reflect the grief shared by all Russians in the wake of Alexander's assassination.

Jewellers' enamel was used to cover the 1,000 sq m (10,760 sq ft) surface of the five domes.

Glazed ceramic tiles enliven the façade.

Twenty dark red plaques of Norwegian granite are engraved in gilt letters with the most outstanding events of Alexander II's reign (1855–81). Among the historic events recorded are the emancipation of the serfs in 1861 and the conquest of Central Asia (1860–81).

Intricate Detailing
The flamboyant Russian Revival style of the exterior provides a dramatic contrast to the Neo-Classical and Baroque architecture which dominates the centre of St Petersburg.

Mosaic portraits of the saints are set in tiers of *kokoshniki* gables. Almost 7,000 sq m (75,300 sq ft) of mosaics embellish the church's extravagant exterior.

Window Frames
The windows are flanked by carved columns of ornate Estonian marble. The casings are in the form of double and triple kokoshniki (tiered decorative arches).

South façade of the Engineer's Castle and statue of Peter the Great

Engineers' Castle ❷

Инженерный замок
Inzhenernyy zamok

Sadovaya ulitsa 2. **Map** 2 F5.
210 4173. 46, 134, T74.
2, 12, 34, 54. 10am–6pm
Wed–Mon. English.

T HE IMPOSING red brick castle overlooking the Moyka and Fontanka rivers was originally named Mikhaylovskiy Castle. It was erected in 1797–1801 by Vasiliy Bazhenov and Vincenzo Brenna for Tsar Paul I. The tsar's obsessive fear of being assassinated led him to surround his new residence with moats and drawbridges, and to build a secret underground passage to the barracks on the Field of Mars *(see p94)*. All these precautions proved futile and, after living in his fortified castle for just 40 days, Paul fell victim to a military conspiracy which resulted in his murder *(see p22)*.

In 1823 the fortress was acquired by the Guards Corps of Engineers and was given its current name. The school's most famous graduate was Dostoevsky *(see p123)*. Today the castle serves as a branch of the nearby Russian Museum.

Paintings of the city's prominent citizens are hung in the portrait gallery and there is a display on the building's military associations. The Church of the Archangel Michael can be accessed via the exhibition and is a good example of Brenna's Neo-Classical style.

In front of the castle stands a bronze statue of Peter the Great on horseback, designed by Bartolomeo Carlo Rastrelli and cast in 1747.

Russian Museum ❸

See pp104–107.

Arts Square ❹

Площадь Искусств
Ploshchad Iskusstv

Map 6 F1. M Nevskiy Prospekt, Gostinyy Dvor.

S EVERAL OF THE CITY'S leading cultural institutions are located on this imposing Neo-Classical square, hence its name. The attractive square was designed by Carlo Rossi in the early 19th century to harmonize with the magnificent Mikhaylovskiy Palace (now the Russian Museum) which stands on its northern side.

On the opposite side of the square is the Great Hall of the St Petersburg Philharmonia, also known as the Shostakovich Hall *(see p43)*. This is where the Philharmonic Orchestra has been based since the 1920s *(see p194)*. Constructed by Paul Jacot in 1834–9, it started as a Nobles' Club where concerts were held. Among the works premiered here were Beethoven's *Missa Solemnis* in 1824 and Tchaikovsky's *(see p45) Pathétique* in 1893.

On the square's western side is the Mussorgsky Theatre of Opera and Ballet *(see p194)*, rebuilt by Albert Kavos in the mid-19th century. In the centre of the square is a sculpture of one of Russia's greatest literary figures, Alexander Pushkin *(see p44)*. The statue was executed by leading post-war sculptor, Mikhail Anikushin.

Grand Hotel Europe's elegant Style-Moderne restaurant *(see p181)*

Grand Hotel Europe ❺

Гранд Отель Европа
Grand Otel Evropa

Mikhaylovskaya ulitsa 1/7. **Map** 6 F1.
119 6000. M Nevskiy Prospekt, Gostinyy Dvor. See Where to Stay p173.

O NE OF RUSSIA'S most famous hotels, the ornate Grand Hotel Europe (1873–5) was designed by Ludwig Fontana. The building owes much of its character to alterations made in the 1910s by Style-Moderne architect Fyodor Lidval.

Before the Revolution, the hotel's magnificent restaurant was a favourite rendezvous for members of the diplomatic corps and secret police. In the 1970s, the hotel café became a popular meeting place for young intellectuals and artists.

Pushkin's statue in front of the Russian Museum, Arts Square

The Church on Spilled Blood, a magical reminder of old Russia ▷

Russian Museum ③

Русский Музей
Russkiy Muzey

THE MUSEUM is housed in the Mikhaylovskiy Palace, one of Carlo Rossi's finest Neo-Classical creations which was built in 1819–25 for Grand Duke Mikhail Pavlovich. Alexander III's plans to create a public museum were realized by his son, Nicholas II, when the Russian Museum opened here in 1898. Today, the museum holds one of the world's greatest collections of Russian art.

Stairs to ground floor

The Benois Wing, named after its main architect Leonty Benois, was added in 1913–19.

Stairs to ground floor

★ **Mother** (1915)
The peasant woman in Kuzma Petrov-Vodkin's painting represents the future, while her Madonna-like pose echoes the Italian Renaissance.

Room 79
usually displays paintings by avant-garde artists such as Chagall, Malevich and Kandinsky.

Entrance to temporary exhibitions

Ticket office

Portrait of Sergey Diaghilev (1906)
Leon Bakst's painting reveals the determination and vitality of the famous impresario and founder of the Ballets Russes. Bakst also designed costumes for the ballets (see p119).

STAR EXHIBITS

★ **The Last Day of Pompeii by Bryullov**

★ **Mother by Petrov-Vodkin**

★ **Barge-Haulers on the Volga by Repin**

Stairs to first floor of Benois Wing

GALLERY GUIDE

The main entrance on Arts Square leads to the ticket office in the basement. The exhibition starts on the first floor. It is arranged chronologically in numbered rooms starting with icons in Room 1. It continues on the ground floor of the main building and Rossi Wing, ending with modern art on the first floor of the Benois Wing.

Folk Art Toy (1930s)
This clay toy from Dykomovo is part of the colourful selection of folk art which also includes lacquer boxes, painted ceramics and textiles.

★ **The Last Day of Pompeii** (1833)
*Karl Bryullov's Classical subject em-
bodies the aesthetic principles of the
Academy of Arts. This vivid depiction
of the eruption of Vesuvius won him
the Grand Prix at the Paris Salon.*

★ **Barge-Haulers on
the Volga** (1870–73)
*Ilya Repin was the most famous
member of the Wanderers, a
group of artists dedicated to social
realism and Russian themes. His
powerful indictment of forced
labour imbues the oppressed
victims with sullen dignity.*

**Stairs to
ground floor**

14
15
16 17 13 12
11
10 9 8 7
1 2 3 6
4 5

**The White
Hall** contains
original Empire-
style furniture
by Carlo Rossi.

**Start of
exhibition**

Rossi Wing

43 42 41 40 39
54 35 34 33 32 31 30 29 28 27 26 25 24
36 38 18 19 20 21 22 23

**Entrance points
from basement
ticket office**

A Meal in the Monastery (1865–76)
*Vasiliy Perov's politically motivated
canvas exposes the hypocrisy of the
Orthodox clergy, with the juxtaposition of good and evil, rich and
poor, false piety and true faith.*

The portico of
eight Corinthian
columns is the
central feature of
Rossi's façade.
Behind is a frieze
of Classical figures,
designed by Rossi
and executed by
Demut-Malinovskiy.

**Stairs to
first floor**

**The main
entrance** is
through a small door
which leads to the
basement with a ticket
office, a cloakroom,
toilets and a café.

KEY

☐	Icons
☐	1700–1860
☐	The Wanderers and Fin de Siècle
☐	20th-century art
☐	Folk art
☐	Temporary exhibitions
☐	Non-exhibition space

Exploring the Russian Museum

Housing one of the world's greatest collections of Russian art, the museum originally comprised official-ly approved works from the Academy of Arts *(see p63)*. When the museum was nationalized after the Revolution, art was transferred from palaces, churches and private collections. By the 1930s, Socialist Realism had become state policy and avant-garde works were stored away, to reemerge with the advent of *perestroika* in the 1980s.

Portrait of E I Nelidova (1773), by Dmitriy Levitskiy

The Angel with the Golden Hair, an icon from the early 12th century

Icons

The museum's fine collection begins with icons dating from the 12th–17th centuries. Russian icons derive from the Orthodox tradition and thus, just like Byzantine icons, tend to be sombre, marked by an absence of movement and a remote, mystic characterization of the saints. A superb example is one of the earliest icons, *The Angel with the Golden Hair*, in which the large, expressive eyes and delicate modelling of the Archangel Gabriel's face convey a sense of ethereal grace.

The Novgorod School *(see p163)* encouraged a much bolder and brighter style with a greater sense of drama and movement. And yet it is the poetically expressive and technically refined work of Andrey Rublev (c.1340–c.1430) that is considered by many to mark the pinnacle of Russian icon painting.

1700–1860

The first secular portraits (which owed much to the static quality of the icons) appeared in the second half of the 17th century. It was, however, under Peter the Great that Russian painting fully cast off from its Byzantine moorings. Peter himself was the first patron to send young artists, often serfs, to study abroad. Secular art gained momentum in 1757 with the establishment of the Academy of Arts *(see p63)* which placed a heavy emphasis on Classical and mythological subjects.

European influence permeates the work of Russia's first important portrait painters, Ivan Nikitin (1688–1741) and Andrey Matveev (1701–39). The art of portraiture matured with Dmitriy Levitskiy (1735–1822), amongst whose best known works is a series of portraits of noble girls from the Smolnyy Institute.

Russian landscape painting was stimulated by the Romantic movement and in particular artists who sought inspiration abroad, including Silvestr Shchedrin (1791–1830) and Fyodor Matveev (1758–1826).

Ivan Aivazovskiy's (1817–1900) vast marine paintings, however, have something purely Russian in their scale and mood. Romanticism also influenced history painters such as Karl Bryullov (1799–1852), as in his depiction of *The Last Day of Pompeii*.

THE WANDERERS AND FIN DE SIÈCLE

In 1863 a group of students, led by Ivan Kramskoy (1837–87), rebelled against the Academy of Arts. Seven years later they went on to set up the Association of Travel-ling Art Exhibitions, and came to be known as the Wanderers *(Peredvizhniki)* or Itinerants. They demanded that painting be more socially relevant and were fundamentally committed to Russian subject matter.

The most versatile of the Wanderers was Ilya Repin *(see p43)* whose bold canvas

Knight at the Crossroads (1882), by Viktor Vasnetsov

The Six-Winged Seraph (1904), by Mikhail Vrubel

Barge-Haulers on the Volga combines a powerful attack on forced labour with a romantic view of the Russian people. *A Meal in the Monastery* by Vasiliy Perov (1833–82) is a satirical and equally effective attack on social injustice.

The nationalist element led history painters such as Nikolay Ge (1831–94) and Vasiliy Surikov (1848–1916) to turn to Russian history for inspiration, treating their subjects with a new psychological acuity, as in Ge's canvas of 1871–2, in which Peter the Great interrogates his sullenly resistant son.

The general Slavic revival also breathed new life into landscape painting, concentrating on the beauties of the Russian countryside. The master of the genre was Isaak Levitan (1860–1900), whose *Golden Autumn Village*, dated 1889, is almost Impressionist in style, a sign perhaps that the ascendancy of the Wanderers was coming to an end.

Viktor Vasnetsov (1848–1926) turned to Russia's heroic, and often legendary, pre-European past, in realistically painted canvases such as the *Knight at the Crossroads*. A haunting metaphor for Russia's uncertain future, the painting reveals that Vasnetsov was unable to avoid the fin-de-siècle melancholy and mysticism which was so potently expressed in the work of the next up-and-coming generation of artists, notably the Symbolists.

20TH-CENTURY ART

THE DARK, brooding canvases of Symbolist Mikhail Vrubel (1856–1910) combine Russian and religious themes with a more international outlook. Vrubel used colour and form to depict emotion and in *The Six-Winged Seraph* he employs a broken, vibrant, surface to express tension.

Another major contribution to 20th-century art was the "World of Art" movement, founded by Alexandre Benois and Sergey Diaghilev in the 1890s *(see p26)*. It rejected the notion of "socially useful art" in favour of a new tenet, "art pure and unfettered", and also opened up Russian painting to Western influences. Many members of the group,

Portrait of the Director Vsevolod Meyerhold (1916), **Boris Grigorev**

including Benois and Leon Bakst, designed stage sets and costumes for Diaghilev's Ballets Russes *(see p119)*.

The Russian avant-garde grew out of these local influences, plus the art of Cézanne, Picasso and Matisse. Mikhail Larionov (1881–1964) and Natalya Goncharova (1881–1962) both made brilliant use of Russian folk art as inspiration for primitivist works such as Goncharova's *Bleaching Canvas* (1908). They often altered their style in response to changing stimuli and later turned to Futurism's cult of the machine, as in Goncharova's *Cyclist* (1913) *(see p40)*.

The link between innovation in painting and the arts in general at this time is strikingly depicted in Boris Grigorev's angular portrait of Meyerhold, himself renowned for his radical approach to theatre.

Kazimir Malevich's (1878–1935) fascination with the juxtaposition of simple geometric shapes inspired the Suprematist movement. Vasily Kandinsky (1866–1944), a leading member of Munich's Blaue Reiter group, was also a key figure in the growth of Russian abstract art.

Marc Chagall (1887–1985), El Lissitskiy (1890–1941) and Alexander Rodchenko (1891–1956) are also represented.

Due to the high demand for the loan of avant-garde works abroad, a changing selection by the major artists is on show.

FOLK ART

FOLK ART became a strong influence on the development of modern Russian art in the 1860s when the wealthy industrialist and patron Savva Mamontov established an artists' colony at Abramtsevo, near Moscow. Vasiliy Polenov (1844–1927), Ilya Repin and Viktor Vasnetsov were among the painters encouraged to work alongside, and learn from, the serf craftsmen on the estate. The museum's collection of folk art is wonderfully diverse and includes exquisitely embroidered tapestries, traditional headdresses, painted tiles, porcelain toys, and lacquered spoons and dishes.

Nevskiy Prospekt ⑥
Невский проспект
Nevskiy prospekt

Map 6 D1–8 D3. M *Nevskiy Prospekt, Gostinyy Dvor. See also pp46–9.*

Russia's most famous street, Nevskiy prospekt, is also St Petersburg's main thoroughfare and artery. In the 1830s, the novelist Nikolai Gogol *(see p42)* declared with great pride: "There is nothing finer than Nevskiy Avenue ... in St Petersburg it is everything ... is there anything more gay, more brilliant, more resplendent than this beautiful street of our capital?". In this respect very little has actually changed, for Nevskiy prospekt's intrinsic "all-powerful" value still prevails today.

Laid out in the early days of the city, it was first known as the Great Perspective Road, running 4.5 km (3 miles) from the Admiralty *(see p78)* to the Alexander Nevskiy Monastery *(see pp130–31)*. In spite of roaming wolves and uncontrollable flooding from the Neva *(see p37)* which made the avenue navigable in 1721, fine mansions, such as the Stroganov Palace *(see p116)* soon started to appear. Shops and bazaars, catering for the nobility, and inns for travelling merchants followed. A magnet pulling rich and poor alike, by the mid-18th century the avenue had become the place to see and be seen, to meet for gossip, business and pleasure.

Today, the street still teems with people until late into the night throughout the year. Many of the city's sights are close to the stretch between the Admiralty and Anichkov Bridge *(see pp46–7)*. Some of the best shops *(see pp186–7)* can be found around Gostinyy dvor and Passazh arcade. Nevskiy prospekt also offers a wealth of cultural interest: the Small Philharmonia concert hall *(see p194)*, the exclusive Grand Hotel Europe *(see p101)*, the city's national library, and a variety of museums, churches, shops, cinemas and eateries. All this ensures that people from all over town regularly visit this thriving street.

Armenian Church portico (1771–9)

Armenian Church ⑦
Армянская церковь
Armyanskaya tserkov

Nevskiy prospekt 40–42. **Map** 6 F1. M *Gostinyy Dvor.* ☐ *9am–10pm.*

Yuriy Velten designed the beautiful blue and white Armenian Church of St Catherine, with its Neo-Classical portico and single cupola. The church, which opened in 1780, was financed by a wealthy Armenian businessman called Ioakim Lazarev, who acquired the money from the sale of a Persian diamond which Count Grigoriy Orlov purchased for Catherine the Great *(see p22)*.

Closed in 1930, the building has now been returned to the Armenian community and visitors are welcome to attend a service or view the restoration work which is under way.

Gostinyy Dvor ⑧
Гостиный двор
Gostinyy dvor

Nevskiy pr 35. **Map** 6 F2. ☎ *312 4165.* M *Gostinyy Dvor.* ☐ *10am–9pm Mon–Sat, 11am–6pm Sun.*

The term *gostinyy dvor* originally meant a coaching inn, but as trade developed around the inns, with travelling merchants setting up their stalls, it later came to mean "trading rows". The original wooden structure of this *gostinyy dvor* was destroyed by fire in 1736. Twenty years later, Bartolomeo Rastrelli

View along the bustle of Nevskiy prospekt, the hub of St Petersburg

designed a new building but the project proved too costly and ambitious. Building recommenced in 1761 and continued until 1785. Vallin de la Mothe created the striking sequence of columned arcades and massive porticos. The prominent yellow building forms an irregular quadrangle which is bounded on one side by Nevskiy prospekt. The combined length of its façades is nearly 1 km (3,300 ft).

In the 19th century the gallery became a fashionable promenade where more than 5,000 people were employed. Serious damage during the Siege of Leningrad *(see p27)* led to major reconstruction, making it more like a modern department store. Even now, with all the changes, it has retained its layout of "stalls" of individual trading units. Today it includes branches of foreign shops and a wide range of goods, making it the city's most important store *(see p187)*.

Style-Moderne stained-glass windows in Yeliseev's food store

Columned arcades, Gostinyy dvor

Yeliseev's **9**
Елисеевский гастроном
Yeliseevskiy gastronom

Nevskiy prospekt 56. **Map** 6 F1.
C *311 9323.* **M** *Gostinyy Dvor.*
O *9am–9pm Mon–Fri, 10am–9pm Sat, 10am–7pm Sun.* ● *Public holidays.*

THE SUCCESSFUL Yeliseev dynasty was founded by Pyotr Yeliseev, an ambitious peasant who, in 1813, opened a wine shop on Nevskiy prospekt. By the turn of the century his grandsons owned a chocolate factory, numerous houses, inns and this famous food store. Housed in the city's most opulent Style-Moderne building, designed by Gavriil Baranovskiy in 1901–3, it is adorned with bronzes, heroic sculptures and huge windows. The equally impressive interior, with its stained-glass windows, marble counters and crystal chandeliers, steals the attention from the delicacies on sale *(see p190)*. A plaque by the main door honours the grandsons.

Anichkov Palace **10**
Аничков дворец
Anichkov dvorets

Nevskiy prospekt 39. **Map** 7 A2.
M *Gostinyy Dvor.* ● *to public except for special events.*

IN THE EARLY days, the broad Fontanka river was lined by palaces accessible mainly by boat. One of them was the Anichkov Palace (1741–50), remodelled in Baroque style in 1754. The palace was a gift from Tsarina Elizabeth to her lover Aleksey Razumovskiy. It was named after Lieutenant Colonel Mikhail Anichkov who set up camp on this site at the time of the founding of the city. Over the years the palace was rebuilt and altered many times, according to the tastes of each successive owner. After Razumovskiy's death, Catherine the Great in turn gave the building to her lover, Prince Potemkin *(see p25)*. In the early 19th century, Neo-Classical details were added by Carlo Rossi.

The palace then became the traditional winter residence of the heir to the throne. When Alexander III became tsar in 1881, however, he continued to live here, rather than move to the Winter Palace as was customary. After his death, his widow Maria Fyodorovna stayed on until the Revolution.

The palace originally had large gardens to the west but these were curtailed in 1816 when Ostrovskiy Square *(see p110)* was created and two Neo-Classical pavilions were added. The elegant colonnaded building overlooking the Fontanka to the east had been another addition to the palace, commissioned by Giacomo Quarenghi in 1803–5. It was initially built as an arcade where goods from the imperial factories were stored before being allocated to the palaces. Later it was converted into government offices.

Quarenghi's addition to the Anichkov Palace from Nevskiy prospekt

Porticoed façade of Aleksandrinskiy Theatre (1828–32), Ostrovskiy Square

Ostrovskiy Square

Площадь Островского
Ploshchad Ostrovskovo

Map 6 F2. **M** *Gostinyy Dvor.* **Russian National Library** ● *to foreigners unless special permission is obtained.* **Theatre Museum** ◻ *11am–6pm Thu–Mon; noon–7pm Wed.* ● *public hols.* ◻ ◻

ONE OF RUSSIA's most brilliant and prolific architects, Carlo Rossi, created this early 19th-century square which is now named in honour of the prominent dramatist Aleksandr Ostrovskiy (1823–86).

The focal point of the square is the elegant Aleksandrinskiy Theatre *(see p194)*, designed in the Neo-Classical style which Rossi favoured. The portico of six Corinthian columns is crowned by a chariot of Apollo, sculpted by Stepan Pimenov.

The building was the new home to Russia's oldest theatre company, set up in 1756. Plays premiered here included Nikolai Gogol's *The Inspector General* (1836) and Anton Chekhov's *The Seagull* (1901). In Soviet times the theatre was renamed the Pushkin Theatre.

In the garden just in front of the theatre is a monument to Catherine the Great, surprisingly the only one to be found in St Petersburg. It was designed principally by Mikhail Mikeshin and unveiled in 1873. The statue depicts Catherine surrounded by states-men and other worthies, and includes the female president (1783–96) of the Academy of Sciences, Princess Yekaterina Dashkova.

On the west side of the square, opposite the Anichkov Palace *(see p109)* is an elegant colon-nade decorated with Classical sculptures. This is the exten-sion of the Russian Library, made by Rossi in 1828–34. Founded in 1795, the library currently holds more than 28 million items. A prized pos-session is the personal library of the French philosopher Voltaire, which Catherine the Great purchased to show her appreciation of her sometime mentor and correspondent.

In the southeast corner of the square, at No. 6, is the Theatre Museum which traces the evolution of the Russian stage from its origins in mid-18th-century serf and imperial theatres. Amid the eclectic array of playbills, photographs, costumes, set designs and other artifacts is the bejewelled costume worn by the famous bass Fyodor Shalyapin in the opera *Boris Godunov*. There are also some bold and imagi-native set designs by one of the great innovators of modern theatre, the director Vsevolod Meyerhold (1874–1940).

Ulitsa Zodchevo Rossi

Улица Зодчего Росси
Ulitsa Zodchevo Rossi

Map 6 F2. **M** *Gostinyy Dvor.*

THERE COULD BE no better memorial to Carlo Rossi than the near perfect architec-tural ensemble of identical arcades and colonnades forming "Architect Rossi Street". The 22-m (72-ft) high buildings stand precisely 22 m (72 ft) apart and are 220 m (720 ft) in length. Viewed from ploshchad Lomonosova, the perspective hypnotically coaxes the eye towards the Aleksandrinskiy Theatre.

At No. 2 is the home of the former Imperial School of Ballet, now named after the teacher Agrippina Vaganova (1879–1951), one of the few dancers not to emigrate after the Revolution. The school began in 1738 when Jean-Baptiste Landé began training orphans and palace servants' children to take part in court entertainment. It moved to its present quarters in 1836 and has since produced many of Russia's most celebrated dan-cers *(see p118)*, including Anna Pavlova and Rudolf Nureyev.

19th-century photograph of ulitsa Zodchevo Rossi (1828–34)

ARCHITECT CARLO ROSSI

Carlo Rossi (1775–1849) was one of the last great exponents of Neo-Classicism in St Petersburg. He found an ideal client in Alexander I, who shared his belief in the use of architecture to express the power of the ruling autocracy. By the time of his death, Rossi had created no fewer than 12 of St Petersburg's impressive streets and 13 of its squares, including Palace Square *(see p83)*. Rossi's status as Alexander I's favourite architect encouraged rumours that Rossi was the offspring of an affair between Tsar Paul I and Rossi's Italian ballerina mother.

all the way along Apraksin pereulok, and in a yard *(see p187)* behind the arcade, toys, car parts, cigarettes, watches, TV sets, alcohol and leather jackets are sold.

Kazan Cathedral ⑮

Казанский собор
Kazanskiy sobor

Kazanskaya pl 2. **Map** 6 E1. 📞 *311 0495.* Ⓜ *Nevskiy Prospekt.* ⭘ *11am–6pm Mon, Tue, Thu, Fri; noon–6pm Sat; 12:30pm–6pm Sun.* 📷

ONE OF St Peterburg's most majestic churches, the Kazan Cathedral was commissioned by Paul I and took over a decade to build (1801–11). The impressive design by serf architect Andrey Voronikhin was inspired by St Peter's in Rome. Its 111-m (364-ft) long, curved colonnade disguises the orientation of the building which runs parallel to Nevskiy prospekt, conforming to a religious stipulation that the main altar face east. Voronikhin originally intended to duplicate the colonnade on the south side.

The cathedral is named after the miracle-working icon of Kazan, Mother of God, which

it once housed. The icon, now in the Prince Vladimir Cathedral on Petrogradskaya, is said to have been responsible for delivering Moscow from the Poles in 1612.

The interior decoration is generally subdued. Its most impressive features are the great 80-m (262-ft) high dome and the massive pink Finnish granite columns with bronze capitals and bases. The nave still houses an exhibition on Christianity, which was set up to supersede a museum of atheism set up by the Communists during a time of religious repression.

The cathedral's completion coincided almost exactly with the war against Napoleon *(see p22).* In 1813 Field Marshal Mikhail Kutuzov (1745–1813), who skilfully masterminded the retreat from Moscow, was buried here in the north chapel with full military honours. Kutuzov has been immortalized in Tolstoy's great novel *War and Peace* (1865–9). His statue and that of his comrade-in-arms, Mikhail Barclay de Tolly (1761–1818), both by Boris Orlovskiy, have stood in Kazanskaya ploshchad outside the cathedral since 1837.

Central corpus of Vorontsov Palace

Vorontsov Palace ⑬

Воронцовский дворец
Vorontsovskiy dvorets

Sadovaya ulitsa 26. **Map** 6 F2. ⬤ *to public.* Ⓜ *Gostinyy Dvor, Sennaya Ploshchad.*

THE MOST EXCLUSIVE military school in the Russian empire, the Corps des Pages, occupied the Vorontsov Palace from 1810–1918. Among those privileged enough to study here were a number of the Decembrists *(see pp22–3)* and Prince Felix Yusupov *(see p121).* Today the palace houses the Suvorov Military Academy.

Designed by Bartolomeo Rastrelli *(see p93),* the handsome palace, which once stood in its own extensive grounds, was built in 1749–57 for Prince Mikhail Vorontsov, one of Tsarina Elizabeth's leading ministers. Rastrelli's graceful wrought-iron railings are among the earliest examples of their kind in Russia.

Apraksin Market ⑭

Апраксин двор
Apraksin dvor

Sadovaya ulitsa. **Map** 6 E2. Ⓜ *Gostinyy Dvor, Sennaya Ploshchad.* ⭘ *9am–5pm.*

FOUNDED in the late 18th century, the market takes its name from the Apraksin family who owned the land it was built on. When fire destroyed the original wooden stalls in 1862, the arcade was erected. By 1900 there were more than 600 outlets selling everything from food, wine and spices to furs, furniture and haberdashery. Today, street stalls extend

Pink granite columns and mosaic floor in main nave, Kazan Cathedral

Stroganov Palace ⑯

Строгановский дворец
Stroganovskiy dvorets

Nevskiy prospekt 17. **Map** 6 E1.
Ⓜ *Nevskiy Prospekt.* ☎ *311 8238.*
◯ *for temporary exhibitions.* 🅿️

THIS BAROQUE masterpiece
was designed in 1752–4
by Bartolomeo Rastrelli *(see
p93).* Commissioned by the
enormously wealthy Count
Sergey Stroganov, the palace
was occupied by his descendants until the Revolution. The
Stroganovs amassed their huge
fortune through the monopoly
they held on salt, which came
from mines in their vast terri-
tories in the north.

The green and white palace,
which overlooks both Nevskiy
prospekt and the Moyka river,
was one of the city's most
impressive private residences.
The magnificent river façade is
decorated with Doric columns,
cornices, pediments and inventive window surrounds.

The Stroganovs were noted
collectors of everything from
Egyptian antiquities and Roman
coins to icons and Old Masters.
The palace was nationalized
after the Revolution and then
preserved for ten years as a
museum of the life of the
decadent aristocracy. When it
was closed, some of the objects
were auctioned in the West,
and the rest were transferred

**Neo-Romanesque portal of the
Lutheran Church (1832–8)**

to the Hermitage *(see pp84–
93).* The Russian Museum *(see
pp104–107)* aims to revive the
idea of a museum of noble
life and, in the meantime, is
opening rooms as restoration
finishes, showing temporary
exhibitions of objects relating
to the Stroganov family.

Lutheran Church ⑰

Лютеранская церковь
Lyuteranskaya tserkov

Nevskiy prospekt 22–24. **Map** 6 E1.
Ⓜ *Nevskiy Prospekt.*

SET BACK a little from Nevskiy
prospekt, the attractive,
twin-towered Lutheran church
is dedicated to St Peter. Built
in its present form during the

1830s, the church served
St Petersburg's ever-growing
German community *(see p57).*
The prize-winning design by
Aleksandr Bryullov is in an un-
usual, Neo-Romanesque style.

From 1936 the church was
used as a vegetable store until,
in the late 1950s, it was converted into a swimming pool.
The basin was carved out of
the nave floor, the gallery
lined with spectator benches
and there was a high diving
board under the apse. The
building has now been handed
back to the German-Lutheran
Church of Russia. Restoration
is under way, but the church is
open and has Sunday services.

Glinka Capella concert hall

Glinka Capella ⑱

Хоровая капелла имени
М. И. Глинки
*Khorovaya kapella imeni
MI Glinki*

Naberezhnaya reki Moyki 20. **Map**
2 E5. ☎ *314 1058.* 🚌 *12, 53.*
◯ *for concerts only.* 🅿️ 🚫
See Entertainment p194.

ENCLOSED WITHIN a courtyard
off the Moyka river is this
ochre-coloured concert hall
with a façade in the French
Classical style of Louis XV. The
Glinka Capella was designed
by Leontiy Benois in 1887–9
as the residence of the Imperial
Court choir. Founded during
the reign of Peter the Great,
the choir is as old as the city
itself. Former directors have
included the distinguished
Russian composers Mikhail
Glinka (1804–57) and Nikolai
Rimsky-Korsakov (1844–1908).

With its excellent acoustics
Glinka Capella can claim to be
one of the best concert halls in
the world. Outside is Singers'
Bridge *(Pevcheskiy most),* aptly
named, which was designed
by Yegor Adam in 1837–40.

Elaborate west façade of the Stroganov Palace overlooking the Moyka river

Personal effects in Pushkin's study, Pushkin House-Museum

than 4,500 volumes in a staggering 14 European and Oriental languages. Among these are works by the authors whom Pushkin most admired, including Shakespeare, Byron, Heine, Dante and Voltaire.

Pushkin House-Museum ⑲
Музей-квартира
А. С. Пушкина
Muzey-kvartira AS Pushkina

Naberezhnaya reki Moyki 12.
Map 2 E5. 311 3531. 12, 53.
11am–5pm Wed–Mon.
public hols.

E VERY YEAR on the anniversary of Alexander Pushkin's death (29 January 1837), loyal devotees of Russia's greatest poet come to lay floral tributes outside his apartment. Pushkin was born in Moscow in 1799, but spent many years of his life in St Petersburg and the museum is one of several places in the city with which the poet is associated.

From the autumn of 1836 until his death, Pushkin lived in this fairly opulent apartment overlooking the Moyka, with his wife Natalya, their four children and Natalya's two sisters. It was here on the couchette in the study that he bled to death after his fateful duel with d'Anthés *(see p83).*

Some half dozen rooms on the first floor have been refurbished in the Empire style of the period. By far the most evocative is Pushkin's study, which is arranged exactly as it was when he died. On the writing table is an ivory paper knife given to the poet by his sister, a bronze handbell and a treasured inkstand *(see p39).* Embellished with the figure of an Ethiopian boy, the inkstand is a reminder of Pushkin's great grandfather, Abram Hannibal. Bought by the Russian ambassador in Constantinople as a

slave in 1706, Hannibal served as a general under Peter the Great. He was the inspiration for the unfinished novel *The Negro of Peter the Great* on which Pushkin was working at the time of his death.

On the wall in front of his desk is a Turkish sabre presented to Pushkin in the Caucasus, where he had been exiled in 1820 for his radical views. Ironically it was there that he spent some of his happiest years. It was there too that he began his most famous work, *Eugene Onegin,* a novel in verse written in 1823–30.

The most impressive feature of the apartment is the poet's library which contains more

Imperial Stables ⑳
Конюшенное Ведомство
Konyushennoe Vedomstvo

Konyushennaya ploshchad 1.
Map 2 E5. 12, 53.
Church daily.

T HE LONG, salmon-coloured building running parallel to the Moyka embankment is the former Imperial stables. Originally built in the first part of the 18th century, the stables were reconstructed by Vasiliy Stasov in 1817–23.

The only part of the building open to the public lies behind the central section of the long south façade, crowned by a silver dome and cross. This is the church where Alexander Pushkin's funeral took place on 1 February 1837. Its Neo-Classical interior is in the form of a basilica and is decorated with yellow marble pillars. The gilded iconostasis of white wood is early 19th-century.

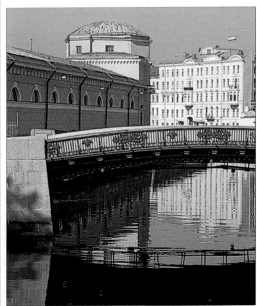
North façade of Imperial Stables (left) and Little Stable Bridge on the Moyka

SENNAYA PLOSHCHAD

THE WESTERN PART of St Petersburg is an area of contrasts, home to some of the city's wealthiest residences and most poverty-stricken dwellings. The palatial architecture along the English Quay is a world away from the decrepit living quarters around bustling Sennaya ploshchad, which have changed little since Dostoevsky *(see p123)* described them. In between lies the old maritime quarter, once inhabited by Peter the Great's shipwrights, many of whom were English. This area extended all the way from the New Holland warehouses to

Coat of arms on Yusupov Palace

St Nicholas' Cathedral, which stands on the site of the naval parade ground. Theatre Square has been a hub of entertainment since the mid-18th century. It is dominated by the prestigious Mariinskiy Theatre and the Rimsky-Korsakov Conservatory, where many of Russia's greatest artists began their careers. Before 1917, the streets leading off the square were home to theatre directors, actors, ballerinas, artists and musicians. Today, performing artists are once more returning to live in this shady backwater, attracted by the peace of the tree-lined canals.

SIGHTS AT A GLANCE

Cathedrals
St Nicholas' Cathedral ❷

Theatres
Mariinskiy Theatre p119 ❶

Historic Buildings and Areas
Main Post Office ❼
New Holland ❺
Rimsky-Korsakov
  Conservatory ❸

Palaces
Yusupov Palace ❹

Streets and Squares
Bolshaya Morskaya Ulitsa ❽
The English Quay ❻
Sennaya Ploshchad ❾

Museums
Railway Museum ❿

KEY

	Street-by-Street map *See pp116–17*
M	Metro
🚊	Tram stop

0 metres   600
0 yards   600

◁ **Gilded Baroque interior of the upper church of St Nicholas' Cathedral**

Street-by-Street: Theatre Square

THEATRE SQUARE WAS ONCE known as Carousel Square and was frequently used as the site for fairs and festivals. During the 19th century when St Petersburg became the cultural capital of Russia, the Mariinskiy Theatre and Rimsky-Korsakov Conservatory were established, and the neighbourhood became home to many artists. Today, the tradition of entertainment is still thriving and Theatre Square remains a focal point for theatrical and musical life *(see p194).*

Atlas on prospekt Rimskovo-Korsakova

Nearby, the tree-lined canal embankments and the gardens surrounding the beautiful St Nicholas' Cathedral are enchanting places to stroll.

The Monument to Rimsky-Korsakov, who taught at the Conservatory for 37 years, was designed by Veniamin Bogolyubov and Vladimir Ingal and erected in 1952.

Yusupov Palace
Historic site of the gruesome murder of Rasputin (see p121), this grand palace belonged to the wealthy Yusupov family. Its opulent interiors include this Italian marble staircase and a tiny Rococo theatre ❹

Rimsky-Korsakov Conservatory
Tchaikovsky, Prokofiev and Shostakovich (see p43) were among the talents nurtured by Russia's first conservatory, founded in 1862 by pianist and composer Anton Rubinstein ❸

Monument to Mikhail Glinka
(see p44)

★ **Mariinskiy Theatre**
This theatre has been home to the world-famous Mariinskiy (Kirov) Opera and Ballet Company since 1860. Hidden behind its imposing façade is the sumptuous auditorium where many of Russia's greatest dancers (see p118) have performed ❶

The Lion Bridge *(Lviny Most)* is one of a number of quaint and curious suspension bridges on the narrow, tree-lined Griboedov canal *(see p34)*. These bridges are well-known meeting places, notably for romantic trysts.

LOCATOR MAP
See Street Finder, map 5

The House of Michel Fokine at No. 109 is where the renowned ballet-master and choreographer lived before the Revolution.

STAR SIGHT

★ **Mariinskiy Theatre**

The Benois House belonged to an artistic dynasty which included the co-founder of the World of Art movement, Alexandre Benois *(see p107)*.

The Belfry, an elegant four-tiered structure with a gilded spire, was built to mark the main entrance to St Nicholas' Cathedral.

NAB KANALA GRIBOEDOVA

GLINKI

SPEKT RIMSKOVO-KORSAKOVA

ULITSA MYASNIKOVA

KANAL GRIBOEDOVA

St Nicholas' Cathedral
A fine example of 18th-century Russian Baroque, the lofty upper church is richly decorated with icons, gilding and this carved iconostasis. The lower church, beautifully lit with candles, is also open for worship **2**

KEY

– – – Suggested route

SADOVAYA ULITSA

0 metres	100
0 yards	100

The former Nicholas market, characterized by its long arcade and steep roof, was constructed in 1788–9. In the 19th century it became an unofficial labour exchange as many unemployed workers gathered here.

Ballet in St Petersburg

ADMIRED THROUGHOUT the world, Russian ballet traces its origins back to 1738 when a French dancing master, Jean-Baptiste Landé, established a school in St Petersburg to train the children of palace employees. The Imperial Ballet School, as it soon became known, flourished under a string of distinguished foreign teachers, culminating in Marius Petipa (1818–1910). Petipa first joined the school in 1847 as a principal dancer and later choreographed over 60 ballets, inspiring such famous dancers as Matilda Kshesinskaya *(see p72)*.

Matilda Kshesinskaya's ballet shoes

Following the 1905 Revolution, a reaction against Classicism led to an increasing number of defections from the Imperial theatres to the new private companies like Sergey Diaghilev's Ballets Russes. The dispersion of talent increased after the Bolsheviks seized power in 1917 and many artists went into exile abroad. Fortunately for Soviet Russia, the distinguished prima ballerina Agrippina Vaganova remained to train the next generation of dancers. St Petersburg's Russian Ballet Academy now bears her name *(see p110)*.

Anna Pavlova's *(1885–1931) most famous role,* The Dying Swan, *was created especially for her by Michel Fokine. In 1912 Pavlova left Russia to form her own touring company, spreading her enthusiasm for ballet throughout Europe.*

Vaslaw Nijinsky *(1890–1950) had one of his greatest roles as the golden slave in* Schéhérazade *which took Paris by storm in 1910. A principal of the Ballets Russes before World War I, he revolutionized male roles. His incomparable technical skills and expressive qualities influenced future generations of dancers.*

Rudolf Nureyev *(1938–93), seen here in* Sleeping Beauty *at the Mariinskiy, defected to the West in 1961. As both choreographer and dancer, Nureyev continued to enthral audiences for over 30 years until his death in 1993.*

The Mariinskiy Ballet, *usually known abroad as the Kirov, is now reviving some of the original productions of the Ballets Russes, including their version of* Giselle, *previously not shown in Russia.*

THE BALLETS RUSSES

The legendary touring company which revolutionized ballet between 1909 and 1929 was the brainchild of the impresario and art critic Sergey Diaghilev (see p43). Diaghilev found a kindred spirit in the choreographer Michel Fokine, who shared his vision of a spectacle that would fuse music, ballet and decor in a seamless artistic whole.

Diaghilev had the pick of dancers from the Mariinskiy and, in 1909, he brought his Ballets Russes to Paris. The company went from strength to strength with successful tours worldwide.

Diaghilev's new company had a remarkable impact on the contemporary art world. The ballets of Fokine, in particular, prepared audiences for greater innovation and experiment. Exciting contributions from costume and set designers Leon Bakst and Alexandre Benois, the composer Igor Stravinsky and the dancers Vaslaw Nijinsky, Anna Pavlova and Tamara Karsavina all played a part in expanding back the artistic frontiers. After Diaghilev's death in 1929, the Ballets Russes fragmented but its ethos and traditions have been preserved in many of today's leading companies.

Early 20th-century programme for the Ballets Russes

One of Russia's most important cultural institutions, the Mariinskiy Theatre

Mariinskiy Theatre ❶

Мариинский театр

Mariinskiy teatr

Teatralnaya ploshchad. **Map** 5 B3.
📞 *114 1211.* 🚎 Э*10, 22, 39Э, 43.*
🚊 *1, 5, 11, 31, 42.* ⬤ *for performances only (see pp194–5).* 📷 🚫

NAMED IN HONOUR of Tsarina Maria Alexandrovna, wife of Alexander II, this theatre is known abroad by its Soviet title, the Kirov, while at home it has reverted to its original name, the Mariinskiy Theatre. The building was erected in 1860 by the architect Albert Kavos, who designed the Bolshoy Theatre in Moscow. It stands on the site of an earlier theatre which was destroyed by fire.

In 1883–96, the Neo-Renaissance façade was remodelled by Viktor Schröter, who added most of the ornamental detail. The sumptuous pale blue and gold auditorium, where so many illustrious dancers have made their debut, creates a dazzling impression. Its architectural decoration of twisted columns, atlantes, cherubs and cameo medallions has remained unchanged since the theatre's completion, and the imperial eagles have recently been restored to the royal box. The ceiling painting of dancing girls and cupids by Italian artist Enrico Franchioli dates from c.1856, while the superb stage curtain was added during Russian ballet's golden age in 1914. Equally remarkable is the glittering festive foyer, decorated with fluted pilasters, bas-reliefs of Russian composers and mirrored doors.

Imperial eagle on the royal box

Although the Mariinskiy is better known abroad for its ballet company, it is also one of the country's leading opera houses. Most of the great 19th-century Russian operas were premiered here, including Mussorgsky's *Boris Godunov* (1874) and Tchaikovsky's *Queen of Spades* (1890). Shostakovich's highly controversial opera *Lady Macbeth of Mtsensk* also opened here in 1934. Widely acclaimed in St Petersburg, this opera was rejected by Stalin and immediately dropped from the repertoire after the composer was denounced in a *Pravda* editorial entitled "Muddle instead of Music".

The Mariinskiy's luxuriant stage curtain, designed by Aleksandr Golovin in 1914

St Nicholas' Cathedral ❷

Никольский собор

Nikolskiy sobor

Nikolskaya ploshchad. **Map** 5 C4. 🚋 *1, 5, 11, 42.* ⏰ *7am–noon, 4–7pm daily.*

THIS STUNNING Baroque cathedral by Savva Chevakinskiy, one of Russia's great 18th-century architects, was built in 1753–62. Founded for sailors and Admiralty employees housed in the neighbourhood, and named after Nicholas, the patron saint of sailors, the cathedral became known as the "Sailors' Church".

The beautiful exterior is decorated with white Corinthian pilasters and surmounted by five gilded cupolas. Nearby, within the cathedral's leafy grounds and overlooking the intersection of the Kryukov and Griboedov canals, is a slender four-tiered bell tower crowned by a spire.

Following the Russian tradition, there are two churches within the cathedral. The lower church, intended for daily use, is lit by icon lamps, candles and chandeliers, creating a magical effect. The icons (1755–7) are the work of the brothers Fedot and Menas Kolokolnikov. In total contrast, the upper church, used mainly on Sundays and festivals, has a brighter, airy feel and a typically Baroque exuberance, with gilt and stucco ornamentation and Italianate paintings.

The pale blue and white Baroque façade of St Nicholas' Cathedral

Islamic arches and coffered ceiling in the Moorish Room, Yusupov Palace

The most impressive feature is the magnificent gilded iconostasis dating from 1755–60.

Rimsky-Korsakov Conservatory ❸

Консерватория имени Римского-Корсакова

Konservatoriya imeni Rimskovo-Korsakova

Teatralnaya ploshchad 3. **Map** 5 B3. ☎ *311 9977.* 🚌 *Э10, 22, 39Э, 43.* 🚋 *1, 5, 11, 31, 42.* ⏰ *for performances only.* 🎫 🎟 *by appt.*

RUSSIA'S OLDEST music school, the conservatory was founded in 1862 by the piano virtuoso Anton Rubinstein (1829–94). The present building was designed in 1896 by Vladimir Nicolas.

Among those to graduate from the school before the Revolution were Tchaikovsky *(see p42)* and Sergey Prokofiev. In the Soviet years, the school continued to flourish, and the greatest musical figure to emerge from this era was composer Dmitriy Shostakovich (1906–75) *(see p43)*.

In the forecourt outside the school are two statues. On the left, a 1952 memorial honours the school's influential teacher, Nikolai Rimsky-Korsakov, after whom the conservatory is now named. On the right, the statue of Mikhail Glinka (1906) by Robert Bach is a reminder that the conservatory stands on the original site where Russia's first opera, Glinka's *A Life for the Tsar*, was premiered in 1836 in the old Kamennyy (Stone) Theatre.

Yusupov Palace ❹

Юсуповский дворец

Yusupovskiy dvorets

Naberezhnaya reki Moyki 94. **Map** 5 B3. ☎ *314 8893.* 🚌 *22, 43.* 🚋 *1, 5, 11.* ⏰ *by appt noon–3pm daily.* 🎫

OVERLOOKING the Moyka, this yellow, colonnaded building (1760s) was designed by Vallin de la Mothe. The palace was acquired in 1830 by the aristocratic Yusupov family to house their superb collection of paintings. Major work was then carried out on the interior by Andrey Mikhaylov and Ippolito Monighetti.

The interiors, notable among them the exotic Moorish Room, with its fountain, colourful mosaics and horseshoe arches, can be viewed by guided tour only. Separate tickets are needed for the tour of the cellars, which house an exhibition on Grigoriy Rasputin, the infamous "holy man" who was murdered here by Prince Felix Yusupov.

The elegant, Rococo-style family theatre seats just 180, and attending a concert *(see p194)* is an experience in itself.

THE GRIM DEATH OF RASPUTIN

The Russian peasant and mystic Grigoriy Rasputin (1869–1916) exercised an extraordinarily powerful influence over the court and government of Russia *(see p26)*. The mysterious circumstances of his dramatic death on 17 December 1916 are legendary. Lured to Yusupov's palace on the pretext of a party, Rasputin was poisoned, then shot by Prince Felix Yusupov and left for dead. Returning to the scene the prince found Rasputin still alive and a struggle ensued before Rasputin disappeared into the courtyard. Pursued by the conspirators he was shot another three times and brutally battered before being dumped in the river. When his corpse was found three days later, clinging to the supports of a bridge, water in his lungs indicated death by drowning.

New Holland ❺

Новая Голландия

Novaya Gollandiya

Naberezhnaya reki Moyki 103. **Map** 5 B3. 🚌 *22, 43.* 🚇 *1, 5, 11, 31, 42.*

CREATED when the Kryukov canal was constructed between the Moyka and Neva rivers in 1719, this triangular island was originally used for storing ship timber. The name is in honour of the Dutch ship-builders who inspired Peter the Great's naval ambitions.

In 1765, the original wooden warehouses were rebuilt in red brick by Savva Chevakinskiy. At the same time Vallin de la Mothe designed the austere but romantic arch facing onto the Moyka which creates an atmospheric entrance to the timber yard. Barges would pass through the arch and into a turning basin beyond, then return loaded with timber

Vallin de la Mothe's impressive arch on the Moyka, leading into New Holland

along the canals towards the Admiralty shipyards. Today the overgrown and inaccessible island holds a certain charm in its isolation.

The English Quay ❻

Английская набережная

Angliyskaya naberezhnaya

Map 5 A2. 🚇 *1, 5, 11, 31.*

THE FIRST English merchants settled here in the 1730s, followed by a huge influx of craftsmen, architects, artists, innkeepers and factory owners. In the 1760s the first English church opened and the embankment came to be known in the 19th century as the English Quay. By the end of the century the area boasted a string of riverside mansions and was one of the city's most fashionable addresses. It has some fine views of the river and several impressive buildings. On naval holidays, ships richly decorated with flags line the shore.

The Neo-Classical mansion (1770s) at No. 10 was the fictional setting for the debutante ball of Natasha Rostova, heroine of Tolstoy's epic novel *War and Peace*. It contrasts sharply with the rusticated façade of No. 28, built in Florentine Renaissance style for the banking family of the barons von Derviz in the 1890s. No. 28 was later occupied by Grand Duke Andrey Vladimirovich, lover of ballet dancer Matilda Kshesinskaya *(see p72)*, and in 1917 it served as headquarters for the Socialist-Revolutionary Party. Its history took a final peculiar turn when it became a Palace of Weddings, or registry office. A little further along, at No. 32, is an elegant edifice built by Quarenghi in 1782–3.

Set back on ploshchad Truda is the palace of Grand Duke Nikolai Nikolaevich (son of Nicholas I), built in 1853–61 by Andrey Stakenschneider. In 1894 it became a school for young ladies of the nobility, but one of the first acts of the 1917 Bolshevik government was to hand it over to the trade unions, who still partly own it.

Back on the embankment, No. 44 is the Rumyantsev House, built in 1826–7. It was intended to be a museum, housing the private collection of Nikolay Rumyantsev, which he bequeathed to the nation. However, the collection was moved to Moscow in 1861, where the library now forms the basis of the Russian State Library. No. 56 is the former English church, an imposing Neo-Classical building by Quarenghi, dating from 1814.

Quarenghi's grand porticoed façade, at No. 32 on the English Quay

Main Post Office ❼

Главпочтамт

Glavpochtamt

Pochtamtskaya ulitsa 9. **Map** 5 C2.
📞 *312 8302.* 🚌 *T8, 22, 43.* 🚎 *5,
22.* ☐ *9am–7:45pm Mon–Sat,
10am–5:45pm Sun.* ● *public hols.*

THE MOST REMARKABLE feature of the Main Post Office is the arched gallery spanning Pochtamtskaya ulitsa. Built as an extension to Nikolay Lvov's main building, the gallery was added by Albert Kavos in 1859. Under the *Pochtamt* (Post Office) sign on the arch is a clock showing the time in major cities around the world.

Inside the post office, behind Lvov's porticoed Neo-Classical façade of 1782–9, is a splendid Style-Moderne hall characterized by decorative ironwork and a glass ceiling over the vast, tiled floor space. The hall was created in the early 20th century when a roof was constructed over what was originally the courtyard stables.

Porticoed façade, Main Post Office

Bolshaya Morskaya Ulitsa ❽

Большая Морская улица

Bolshaya Morskaya ulitsa

Map 5 C2. 🚌 *22, 43.*

ALWAYS ONE of St Petersburg's most fashionable streets, shady Bolshaya Morskaya ulitsa is the choice of the artistic elite to this day. It has some exceedingly handsome 19th-century mansions hidden away between St Isaac's Square (*see p79*) and Pochtamtskiy most.

Stone atlas at No. 43 Bolshaya Morskaya ulitsa (1840)

The mansion at No. 61 was built by Albert Kavos in the 1840s for the St Petersburg Stage Coach Company. No. 52, nearby, was acquired by the Russian Union of Architects in 1932. Built by Aleksandr Pel in 1835–6, it was formerly the residence of the celebrated patron of the arts Aleksandr Polovtsov, who built up the impressive collection of the Stieglitz Museum (*see p127*). The striking late 19th-century interiors with mahogany panelling, tapestries and carved ceilings were designed by Maximilian Mesmacher and Nikolay Brullo and can be admired from the Nikolay restaurant within (*see p180*).

Just across the street, No. 47 is a particularly fine example of Style-Moderne architecture with sculpted stone rosettes,

delicate iron tracery and a beautiful mosaic frieze of pink flowers. This is the work of Mikhail Geisler and Boris Guslistiy, dating from 1901–2. It was in this mansion that the celebrated émigré novelist Vladimir Nabokov (1899–1977) grew up, and there are plans to open a museum to him. Admired for his linguisitic ingenuity in both English and Russian, Nabokov hit the headlines across the world with the publication of *Lolita*, his *succès de scandale* of 1959.

Next door at No. 45 is the Union of Composers, the former home of socialite Princess Gagarina who lived here in the 1870s. The mansion was reconstructed in the 1840s by Auguste-Ricard de Montferrand, and it retains elements of the original 18th-century building.

Montferrand also built the former residence of millionaire industrialist Pyotr Demidov at No. 43. A mass of Renaissance and Baroque elements, with atlantes, vases, winged glories and rustication, the façade also has Demidov's coat of arms.

Sennaya Ploshchad ❾

Сенная площадь

Sennaya ploshchad

Map 6 D3. Ⓜ *Sennaya Ploshchad,
Sadovaya.*

CORRUGATED KIOSKS fill the centre of this vast square, which is one of the oldest in the city. The local traders, seen by some as the guardians of *perestroika* and by others as a blot on the landscape, sell everything from chocolates and soft drinks to flowers, toiletries and vodka. The square's name, meaning Haymarket, derives from the original market of livestock and fodder which opened here in the 1730s.

Style-Moderne mosaic frieze at No. 47 Bolshaya Morskaya ulitsa (1901–2)

FYODOR DOSTOEVSKY

One of Russia's greatest writers, Fyodor Dostoevsky *(see pp43–4)* was born in 1821 in Moscow but spent most of his adult life in St Petersburg, where many of his novels and short stories are set. A defining moment in his life occurred in 1849 when he was arrested and charged with revolution-ary conspiracy. After eight months of solitary confine-ment in the Peter and Paul Fortress *(see pp66–7)*, Dostoevsky and 21 other "conspirators" from the socialist Petrashevsky Circle were subjected to a maca-bre mock execution before being exiled to hard labour in Siberia until 1859. The sinister experience is re-called in his novel *The Idiot* (1868). He died in 1881.

The oldest building, at the centre of the square, is the former guardhouse, a single-storey Neo-Classical building with a columned portico, which dates to 1818–20. The guardsmen's duties ranged from supervising the traders to flogging serfs, mostly for minor misdemeanours. By that time the neighbourhood had become synonymous with dirt, squalor, crime and vice. At No. 3 is the site of "Vyazemskiy's Monastery", the nickname for a notori-ous tenement overrun with pubs, gambling dens and brothels in the 1850s and '60s.

This was the squalid world so vividly evoked in Fyodor Dostoevsky's masterpiece *Crime and Punishment*. As the

Guardhouse and 1950s apartment blocks in bustling Sennaya ploshchad

contemptuous hero of the novel, Raskolnikov, wanders around the market, he ab-sorbs the "heat in the street.... the airlessness, the bustle and the plaster, scaffolding, bricks and dust.... that special St Petersburg stench.... and the numerous drunken men" which "completed the revol-ting misery of the picture". The novel was finished in 1866 while Dostoevsky was living at Alonkin's House, (No. 7 Przhevalskovo ulitsa), to the west of the square.

During the Soviet era the square was given a new image, stallholders were banished, trees were planted and it was optimistically renamed Peace Square (ploshchad Mira). The five-storey, yellow and white apartment blocks that surround the square today were also built then, in Stalin's version of Neo-Classicism. Sadly, in 1961, the square's most attrac-tive monument, the Baroque Church of the Assumption, built in 1765, was pulled down to make way for one of the city's earliest metro stations.

Railway Museum ⑩

Музей железнодорожного транспорта

Muzey zheleznodorozhnovo transporta

Sadovaya ulitsa 50. **Map** 6 D4.
◾ *315 1476.* Ⓜ *Sennaya Ploshchad, Sadovaya.* ◯ *11am–5:30pm Sun–Thu.* 🖼 *on Sun and school hols.* ◪ *English.*

MORE THAN 6,000 fascinating exhibits illustrate the history of the Russian railway system since 1813. The most interesting sections of the museum deal with the earliest railways, including Russia's first from Tsarskoe Selo to St Petersburg which began run-ning in 1837, and the 650-km (404-mile) line from Moscow to St Petersburg (1851).

Exhibits include models of the first Russian steam engine, built by the Cherepanovs in 1834, and of an armoured train used by Trotsky in the defence of the city during the Civil War *(see p27)*. An insight into lux-ury travel in the late tsarist period can be gained from the walk-through section of a first-class sleeping compartment with velvet upholstery and Style-Moderne decoration.

Model of 1830s engine for the Tsarskoe Selo railway, Railway Museum

FURTHER AFIELD

WHILE THE majority of St Petersburg's sights are centrally located, the outlying areas of the city have a number of places of architectural, cultural and historical importance.

Ceramic tile from 1770s stove, Stieglitz Museum

To the east is the Smolnyy district, taking its name from the tar yard which supplied the city's embryonic shipbuilding industry in the 18th century. The highlight of this area is Rastrelli's dazzling Baroque Smolnyy Convent. Nearby, the Smolnyy Institute is famed for its historic role as the Bolshevik headquarters during the October Revolution (see pp28–9).

Southeast of the centre lies the Alexander Nevsky Monastery where many of Russia's celebrated artists, architects and composers are buried.

The southern suburbs offer a strikingly different perspective of the city, with rows of pompous 1930s–50s houses, a reminder that Stalin sought to destroy the city's historical heart by relocating the centre from the old imperial district to the area around Moskovskaya ploshchad. The south also has the Chesma Church and the 1970s Victory Monument, a memorial to the suffering of St Petersburgers during the Siege of Leningrad.

SIGHTS AT A GLANCE

Palaces
Sheremetev Palace **9**
Tauride Palace **6**
Yelagin Palace **1**

Museums
Dostoevsky House-Museum **10**
Stieglitz Museum **4**

Churches
Alexander Nevsky Monastery **11**
Cathedral of the
   Transfiguration **5**
Chesma Church **12**
Smolnyy Convent **7**

Historic Buildings and Monuments
Finland Station **3**
Piskarevskoe Memorial
   Cemetery **2**
Smolnyy Institute **8**
Victory Monument **13**

KEY

	Central St Petersburg
	Greater St Petersburg
✈	Airport
🚉	Railway station
⛴	Ferry port
▬	Major road
▭	Minor road

0 kilometres 3

0 miles 3

◁ **The Baroque Sheremetev Palace on the east bank of the Fontanka river**

East façade of Yelagin Palace with Srednaya Nevka river in foreground

Yelagin Palace ❶

Елагин дворец
Yelagin dvorets

Yelagin ostrov 1. 📞 *239 0080.*
Ⓜ *Chernaya Rechka.* 🚌 *71, 134.*
🚃 *34.* 🚎 *17, 26.* 🕐 *10am–6pm*
Wed–Sun. 📷 ♿ *to ground floor.* 🎫

ONE OF THE northernmost
islands of St Petersburg,
Yelagin Island is named after
a court official who built a
palace here at the end of the
18th century. Alexander I then
bought the island in 1817 for
his mother, Maria Fyodorovna,
and commissioned Carlo Rossi
to rebuild the palace. The magnificent Neo-Classical palace
(1818–22), enlivened on the
east façade by a half rotunda
flanked by Corinthian porti-
coes, is part of an ensemble
which includes an orangery,
a horseshoe-shaped stable
block and porticoed kitchens.
   The palace interior was destroyed by fire during World
War II but is now undergoing
restoration. The Oval Hall is
resplendent with statuary and
trompe l'oeils while the rooms
leading from it are exquisitely
decorated with stucco, *faux
marbre* and painted friezes,
executed by a collective of
gifted artists and craftsmen.

**Statue of Mother Russia (1956–60),
Piskarevskoe Memorial Cemetery**

In the Soviet period, the whole
of the wooded island became
the Central Park of Culture and
Rest *(see pp136–7)*. Festivals
and public entertainments are
held here, and temporary
exhibitions are put on in the
palace's household quarters.

Piskarevskoe Memorial Cemetery ❷

Пискаревское мемориальное
кладбище
*Piskarevskoe memorialnoe
kladbishche*

Prospekt Nepokorennykh 74.
📞 *247 5716.* Ⓜ *Akademicheskaya.*
🚌 *Э71, Т94, 123, 178, Э178.*
🕐 *10am–6pm daily.* ♿ 🎫

THIS VAST, BLEAK cemetery is
a most impressive memo-
rial to the 670,000 Leningraders
who died during the Siege of
1941–4 *(see p27)*. With dimin-
ishing food rations and no
electricity, water or heating,
the citizens of Leningrad perished in vast numbers from
starvation, cold and disease.
Thousands of corpses were
dragged on sledges to collection points from where they
were taken for burial to mass
cemeteries on the outskirts of
town. Piskarevskoe was the
largest, with 490,000 burials.
   Today the cemetery is a
place of pilgrimage for those
who lost relatives and friends
during those desperate times.
The memorial complex, de-
signed by Yevgeniy Levinson
and Aleksandr Vasiliev, opened
in 1960, on the 15th anniversary of the end of the war.
Two memorial halls, one of
which contains an exhibition
on the Siege, flank the stairs
down to a 300-m (984-ft) long
avenue, which culminates in
a towering, heroic bronze
statue of Mother Russia by Vera

Isayeva and Robert Taurit. On
the wall behind are verses
composed by Olga Bergholts,
herself a survivor of the Siege.
The funereal music broadcast
over the whole cemetery adds
to the sombre atmosphere.
   On either side of the avenue
are 186 grassy mounds, each
with a granite slab marking
the year and indicating, with
a red star or hammer and
sickle, whether those interred
were soldiers or civilians.

Locomotive 293, Finland Station

Finland Station ❸

Финляндский вокзал
Finlyandskiy vokzal

Ploshchad Lenina 6. **Map** 3 B3.
📞 *168 7687.* Ⓜ *Ploshchad Lenina.*
See also p221.

ON THE NIGHT of 3 April
1917, the exiled Vladimir
Lenin and his Bolshevik com-
panions arrived at Finland
Station after travelling from
Switzerland on a sealed train.
A triumphant reception await-
ed their return to Russia and,
on leaving the station, Lenin
spoke to cheering crowds of
soldiers, sailors and workers.
A statue erected outside the
station in 1926 depicts Lenin
delivering his speech.
   The modern terminal was
opened in the 1960s. On platform 5 there is a huge glass
case containing Locomotive
293 which Lenin rode when
fleeing the capital for a second
time in July 1917. After spending the summer as a fugitive
in Russian Finland, Lenin
returned on the same train
and spurred on the October
Revolution *(see pp28–9)*.

Stieglitz Museum ❹

Музей Штиглица

Muzey Shtiglitsa

Solyanoy pereulok 13. **Map** 3 A5.
📞 *273 3258.* 🚌 *46, 134.* 🚎 *2, 34, 54.* 🕐 *11am–6pm (Oct–May: 11am–5pm) Tue–Sat.* 📷 ✔

THE MILLIONAIRE industrialist Baron Aleksandr Stieglitz founded the Central School of Industrial Design in 1876. His aim was to train Russian students in applied arts and design by surrounding them with a collection of top quality original works which they could study.

19th-century crystal vase, Stieglitz Museum

With a large budget and the good taste of Stieglitz's son-in-law, Aleksandr Polovtsov *(see p122)*, the collection, unusual in covering both Western European and Oriental art, soon outgrew the school and in 1896 a Museum of Applied Arts opened next door. This magnificent building, designed by Maximilian Messmacher, was inspired by Italian Renaissance palaces. Inside, the halls and galleries were decorated in an impressive variety of national and period styles, echoing French and German Baroque and, above all, Italian Renaissance monuments, such as St Mark's Library in Venice, the Raphael Loggias of the Vatican and the Villa Madama, also in Rome.

After the Revolution the school was closed and the museum became a branch of the Hermitage *(see pp84–93)*. Serious damage to the building was inflicted during the Siege of Leningrad *(see p27)* and restoration continues. At the end of the war the school was revived to train gilders and carvers for the huge restoration programme needed to repair the damaged city. Situated on the ground floor, the exhibition features opulent displays of glassware, ceramics and majolica, as well as porcelain from all the great European manufacturers. One room, decorated in the style of the medieval Terem Palace in the Kremlin, provides a superb backdrop for a collection of colourfully embroidered dresses and headgear made by Russian peasant women.

Some pieces of decorative metalwork including locks, keys and craft tools date back to the Middle Ages. The workmanship seen on the wooden furniture is breathtaking. The Neo-Gothic cabinet is a beautiful example. Its finely inlaid doors, depicting church naves in skilful perspective, open to reveal sculpted biblical scenes.

The guided tour concludes with a visit to the stunning Grand Exhibition Hall with its curving staircase of Italian marble and magnificent glass roof.

Cathedral of the Transfiguration ❺

Спасо-Преображенский собор

Spaso-Preobrazhenskiy sobor

Preobrazhenskaya ploshchad 1. **Map** 3 B5. 📞 *272 3662.* Ⓜ *Chernyshevskaya.* 🚌 *46, 134, 136, Э136.* 🚎 *49.* 🚎 *14, 90, 25.* 🕐 *8am–8pm daily.*

DESPITE ITS monumental Neo-Classicism, and the surrounding fence made of guns captured during the Russo-Turkish war *(see p22)*, Vasiliy Stasov's church has an intimate air as it nestles in its leafy square. The original church on this site was built by Tsarina Elizabeth to honour the Preobrazhenskiy Guards, but it was rebuilt after a fire in 1825. Today, the church is famous for its excellent choir, which is second only to that in the Alexander Nevsky Monastery *(see pp130–31)*.

Dolls in 17th–19th century Russian folk costumes, in front of the Terem Room, Stieglitz Museum

Tauride Palace
Таврический дворец
Tavricheskiy dvorets

Shpalernaya ulitsa 47. **Map** 4 D4.
M *Chernyshevskaya*. 📷 *46, T74,
135, Э136*. ● *to public.*

THIS FINELY proportioned palace by Ivan Starov was built in 1783–9 as a present from Catherine the Great to her influential lover Prince Grigoriy Potemkin *(see p25).* Potemkin had successfully annexed the Crimea (Tauris) to Russia in 1783 and was given the title of Prince of Tauris, hence the palace's name.

Uncompromising in its lack of external ornamentation, the long, yellow building with its distinctive six-columned portico was one of Russia's first Neo-Classical designs. Sadly, the magnificent interiors have been badly damaged both by Catherine's son, Paul I, who turned the palace into a barracks, and by the many reconstructions undertaken.

The palace has played a vital role in 20th-century cultural and political life. In 1905, the impresario Sergey Diaghilev *(see p43)* organized the first ever exhibition of Russian 18th-century portraiture here. The following year the palace hosted Russia's first parliament, the State Duma. After the February Revolution of 1917 it became the seat of the Provisional Government, then the Petrograd Soviet of Workers' and Soldiers' Deputies. Today it is still a government building.

The lovely gardens, with winding streams, bridges and an artificial lake, are among the city's most popular parks.

Façade of the Smolnyy Cathedral with adjacent convent buildings

Smolnyy Convent
Смольный монастырь
Smolnyy monastyr

Ploshchad Rastrelli 3/1. **Map** 4 F4.
📞 *278 1461.* 📷 *46, 58, 134, 136,
Э136.* 🕙 *10am–5pm Fri–Wed.* 💷
&. 🎫 *English.*

THE CROWNING GLORY of this architectural ensemble is the stunning cathedral with its dome and four supporting cupolas topped by golden orbs.

As a symbol of her majesty, Tsarina Elizabeth founded the convent where many young noblewomen were to be educated. It was designed in 1748 by Bartolomeo Rastrelli *(see p93),* who conceived a brilliant fusion of Russian and Western Baroque styles. Work advanced extremely slowly; 50,000 wooden piles were used to secure the foundations in the marshy soil and the architect's model alone, now in the Academy of Arts *(see p63),* took seven years to build.

Catherine the Great disliked Rastrelli's work and had little sympathy for the late Elizabeth. When she came to power in 1762, funding for the project stopped. It was only in 1835 that Nicholas I commissioned the Neo-Classical architect Vasiliy Stasov to complete the cathedral. His austere white interior contrasts dramatically with the luxuriant exterior.

Exhibitions and Sunday services are now held here, as well as regular weekly concerts *(see p194).* There are spectacular views of the city from the cathedral tower.

Smolnyy Institute
Смольный Институт
Smolnyy Institut

Ploshchad Proletarskoy Diktatury.
Map 4 F4. 📞 *276 1461.* 📷 *T8, 22,
T26, 136.* 🚋 *5, 7, 11, 15, 16, 49.*
Lenin Museum 🕙 *10am–5pm Mon–
Fri by appt only.* 💷 &. 🎫 *English.*

GIACOMO QUARENGHI considered this Neo-Classical building to be his masterpiece. Built in 1806–8 to house the school for young noblewomen, which had outgrown its premises at the Smolnyy Convent, the institute is famed for the part it played in the October Revolution *(see pp28–9).*

It was from here, on 25 October 1917, that Lenin directed the Bolshevik coup d'état while the second All-Russian Congress of Soviets was convening simultaneously in the Assembly Hall. The Congress subsequently confirmed Lenin in power and this became his seat of government until March 1918. With the Germans advancing and the outbreak of civil war *(see p27),* the government left for Moscow and the Institute was taken over by the Leningrad Communist Party. On 1 December 1934, the First

View of Tauride Gardens and the Tauride Palace beyond the lake

Isaak Brodskiy's 1927 painting of Lenin, Smolnyy Institute Assembly Hall

Secretary of the party, Sergey Kirov *(see p72)*, was assassinated here, an event that lit a slow fuse on Stalin's purges of the late 1930s *(see p27)*.

The rooms where Lenin lived and worked during the Revolution can be viewed by appointment. The rest of the institute now houses the Mayor's Office. The imperial eagle has replaced the hammer and sickle on the pediment, but the statue of Lenin outside has survived from 1927.

Sheremetev Palace ➒
Шереметьевский дворец
Sheremetevskiy dvorets

Naberezhnaya reki Fontanki 34. **Map** 7 A1. **☎** *272 3898.* **M** *Gostinyy Dvor.* **🚎** *3, 8, 15.* **🚊** *5, 12, 14, 28, 34, 90.* **◯** *noon–6pm Wed–Sun.* 📷 ✓

THE SHEREMETEV family lived on this site from 1712 – when the first palace was built here by Field Marshal Boris

Sheremetev – until the Revolution. The palace is also known as the Fountain House, or *Fontannyy dom*, because of the many fountains that once adorned its grounds. The existing Baroque building dates essentially from the 1750s when it was designed by Savva Chevakinskiy and Fyodor Argunov, although numerous later alterations were made.

Sheremetev's descendants were fabulously wealthy, at one time owning some 200,000 serfs. They were also among Russia's leading artistic patrons and the palace is now home to the Museum of Musical Life *(Muzey Muzikalnoy zhizhni)*, which chronicles their contribution to music in the city. In the 18th and 19th centuries, serf composers, musicians and actors from rural estates owned by the family performed in many concerts and plays at the palace. Among those to praise the fine Sheremetev choir was the composer Franz Liszt.

The museum's exhibits include a variety of period instruments and a number of scores, some of which are compositions by the Sheremetevs themselves.

One of Russia's greatest 20th-century poets, Anna Akhmatova, lived in one of the service blocks of the palace from 1933 to 1941 and then again between 1944 and 1954. Her flat is open to the public as the Anna Akhmatova Museum (*Muzey Anny Akhmatovoy*) and is reached through the courtyard of No. 53 Liteynyy prospekt. By the time she moved into the palace, it had been divided into dingy communal apartments. The rooms where she lived and worked display some of her personal possessions, which trace her intriguing life. Recordings of the poetess reading her own poems can also be heard.

ANNA AKHMATOVA

By 1914 Anna Akhmatova (1889–1966) was a leading light of Russia's "Silver Age" of poetry *(see p44)*. Tragedy gave her work a new dimension when first her husband was shot by the Bolsheviks, and then, in the 1930s, her son and her lover were arrested in Stalin's purges. Anna herself was placed under police surveillance and officially silenced for more than 15 years. Her most famous poem, *Requiem* (1935–61), inspired by her son's arrest, was written in fragments and distributed amongst friends to memorize. Anna was partially rehabilitated late in her life and received honorary awards abroad in 1965.

Pilastered façade of Sheremetev Palace on the Fontanka embankment

Dostoevsky House-Museum ⑩

Музей Достоевского
Muzey Dostoevskovo

Kuznechnyy pereulok 5/2. **Map** 7 B3.
📞 *311 4031*. **M** *Vladimirskaya*.
🚌 *16, 28, 34, 49, 90*. ⏰ *11am–6pm Tue–Sun*. 🎧 🎫

THIS EVOCATIVE museum was the final home of the famous Russian writer, Fyodor Dostoevsky *(see p44)*, who lived here from 1878 until his death in 1881. Dostoevsky was then at the height of his fame, and it was here that he completed his last great novel, *The Brothers Karamazov*, in 1880. Gambling and debts, however, confined him to a fairly modest lifestyle in this five-roomed apartment.

Although Dostoevsky's public persona was dour and humourless, he was a devoted and affectionate husband and father. The delightful nursery contains a rocking horse, silhouettes of his children and the book of fairy tales which he read aloud to them. In Dostoevsky's study are his writing desk and a reproduction of his favourite painting, Raphael's *Sistine Madonna*.

Chesma Church (1777–80), a very early example of Neo-Gothic in Russia

Chesma Church ⑫

Чесменская церковь
Chesmenskaya tserkov

Ulitsa Lensoveta 12. **M** *Moskovskaya*.
🚌 *16*. 🚊 *29, 45*. ⏰ *10am–7pm daily*.

THERE IS LITTLE Russian about the highly unusual Chesma Church, which was designed by Yuriy Velten in 1777–80. Its fanciful terracotta-coloured façade is decorated with thin vertical stripes of white moulding which direct the eye upwards to its zig-zagged crown and Neo-Gothic cupolas.

The name commemorates the great Russian naval victory over the Turks at Chesma in the Aegean in 1770. During the Communist era the church became a museum to the battle, but today the building is once again open as a church.

On the opposite side of ulitsa Lensoveta is the Neo-Gothic Chesma Palace (1774–77), formerly *Kekerekeksinen*, or Frog Marsh Palace. Also designed by Velten, it served as a staging post for Catherine the Great en route to Tsarskoe Selo *(see pp150–53)*. Wedgwood's famous dinner service with its frog emblem, now in the Hermitage *(see p91)*, was designed specially for the Chesma Palace.

The palace achieved notoriety when Rasputin's body lay in state here after his murder in 1916 *(see p121)*. Now substantially altered, it serves as a home for the elderly.

Alexander Nevsky Monastery ⑪

Александро-Невская лавра
Aleksandro-Nevskaya lavra

Ploshchad Aleksandra Nevskovo. **Map** 8 E4. 📞 *274 2635*. **M** *Ploshchad Aleksandra Nevskovo*. 🚌 *8, 58, T73*. 🚊 *1, 11, 14, 16, 22, 33*. 🚊 *7, 39, 44, 65*. **Cemeteries** ⏰ *10am–7pm Fri–Wed (10am–4pm Dec–Apr)*. 🎧 *cemeteries only*. 🎫

FOUNDED BY Peter the Great in 1710, this monastery commemorates Alexander Nevsky, the prince of Novgorod, who defeated the Swedes on the Neva river in 1240. Peter himself had just defeated them, in 1709, in the course of the Great Northern War *(see p18)*.

From the entrance, a path runs between two large, walled cemeteries, then across a stream and into the main monastic complex. The earliest building, to the left of the gate, is the Church of the Annunciation (1717–22), designed by Domenico Trezzini. The church, currently closed to the public, was once the burial place for non-ruling members of the Russian royal family. A series of red and white, mid-18th-century monastic buildings, including the Metropolitan's House (1755–8), surround the courtyard. Among the trees in the courtyard lie the graves of atheist Soviet scholars and leading Communists.

Dominating the essentially Baroque complex is the twin-towered and domed Neo-Classical Holy Trinity Cathedral, constructed by architect Ivan Starov in 1776–90. The wide nave inside is flanked by Corinthian columns with statues by Fedot Shubin. This leads to the impressive red agate and white marble iconostasis, which features copies of works by Van Dyck, Rubens and others. To the right of the iconostasis is a silver reliquary that contains the remains of Alexander Nevsky, transferred

Dostoevsky's tombstone

Reliquary with Alexander Nevsky's remains, Trinity Cathedral

Victory Monument ⑬

Монумент Защитникам
Ленинграда
*Monument Zashchitnikam
Leningrada*

Ploshchad Pobedy. **Ⓜ** *Moskovskaya.*
🚌 T2, 3, 11, 13, T13, T18, T20, 39,
Э39, 55, 64, 64A, T75, Э90, T90, 287,
Э287, 290, 431, 472, Э530. **Memorial
Hall** ⬜ 10am–5pm Thu–Tue. 📷

ERECTED IN 1975 to coincide
with the 30th anniversary
of the end of World War II, this
sombre memorial stands on the
site of a temporary triumphal
arch built to greet the returning
troops. Named the Monument
to the Heroic Defenders of
Leningrad, it commemorates

not only the estimated 670,000
victims of the Siege *(see p27)*,
but also the survivors. It was
designed by Sergey Speranskiy
and Valentin Kamenskiy and
sculpted by Mikhail Anikushin.
A 48-m (157-ft) high obelisk
of red granite rests near a vast,
circular enclosure which sym-
bolizes the vice-like grip of
the siege. Heroic-style, larger-
than-life sculptures of soldiers,
sailors and grieving mothers
surround the monument.

An underpass on Moskovskiy
prospekt leads to the gloomy,
subterranean Memorial Hall.
Here solemn music gives way
to the persistent beat of a
metronome, the wartime radio
signal, intended to represent

the city's defiant heartbeat.
The subdued lighting com-
prises 900 dim, orange lamps,
one for each day of the Siege.
On the marble walls are tablets
inscribed with the names of
the 650 Heroes of the Soviet
Union who were awarded the
title after the war, while, on
the far wall, a mosaic depicts
the women of the city greeting their soldier menfolk at
the end of the grim conflict.

Around the hall a small
display of artifacts, including
Shostakovich's violin *(see p43)*,
records the contribution of
different sections of the community to the war effort, while
an illuminated relief map
illustrates the battle lines.

Heroic partisans facing south towards the enemy during the Siege of Leningrad, detail of Victory Monument

to the previous church on
this site in 1724. Behind the
reliquary hangs a painting of
Nevsky, who has been venerated as a saint in Russia since
the mid-16th century.

Many of the nation's leading
cultural figures are buried in
the two monastic cemeteries
near the main entrance. The
city's oldest graveyard, the
Lazarus Cemetery, to the east,
contains the graves of the
polymath Mikhail Lomonosov
(see p45) and a number of
prominent architects, including
Andrey Zakharov, Thomas de
Thomon, Giacomo Quarenghi,
Carlo Rossi *(see p110)* and
Andrey Voronikhin. Clustered
together along the northern
wall of the Tikhvin Cemetery
(to the west) are the tombs of
some of Russia's most famous
composers. Many of their
tombs are inscribed with musical motifs. Fyodor Dostoevsky
(see p44) is also buried here,
to the right of the entrance.

TOMBS OF INTEREST AT TIKHVIN CEMETERY

1 Mikhail Glinka
  (Composer, 1804–57)
2 Ivan Krylov
  (Poet, 1768–1844)
3 Marius Petipa
  (Choreographer, 1818–1910)
4 Pyotr Klodt
  (Sculptor, 1805–67)
5 Ivan Kramskoy
  (Painter, 1837–87)
6 Pyotr Tchaikovsky
  (Composer, 1840–93)
7 Modest Mussorgsky
  (Composer, 1839–81)
8 Nikolai Rimsky-Korsakov
  (Composer, 1844–1908)
9 Fyodor Dostoevsky
  (Writer, 1821–81)

**Main
entrance**

KEY

✝ Gate church

0 metres   50
0 yards   50

TWO GUIDED WALKS

ST PETERSBURG IS a very manageable city to explore on foot, and many of its sights are best appreciated in this way. The two walks chosen present different sides of the city's character. However, since St Petersburg is dominated by its location on a group of islands at the mouth of the Neva river, water plays a central part in both.

The first walk follows two of the many waterways, the Moyka river and the Griboedov canal, which criss-cross the heart of the city presenting the magnificent scale of St Petersburg as it was built in the 18th and 19th centuries. It shows the contrasts of rich palaces and overcrowded apartment blocks, gilded bridges and the dilapidation of the area around Sennaya

19th-century urn on the steps of Yelagin Palace

ploshchad. An alternative way to appreciate the canals is to take a boat trip *(see pp218–19)*, which delivers another perspective on the city's glorious historical buildings.

The second walk explores the world where Petersburgers have spent much of their free time since the 18th century. The Yelagin and Kamenyy islands, to the north of the centre, were once the preserve of the rich, who spent the hot summers in the cool of their *dachas*, the marvellously varied architecture of which can still be admired today. Now the islands offer a calm retreat for all. Locals come to walk and row boats in summer, collect leaves in autumn, ski and skate in winter, or simply to breathe the fresh air in spring.

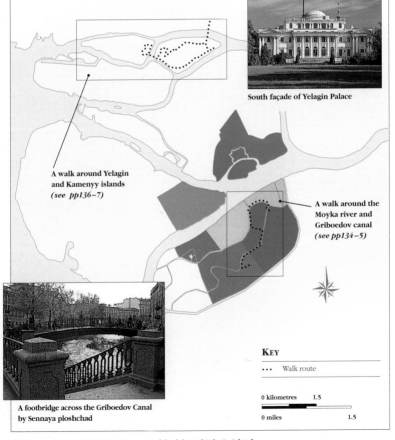

South façade of Yelagin Palace

A walk around Yelagin and Kamenyy islands *(see pp136–7)*

A walk around the Moyka river and Griboedov canal *(see pp134–5)*

A footbridge across the Griboedov Canal by Sennaya ploshchad

KEY

•••   Walk route

0 kilometres   1.5

0 miles   1.5

◁ **Peace and tranquillity enjoyed on one of the lakes of Yelagin Island**

A Walk along St Petersburg's Waterways

A STROLL ALONG the embankments of the Moyka river and the Griboedov canal is a chance to appreciate the history and splendid architecture of this beautiful city. The two waterways present interesting contrasts. The Moyka winds past the Imperial Summer and Winter Palaces and the lavish mansions of the aristocracy, while the Griboedov is lined with 19th-century apartments, once home to merchants, civil servants and, towards Sennaya Ploshchad *(see p122)*, the working class. The walk also includes a short stretch of the majestic Nevskiy prospekt.

TIPS FOR WALKERS

Starting point: Church on Spilled Blood. **Length**: 5.8 km (3 miles). **Getting there**: Nevskiy Prospekt metro. **Stopping-off points**: Café Minutka, Nevskiy prospekt 20; Bistro Layma, nab kanala Griboedova 16.

View of the Church on Spilled Blood and the Griboedov canal

The Moyka River
Begin the walk at the recently restored Church on Spilled Blood ① *(see p100)*, built over the spot where Alexander II was assassinated in 1881 *(see p26)*. From here, walk around the church beside the park, crossing the canal bridge to Konyushennaya ploshchad. The square is embraced by the elongated façade of the former Imperial Stables ② *(see p113)*. Straddling the junction of the Griboedov canal and the Moyka river are two ingeniously linked bridges, the Malo-Konyushennyy most (Little Stable Bridge) and Teatralnyy most (Theatre Bridge) *(see p37)*. Cross over these bridges to the north bank of the Moyka and the expansive façade of the Adamini House ③, designed by Domenico Adamini in 1823–7. Between 1916 and 1919 the basement was used

by an artists' and writers' club known as "The Bivouac of the Comedians". Visitors included the avant-garde theatre director Vsevolod Meyerhold and the poets Aleksandr Blok and Anna Akhmatova *(see p44)*.

Turn left onto naberezhnaya reki Moyki and walk past the Round Market ④ built in 1790 by Giacomo Quarenghi, who had shopping arcades as one of his specialities. Continue along the embankment, passing Adam's Bolshoy Konyushennyy most (Great Stables Bridge) to Prince Abamelek-Lazarev's former mansion ⑤ built in 1913–15. The handsome façade, with Corinthian pilasters and graceful reliefs of dancing figures, is by Ivan Fomin. On the opposite bank is the 17th-century apartment block where Pushkin spent the last few months of his life. His flat is now a museum ⑥ *(see p113)*.

At the intersection of Millionaya ulitsa and the beautiful Winter Canal (Zimnaya Kanavka) are the former barracks of the elite First Regiment of the Preobrazhenskiy Life-Guards. This prestigious corps was formed by Peter the Great in the 1690s.

Quarenghi's arcaded Round Market (1790), overlooking the Moyka river

KEY

• • • Tour route

M Metro station

(map showing: SUVOROVSKAYA PLOSHCHAD, PLOSHCHAD, LETNIY SAD, MARSOVO POLE, Fontanka Фонтанка, ORTSOVAYA NAB, NAB LEBYAZHEVO, Adamini House, MALO-KONYUSHENNYY MOST, NAB REKI MOYKI, Moyka Мойка, KONYUSHENNYY MOST, KONYUSHENNAYA, MIKHAYLOVSKIY SAD, SADOVAYA ULITSA, INZHENERNAYA ULITSA, PLOSHCHAD ISKUSSTV, ITALYANSKAYA ULITSA, NAB KANALA GRIBOEDOVA, Kanal Griboedova Канал Грибоедова, MIKHAYLOVSKAYA UL, Gostinyy Dvor, KAZANSKIY MOST, НЕВСКИЙ ПРОСПЕКТ, Gostinyy Dvor, Kazan Cathedral, DUMSKAYA ULITSA, PER KRYLOVA, MAL SADOVAYA UL, SADOVAYA ULITSA, UL LOMONOSOVA, BANKOVSKIY MOST)

View of the tree-lined Griboedov canal

Across the Winter Canal is the New Hermitage ⑦ *(see p84)*. Ten granite atlantes bear the weight of the elaborate porch. Returning to the Moyka, the route passes a green, three-storey house ⑧, built by F Demertsov for Alexander I's military advisor and sometime chief minister, Count Aleksey Arakcheev. The Moyka now makes a curve behind the majestic buildings of Palace Square *(see p83)* which includes the Staff of the Guards Corps ⑨ and the huge crescent of Carlo Rossi's imposing yellow General Staff Building ⑩. Cross the Pevcheskiy most (Singers' Bridge) *(see p37)* ⑪ and follow the Moyka down to the Politseyskiy most (Police Bridge). The yellow building on the other side of the Moyka is the Literary Café ⑫, renowned as a meeting-place for writers in Pushkin's day *(see p83)*.

Nevskiy Prospekt

Turn left onto St Petersburg's main street, where a range of architectural styles can be seen. On the left, the elegant façade of Paul Jacot's Dutch Church building ⑬ *(see p47)* hides a series of shops. Across

Griffons on Bank Bridge (1826), Griboedov canal

the road, the beautifully embellished façade of the Baroque Stroganov Palace ⑭ *(see p112)* contrasts starkly with the triple-arched glass frontage of the Style-Moderne Fashion House ⑮ *(see p47)*. The magnificent colonnaded forecourt of the Kazan Cathedral ⑯ *(see p111)* can be seen further along.

The Griboedov Canal

Cross Nevskiy prospekt by the attractive Dom Knigi *(see p47)* and follow the Griboedov south. When you reach Georg von Traitteur's Bankovskiy most *(see p35)* ⑰, decorated with golden griffons, cross the canal and continue past the wrought-iron railings to the rear of the former Assignment Bank ⑱ (now occupied by an Economics University). Further south the humped Kamennyy most (Stone Bridge) has survived since 1776 despite an attempt by the revolutionary group, Peoples' Will, to blow it up as Tsar Alexander II passed in his carriage. Across the Demidov most, on the corner of Kaznacheyskaya ulitsa ⑲ (No.1), is the apartment where Dostoevsky wrote *Notes from the House of the Dead* (1861). He was living on the same street when he wrote *Crime and Punishment*. Also with literary associations, the former Zverkov House ⑳ was where the novelist and dramatist Nikolai Gogol *(see p44)* lived in the 1830s.

The walk ends in Sennaya ploshchad *(see p122)*, where there are two metro stations.

Apartment block where Dostoevsky lived, on the Griboedov canal

A Walk around Kamennyy and Yelagin Islands

An AREA OF ROLLING parkland, birch and lime groves and fine river views, the northern islands of the Neva delta offer a retreat from city life. The imperial family built palaces on Kamennyy and Yelagin islands at the end of the 18th century and were soon joined by wealthy aristocratic families. Before the Revolution, many government ministers, industrial magnates and celebrities built themselves a *dacha* here. Today these neglected houses, some intimate, some palatial, in styles ranging from Neo-Gothic to Neo-Classical and Style Moderne, are being returned to their former glory by the new business elite.

the fashionable architect, Vladimir Apyshkov, to build this splendid Style-Moderne mansion in 1913–14.

Continue west, and cross the canal bridge to reach the wooden Kamennoostrovskiy Theatre ⑥ which took only 40 days to erect in 1827. Though in need of a coat of paint, its Neo-Classical portico, rebuilt by Albert Kavos in 1844, is still impressive. The banks of the Krestovka river, with views across to the boatyards of Krestovskiy Island, are ideal for a picnic. Return to the path and cross 1-y Yelagin most to Yelagin Island.

Yelagin Island
This island is an oasis of calm, popular with Petersburgers wishing to escape the city. A tollgate marks the entrance to the grounds of Carlo Rossi's

Wooden façade of Dolgorukov Mansion

3-Y YELAGIN MOST

2-Y Severnyy prub

4-Y Severnyy prub

5-Y Severnyy prub

Srednaya Nevka Средняя Невка

Yelagin Palace ⑦

YELAGIN OSTROV

4-Y Fzhnyy prub

TSENTRALNIY PARK KULTURIY I OTDYKHA IM KIROVA

3-Y Fzhnyy prub

2-Y Fzhnyy prub

2-Y YELAGIN MOST

1-Y Fzhnyy prub

South Kamennyy Island

Begin at Chernaya Rechka metro station and head south to Bolshaya Nevka river, then crossing over to Kamennyy Island, an area of recreation and relaxation. Just across the main road is the small redbrick Church of St John the Baptist ①, designed in Neo-Gothic style by Yuriy Velten in 1776–8. Nearby a yellow gateway leads to the grounds of Kamennoostrovskiy Palace ② (now a retirement home) from where Alexander I led the Russian campaign of 1812 against Napoleon *(see p26)*.

Follow Kamennoostrovskiy prospekt to the Malaya Nevka river, then turn right on to naberezhnaya Maloy Nevki where there is an imposing wooden mansion ③ at No. 11 with a white-columned portico. The Dolgorukov Mansion was built in 1831–2 by Smaragd Shustov for the Dolgorukovs,

one of Russia's oldest aristocratic families. The two sphinxes guarding the granite embankment date to 1824. From this point you can see across to Aptekarskiy or Apothecary's Island, named after the medicinal herb gardens founded by Peter the Great. St Petersburg's Botanical Gardens are still located there. Continue along the path, which turns into naberezhnaya reki Krestovki. Standing in the middle of the path are the remains of Peter the Great's oak tree ④, said to have been planted by the tsar in 1718. The house on the left, towards the Malo-krestovskiy most, is the former home of Sergey Chaev ⑤, the chief engineer of the Trans-Siberian railway. Chaev commissioned

The tower of the Church of St John the Baptist (1776–8)

Kamennoostrovskiy Theatre (1827)

graceful Yelagin Palace ⑦ (see p126). The western spit of the island is ideal for viewing the often spectacular sunsets over the Gulf of Finland, especially during the White Nights (see p51). Across 2-y Yelagin most, leading south to Krestovskiy Island, are Petrovskiy Stadium and the Maritime Victory Park, while to the north, 3-y Yelagin most leads to Primorskiy prospekt and the Buddhist Temple, erected by Gavriil Baranovskiy in 1909–15 and inspired by traditional Tibetan architecture.

North Kamennyy Island

Return to Kamennyy Island across 1-y Yelagin most, taking the left fork on to Teatralnaya alleya from where you can see the former mansion of Aleksandr Polovtsov ⑧, minister of foreign affairs under Nicholas II. This splendid Neo-Classical mansion with Style-Moderne touches was built by Ivan Fomin in 1911–13. Leave Teatralnaya alleya and cut through the quiet and restful park, passing between the ponds and the canal. Near the junction with Bolshaya alleya are two more early 20th-century mansions. Follenveider's mansion ⑨ on the left, with its distinctive

Early 20th-century Polovtsov Mansion

tented tower, was designed by Roman Meltser in 1904 and now belongs to the Danish consulate. Yevgeniya Gausvald's dacha ⑩ dates from 1898 and stands as one of the earliest Style-Moderne buildings in St Petersburg. It was designed by Vasiliy Schöne and Vladimir Chagin.

Finally, the last stage of the walk leads along the 2-ya Berezovaya alleya, back to the starting point at Ushakovskiy most and Chernaya Rechka metro.

KEY

••• Walk route

Ⓜ Metro station

TIPS FOR WALKERS

Starting point: Chernaya Rechka metro station (see p215).
Length: 6 km (3.5 miles).
Stopping-off points: Café in former stables of Yelagin Palace (summer only) and plenty of places to picnic.

The tree-shrouded grassy banks of the Krestovka river

BEYOND
ST PETERSBURG

BEYOND ST PETERSBURG

T HE COUNTRYSIDE *around St Petersburg is typical of northwest Russia. Among its flat sweeps of land, pine forests and lakes there are sights of cultural interest, including the imperial palaces and the walled medieval city of Novgorod. Venturing away from St Petersburg allows a richer and deeper insight into this splendid land.*

Before St Petersburg was founded in 1703, the surrounding landscape was a marshy and inhospitable wilderness, inhabited by wolves. Nevertheless, the area from the Gulf of Finland to Lake Ladoga was of strategic importance for trading and thus one of the reasons for continuous wars between Sweden and Russia. At the time the only city of importance here was Novgorod, an independent and quite wealthy principality *(see p17)*. It has retained its medieval atmosphere, so different from the imperial palaces adorning the countryside south of St Petersburg. They each reflect the tastes of their owners. Peter the Great's fine residence, Peterhof, is dominated by water; the Gulf and the fountains mirror his maritime interest. Elizabeth wanted vibrant colour and excess to

Muse of love and poetry, Pavlovsk

accommodate her extravagant balls, hence the grand Baroque palace at Tsarskoe Selo. Catherine the Great's love of intimacy led her to add private apartments to Tsarskoe Selo, and the exquisite Chinese Palace at Oranienbaum. Paul I's military mania made him turn Gatchina into a castle, while his wife Maria Fyodorovna created a feminine, elegant residence at Pavlovsk. All the palaces except Oranienbaum suffered devastating damage during World War II *(see p27)*. A great deal of effort has been made to restore them painstakingly over the last 50 years.

While the aristocracy indulged in their extravagances, the middle classes had more modest country houses. The comfortable *dacha* of the artist Repin, northwest of the city, gives visitors a feel of his more bohemian lifestyle.

The Novgorod Kremlin with the Cathedral of St Sophia and its belfry

◁ The gilded maze of the main staircase at Peterhof's Grand Palace

Exploring St Petersburg's Surroundings

MOST ST PETERSBURGERS leave the city to spend time at their *dacha* or country house for weekends and holidays. But there are several ways of experiencing the countryside around St Petersburg. There are many stunning imperial palaces, spread out like pearls in a necklace south of the city. Each one of them offers splendid interiors as well as beautifully laid out parks and gardens with lakes. Around the artist's studio at Repino is a more typical Baltic landscape, with pine and fir trees stretching down to the pebbly beaches of the Gulf of Finland.

Further away to the south, the medieval town of Novgorod is a great representative of an old Russian city, complete with a walled kremlin and onion-domed churches.

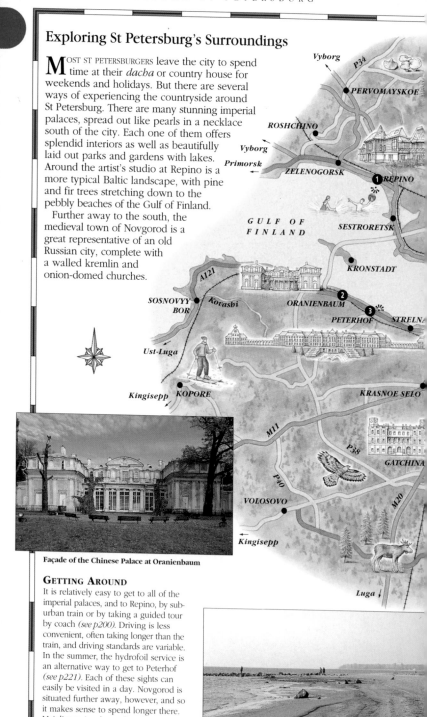

Façade of the Chinese Palace at Oranienbaum

GETTING AROUND

It is relatively easy to get to all of the imperial palaces, and to Repino, by suburban train or by taking a guided tour by coach *(see p200)*. Driving is less convenient, often taking longer than the train, and driving standards are variable. In the summer, the hydrofoil service is an alternative way to get to Peterhof *(see p221)*. Each of these sights can easily be visited in a day. Novgorod is situated further away, however, and so it makes sense to spend longer there. Mainline trains depart from Moscow railway station *(see p221)* for Novgorod.

Coastal landscape along the Gulf of Finland

Priozersk

● VASKELOVO

P33

Morye

● TOKSOVO

● BORISOVA GRIVA

PARGOLOVO

Okhta

● VSEVOLOZHSK

LAKE LADOGA

● **ST PETERSBURG**

M18

● SCHLÜSSELBURG

● KIROVSK

Novaya Ladoga

M10

TSARSKOE SELO
5

6
PAVLOVSK

● MGA

Nazma

● TOSNO

Mga

P38

Novgorod Moscow

P40

Tosna

SIGHTS AT A GLANCE

Gatchina **4**
Novgorod **7**
Oranienbaum **2**
Pavlovsk **6**
Peterhof **3**
Repino **1**
Tsarskoe Selo **5**

LOCATOR MAP
Novgorod is 190 km (118 miles) south of St Petersburg.

ST PETERSBURG

NOVGOROD

Gilded cupolas of the chapel of Catherine Palace at Tsarskoe Selo

| 0 kilometres | 20 |
| 0 miles | 10 |

NOVGOROD

↗ St Petersburg

M10

● LYUBOLYADY

P47

● KRECHEVITSY

● NOVGOROD
7

BELAYA GORA

● PANKOVKA

A116

PROLETARIY

Ostrov

Ozero Ilmen

Moscow →

KEY

▬ Major road

▬ Minor road

▬ Scenic route

+++ Railway

— River

☆ Viewpoint

Repino ❶
Репино
Repino

47 km (29 miles) NW of St Petersburg.
🚊 *from Finland Station.* 🚌 *411 from
Chernaya Rechka metro.* **Penaty**,
Primorskoe shosse 411. 📞 *231 6828.*
⭕ *10:30am–6pm Wed–Mon (Oct–Apr:
10:30am–5pm).* 🈂️ ♿ *ground floor.*

Studio of the eminent artist Ilya Repin at his home in Repino

O NLY ABOUT AN HOUR'S drive
from St Petersburg on
Primorskoe shosse, the northern coastal road, is a region
of lakes, pine-scented forests
and sandy beaches. Among
the green-painted *dachas* and
sanatoria is Repino, a resort
named after one of Russia's
greatest artists, Ilya Repin
(see p43), who lived here for
over 30 years until his death
in 1930 at the age of 86. His
extraordinary *dacha*, with its
steeply pitched glass roof and
angled windows, was restored
after damage in World War II
and is now open as a museum.

Named Penaty in honor of
the Roman household gods,
penates, the house was redesigned by Repin himself to
accommodate all that an artist
might need, including a glass-
panelled veranda downstairs,
which was used as a winter
studio. On display in the first
floor studio are the artist's
brushes and a number of his
works, including an unfinished
portrait of Pushkin *(see p44)*
and Repin's last self-portrait.

Works by the artist adorn the
dining room, including portraits
of the singer Fyodor Shalyapin
and writer Maxim Gorky who
were among Repin's many visitors. A specially constructed
revolving dining table enabled
guests to serve themselves
and to store away their used

dishes, since there were no
servants. Anyone failing to
obey this household rule had
to give an impromptu speech
from the lectern in the corner.

In the garden, two small
wooden follies are hidden
among the trees, and Repin's
grave is marked by a simple
cross on the top of a hillock.

Oranienbaum ❷
Ораниенбаум
Oranienbaum

Oranienbaum, 40 km (25 miles) W of
St Petersburg. 📞 *422 4796.* 🚊 *from
Baltic station.* **Grounds** ⭕ *9am–
10pm (Oct–Apr: 9am–8pm).* **Palaces
& Sliding Hill Pavilion** ⭕ *11am–
5pm Mon, Wed–Sun (times vary slightly
for individual buildings).* **Chinese
Palace** ⬤ *Oct–Apr.* 🈂️ 🎫

A S THE EXTRAVAGANT project of
Peter the Great's closest
friend and main political advisor, Aleksandr Menshikov *(see
p62)*, Oranienbaum was far
more ambitious in conception
than Peter's palace at Peterhof
(see pp146–9), which lies just
12 km (7 miles) to the west.
The grandiose plan bankrupted

Menshikov and, when he fell
from grace in 1727, the estate
entered the state treasury.

The Baroque appearance of
Oranienbaum's Great Palace
has changed little since it was
constructed in 1710–25. Built
by Gottfried Schädel and
Giovanni-Maria Fontana, its
sweeping wings culminate in
two remarkable pavilions.
Parts of the palace and the
east (Japanese) pavilion are
now open to the public.

From 1743 to 1761 the estate
became the residence of the
heir to the throne, the future
Peter III, who built himself a
miniature fortress with a small
lake for his "navy" and a
parade ground where he was
fond of playing war games
with soldiers. Peter also commissioned Antonio Rinaldi to
build him a modest palace.

Peter's wife, Catherine (later
Catherine the Great), abhorred
her isolated existence here,
but after Peter's murder *(see
p22)* she recovered her spirits
and created what she described
as her "personal *dacha*". Built
by Rinaldi in the 1760s and
known as the Chinese Palace,
it is famous for its fabulous
Rococo interiors and voguish
displays of chinoiserie.

The most unusual building
at Oranienbaum is Rinaldi's
Sliding Hill Pavilion, built in
1762 on Catherine's initiative.
Wooden sledging hills were a
common source of amusement
among the Russian nobility.
Catherine's visitors would climb
the blue and white pavilion
before descending by sledge
or toboggan along a roller
coaster run. The track, 500 m
(1,640 ft) long, was originally
flanked by a colonnade. Sadly,

Façade of Menshikov's Great Palace (1710–25), Oranienbaum

this collapsed in 1813 but there is a model in the pavilion.

A pleasant few hours can be spent wandering through the extensive grounds with their secluded paths, pine woods, ponds and bridges.

Oranienbaum was the only palace in the area to escape German occupation during World War II *(see p141)*. In 1948, the estate was renamed Lomonosov in honour of the famous 18th-century polymath *(see p45)* who established a glass and mosaic factory nearby. The complex has reverted to its original name, an allusion to the exotic orange trees planted here by Menshikov.

Chinoiserie decorations in Catherine the Great's Chinese Palace, Oranienbaum

Peterhof ❸

See pp146–49.

Gatchina ❹
Гатчина
Gatchina

45 km (28 miles) SW of St Petersburg. 🚉 from Baltic Station. 🚌 431 from pl Pobedy. 【 8 271 13492. ◯ 10am–6pm Tue–Sun. 🅰 🎫 English.

IN 1765, Catherine the Great presented the village of Gatchina to her lover, Prince Grigoriy Orlov. He commissioned Antonio Rinaldi to build a Neo-Classical palace which was completed in 1781. When Orlov died, two years later, Catherine transferred the estate to her son and heir Paul (later

Austere central section of Gatchina palace

Paul I). Paul asked his favourite architect Vincenzo Brenna to re-fashion the palace to match his pronounced martial tastes. Brenna's large-scale alterations included the construction of an additional storey and a moat with a drawbridge.

The next Romanov to spend any time here was Alexander III who made it his permanent family residence in the late 19th century. The estate provided a safe and remote haven from the sporadic social unrest which was threatening the capital *(see p26)*. The imperial family led a simple and secluded existence here. In keeping with the increasingly bourgeois tastes of the nobility in the whole of Europe, they scorned the state rooms, confining themselves instead to the cosy and more intimate servants' quarters.

In 1917, immediately after the Bolshevik party had seized power, the proclaimed leader of the Provisional Government,

Aleksandr Kerensky, fled to Gatchina where he made a last ditch attempt to rally his supporters. After a week, he deserted his troops and slipped away into exile *(see p27)*.

After World War II, in which the palace was badly damaged, Gatchina was used for many years as a military academy. The lengthy and thorough restoration process is still under way. Of the restored rooms, the three most impressive are the Marble Dining Room, Paul I's gloomy bedroom at the top of one of Brenna's towers and the magnificent White Ballroom. There is also a display of weaponry on the ground floor.

The delightful grounds are the wildest of all the palace parks. Among the attractions are the circular Temple of Venus (1792–3) on the secluded Island of Love and the Birch House (1790s). At first glance the latter appears to be nothing more than a pile of logs, but it actually conceals a suite of exquisite rooms.

The lake has boats for hire and its clean water makes it an ideal spot for swimming in the summer. Since there are few facilities in the town itself, bring a picnic and enjoy the idyllic views and tranquillity.

Tsarskoe Selo ❺

See pp150–53.

Gatchina's sumptuous White Ballroom with its pseudo-Egyptian statues

Peterhof ❸

Петергоф
Petergof

WITH ITS COMMANDING views of the Baltic, Peterhof is a perfect expression of triumphalism. Originally designed by Jean Baptiste Le Blond, the Great Palace (1714–21) was transformed during the reign of Tsarina Elizabeth when Bartolomeo Rastrelli added a third storey and wings with pavilions at either end. He tried to preserve Le Blond's early Baroque exterior, but redesigned the interiors, indulging his love for gilded Baroque decoration. Peterhof stands at the centre of a magnificent landscaped park, with both French and English gardens.

View from palace of Grand Cascade leading down to the Gulf of Finland

Neptune Fountain

Oak Fountain

Mezheumnyy Fountain

The Upper Gardens are framed by borders and hedges and punctuated with ornamental ponds.

The Imperial Suite

The imperial suite lies in the palace's east wing. Peter's Oak Study is one of the few rooms to have survived unaltered from Le Blond's design. Some of the oak panel designs are originals (1718–21) by Nicholas Pineau.

Cottage Palace

Orangery

Roman Fountain

★ **The Grand Cascade**

The dazzling cascade (1715–24) is a sequence of 37 gilded bronze sculptures, 64 fountains and 142 water jets (see p149), descending from the terraces of the Great Palace to the Marine Canal and the sea.

Pyramid Fountain

Monplaisir

Adam Fountain

| 0 metres | 25 |
| 0 yards | 25 |

PETER THE GREAT'S PALACE

After his victory over the Swedes at Poltava in 1709, Peter the Great decided to build a palace "befitting to the very highest of monarchs". A visit to Versailles in 1717 furthered Peter's ambitions and he employed more than 5,000 labourers, serfs and soldiers, supported by architects, water-engineers, landscape gardeners and sculptors. Work proceeded at a frenetic pace from 1714 until Peterhof was officially opened in 1723.

Le Blond's Great Palace was completed in 1721 and has changed considerably over the decades. Catherine the Great commissioned Yuriy Velten to redecorate some of Rastrelli's interiors in the 1770s, including the Throne Room and the Chesma Room.

Jean Baptiste Le Blond's original two-storey Great Palace

VISITORS' CHECKLIST

Petrodvorets, 30 km (19 miles) W of St Petersburg. ☎ 427 9527.
🚃 from Baltic station (see p220) to Novyy Petergof. 🚤 Hermitage (May–Oct) (see p220). **Great Palace** ◻ 10:30am–5pm Tue–Sun. **Other pavilions** ◻ May–Sep: 10:30am–5pm Tue–Sun; Oct–Apr: 10.30am–4pm Sat & Sun. **Fountains** ◻ May–Sep: 10am–6pm. 🖋 📷 📁 🍴 💳

★ Main Staircase
Caryatids and gilded carvings adorn Rastrelli's glittering staircase. The ceiling fresco depicts Aurora and Genius chasing away the night.

Golden Hill Cascade

Marly and Hermitage

Eve Fountain

STAR FEATURES

★ Grand Cascade

★ Main Staircase

★ The State Rooms

Hydrofoil and Gulf of Finland

The Marine Canal enabled the tsars to sail from the Gulf of Finland up to the Great Palace.

★ The State Rooms
The highlight of the State Rooms is the opulent Throne Room, redesigned by Yuriy Velten in 1770. The relatively restrained stucco ornamentation, red velvet hangings and parquet floor provide an exquisite setting for portraits of Russia's imperial family.

Exploring Peterhof Park

THE GROUNDS AT PETERHOF include the Upper, Lower and Alexandria parks, covering an area of around 607 hectares (1,500 acres). As well as the numerous palaces and fountains, there are tree-lined avenues, wooded paths and the Baltic shore. Le Blond designed the grounds next to the Great Palace to be laid out in the formal French style with geometrically arranged flower beds, sculptures, summerhouses and pergolas. The trees and shrubs, including limes, elms, maples and roses, were imported from all over Russia and abroad.

Cottage Palace in Alexandria Park

Monplaisir palace (1714–22), overlooking the Gulf of Finland

Monplaisir

This delightfully unpretentious palace was designed in 1714 by Johann Braunstein. Even after the Great Palace was built, Peter continued to live and entertain at Monplaisir where his guests were usually subjected to a punishing regime of heavy drinking. At breakfast the coffee cups were filled with brandy and by nightfall guests were often discovered wandering drunk in the park.

While not as lavish as those of the Great Palace the interiors are still impressive, in particular the wood-panelled Ceremonial Hall. A painting on its vaulted ceiling depicts Apollo surrounded by characters from a masque. Russian icon painters skilfully carried out the decoration of the exquisite Lacquered Study in the Chinese style then in vogue. Peter's collection of canvases by Dutch and Flemish artists hang in the rooms and there are wonderful views of the gulf from the tsar's Naval Study.

Adjoining Monplaisir is the Catherine Wing, which was built for Tsarina Elizabeth by Rastrelli in 1747–54. Catherine

the Great was staying here in 1762 when her lover, Count Orlov, arrived with news of the coup which was to bring her to the throne *(see p24)*.

Marly Palace

Named after Marly-le-Rois, the king of France's hunting lodge which Peter the Great visited on a tour of Europe in 1717, this beautifully proportioned country residence was built for the tsar's guests. The rooms open to the public

Elaborate tiled kitchen in the Marly Palace (1720–3)

include the Oak and Plane Tree studies, Peter's bedroom and the Dining Room. It is set in its own formal garden with sculptures, fountains, a large pond and Niccolò Michetti's Golden Hill Cascade, which was added in 1731–7.

The Hermitage

Standing in splendid isolation on the shores of the gulf, this elegant pavilion (1721–5), by Braunstein, was conceived as a private dining venue for the tsar and his friends. To highlight the need for solitude, the building was raised on a plinth and surrounded by a moat that was crossed by a small drawbridge. The stuccoed façade is decorated with Corinthian pilasters, elaborate wrought-iron balconies and enlarged windows. All the servants were confined to the ground floor and a mechanical device took meals up from the kitchen.

Cottage Palace

The romantic landscaped grounds of Alexandria Park, named after Alexandra, wife of Nicholas I, provide a perfect setting for the Cottage Palace. The Neo-Gothic house is more imposing than the term cottage suggests. The Scottish architect, Adam Menelaws, designed it in 1826–9 for Nicholas I and his wife, who wanted a domestic environment in keeping with their bourgeois tastes.

The Gothic theme is pursued throughout, most effectively in the Great Drawing Room with the rose window motif in the carpet and the lace-like tracery of the stuccoed ceiling. The exquisite 5,200-piece crystal and porcelain dinner service in the Dining Room was made for the royal couple at the Imperial Porcelain factory.

The Fountains at Peterhof

JEAN-BAPTISTE LE BLOND submitted his "water plan" to Peter the Great in 1717, by which time the tsar had begun sketching his own ideas. The centrepiece is the Grand Cascade, fed by the underground springs of the Ropsha Hills about 22 km (14 miles) away. The cascade is a celebration of the triumph of Russia over Sweden *(see p19)*, symbolized by Mikhail Kozlovskiy's glorious

Detail of the Mezheumnyy Fountain

sculpture of Samson rending the jaws of a lion. An imaginative variety of fountains, mostly concentrated in the Lower Park, includes triton and lion fountains, dragon fountains with checker-board steps, and smaller fountains with fish-tailed boys blowing sprays of water through conches. Most playful are trick fountains such as the Umbrella which "rains" on those who come too close.

The Adam Fountain, sculpted by Giovanni Bonazza, was commissioned by Peter in 1718, along with a similar statue of Eve. The two fountains suggest the earthly paradise the tsar had recreated at Peterhof.

The Neptune Fountain predates Peterhof by more than 50 years. The Baroque sculpture was erected in 1658 in Nuremberg to mark the end of the Thirty Years War and was sold to Tsar Paul I in 1782 because there was not enough water to make it work.

The Roman Fountains were designed by Ivan Blank and Ivan Davydov in 1738–9. The two-tiered marble fountains were inspired by one in St Peter's Square in Rome.

The Grand Cascade was originally adorned with lead statues which weathered badly and were recast in bronze and gilded after 1799. Shubin, Martos and other noted sculptors worked to create this stunning cascade.

The Pyramid Fountain (1720s) is one of a number of fountains whose jets create a special shape. Over 500 jets of water rise in seven tiers to create an "obelisk" commemorating the Russian victory over Sweden.

Tsarskoe Selo ❺

Царское Село

Tsarskoe Selo

THE LAVISH imperial palace at Tsarskoe Selo was designed by Rastrelli *(see p93)* in 1752 for Tsarina Elizabeth. She named it the Catherine Palace in honour of her mother, Catherine I, who originally owned the estate. The next ruler to leave her mark on the palace was Catherine the Great, and during her reign she commissioned the Scotsman Charles Cameron to redesign the Baroque interiors according to her more Neo-Classical taste. Cameron also built the ensemble for taking traditional Russian cold and warm baths, containing the Agate Rooms, and the Cameron Gallery. Post-war restoration of the palace continues and 20 state rooms are now open, as well as the beautiful park.

★ The Great Hall
Light streams into Rastrelli's glittering hall illuminating the mirrors, gilded carvings and the vast ceiling painting, The Triumph of Russia *(c.1755), by Giuseppe Valeriani.*

The Great Staircase (1860), by Ippolito Monighetti, ascends to the state rooms on the first floor.

Atlantes
The stunning 300-m (980-ft) long Baroque façade is adorned with a profusion of atlantes, columns, pilasters and ornamented window framings.

Entrance

| 0 metres | 25 |
| 0 yards | 25 |

The Agate Rooms *(see p152),* part of the imperial *banya* (baths) are faced inside with semi-precious stones from the Urals.

The Cameron Gallery *(see p152)*

The Cavaliers' Dining Room
The table is laid for Tsarina Elizabeth's gentlemen-in-waiting, in the refined gold and white room created by Rastrelli.

The Royal Chapel is richly decorated in dark blue and gold. Built by Chevakinskiy in the 1740s, it contains an elaborate six-tiered iconostasis.

VISITORS' CHECKLIST

Tsarskoe Selo (Pushkin), 25 km (16 miles) S of St Petersburg. 🚃 from *Vitebsk station to Detskoe Selo*, then bus 371 or 382 (see p220).
Catherine Palace 📞 465 5308. ⬛ *10am–5pm Wed–Mon.* ⬤ *last Mon of month.* 🎦 ✔
⬛ 📷 ⬛ **Agate Rooms** ⬜ *10am–4:30pm Thu–Mon.*
Cameron Gallery ⬤ temporarily. **Park** ⬜ *daily.* 🎦 *mid May–Sep.*

★ Amber Room
The original amber panels (1709) by Andreas Schlüter were a gift from Friedrich Wilhelm I of Prussia to Peter the Great. The room is slowly being recreated from photos, complete with carved reliefs and panels in Florentine mosaic.

The Blue Drawing Room is characterized by blue floral motifs painted on silk. Among the royal portraits hanging here is a painting of Peter the Great by Ivan Nikitin, dating from around 1720.

To the Lycée and the Church of the Sign *(see p153)*

The Picture Gallery displays canvases by Italian, French, Dutch and Flemish masters of the 17th and 18th centuries.

★ Green Dining Room
Cameron's restrained Neo-Classical style contrasts with the Baroque flamboyance of Rastrelli's work. The exquisite stucco bas-reliefs, sculpted by Ivan Martos, were based on motifs from frescoes discovered in Pompeii.

The French-style formal gardens were laid out in the 1740s. Their formality and symmetry contrasts with the naturalistic English-style landscaping of the park *(see p152)*, created in 1768.

Small Enfilade
A varied selection of furniture and objets d'art *make up the exhibition in these unrestored rooms. Chinese lacquer furniture and Oriental rugs were among the treasures used to furnish the palace in the 19th century.*

STAR FEATURES

★ **The Great Hall**

★ **Amber Room**

★ **Green Dining Room**

Exploring Tsarskoe Selo

THE MAGNIFICENT PARKS and gardens of Tsarskoe Selo (the Tsar's Village) were created out of dense forest by thousands of soldiers and labourers. Work began on the formal gardens in 1744 but later, in 1768, Catherine the Great commissioned one of Russia's first landscaped parks. The 567 hectares (1,400 acres) of grounds are dotted with captivating pavilions set around the central lake. The grounds and the town of Tsarskoe Selo, to the northeast of the palace, are also a delight to explore.

Formal gardens in front of Catherine Palace, Catherine Park

Catherine Park

The formal gardens to the southeast of the palace are laid out geometrically with radiating avenues, parterres and terraces, decorous ponds, hedges, elegant pavilions and Classical statuary. Nearest to the palace are Cameron's sumptuous **Agate Rooms** (1780–87). Their heavily rusticated lower storey contrasts with the upper tier, modelled on a Renaissance villa. The building takes its name from the agate, jasper, malachite and other semi-precious stones covering the interior.

The impressive **Cameron Gallery**, built in 1783–7, has a rusticated stone ground floor, surmounted by a Neo-Classical peristyle of 44 Ionic columns. Ranged along the colonnade are bronze busts of ancient philosophers, poets and rulers. In 1792–4 Cameron added a long stone ramp to facilitate access to the gardens for the ageing Catherine the Great.

Girl with a Pitcher by Pavel Sokolov (1816)

The Neo-Classical **Lower and Upper Baths** were built by Ilya Neyelov in 1777–80. The domed Lower Baths were for the use of courtiers while the exquisite Upper Baths were reserved for members of the imperial family.

Construction work on Rastrelli's **Grotto** began in 1749, but the original decoration of the interior with more than 250,000 shells continued well into the 1770s.

The gardens' main avenue leads to the **Hermitage** (1756), a Baroque pavilion built by Rastrelli, where Elizabeth would entertain small groups of guests for dinner.

The romantic landscaped area of the lower park was begun in 1768 by master gardeners such as John Bush, who worked under the overall supervision of the architect, Vasiliy Neyelov. A 16-km (10-mile) waterway was built to feed the numerous canals, cascades and man-made lakes,

including the *pièce de résistance,* the **Great Pond**. From Giacomo Quarenghi's pavilion (1786) on the island, musicians would serenade Catherine and her courtiers as they floated by in gilded gondolas.

A naval theme links Vasiliy Neyelov's Dutch, Neo-Gothic **Admiralty** (1773–7) with the 25-m (82-ft) high **Chesma Column** which is decorated with ships' prows. The column, designed by Antonio Rinaldi in 1771, commemorates the Russian victory over the Turks in the Aegean.

The reflection of the pink dome and minaret of the **Turkish Bath** shimmers in the placid waters on the far side of the lake. Nearby is Neyelov's colonnaded **Marble Bridge** (1770–76). Perched on a rock overlooking the pond is the **Girl with a Pitcher**, a statue by Pavel Sokolov. The figure inspired Pushkin to write his memorable poem, *Fountain at Tsarskoe Selo*, in which he muses on the girl who has broken her urn and now "sits timelessly sad over the timeless stream".

Evidence of the 18th-century craze for chinoiserie can be found on the border with the wilder Alexander Park where Cameron built his **Chinese Village** in 1782–96. Other examples are Yuriy Velten's **Creaking Pavilion**, so-called because it was designed to creak when visitors entered, and Neyelov's **Great Caprice** (1770s), a hump-backed bridge surmounted by a pagoda-like columned structure.

The Moorish-style Turkish Baths (1852) by Ippolito Monighetti

Creaking Pavilion (1778–86)

The Town of Tsarskoe Selo
This town of some 80,000 in-habitants was developed in the 19th century as a summer resort for the aristocracy. In 1937, it was renamed after the poet Alexander Pushkin *(see p43)* who was educated at the local **Lycée** in 1811–17, in room No. 14. One of Russia's most prestigious schools, it was founded by Alexander I

in 1811 to educate members of the nobility. In 1998 the town took back its original name.

The attractive **Church of the Sign,** dating to 1734, is one of the town's oldest buildings. In a garden next door a statue by Roman Bach depicts Pushkin dressed in the Lycée uniform.

Pushkin and his new bride, Natalya, spent the summer of 1831 in the delightful wooden house, now named **Pushkin's Dacha.** The writer, Nikolai Gogol, was amongst the many friends they entertained here.

On the town's western edge is the **Alexander Palace,** commissioned by Catherine for her grandson, the future Alexander I. Designed in 1792 by Giacomo Quarenghi, the austere, Neo-Classical building has a colonnaded façade and protruding wings. It was the residence of Russia's last tsar, Nicholas II, and his family who lived here from 1904 until they were placed under house arrest

in 1917 *(see p28).* The exhib-ition inside includes Nicholas' magnificent Style-Moderne study, designed by Melzer.

Lycée
10:30am–4:30pm Wed–Mon.

Pushkin's Dacha
10:30am–4:30pm Wed–Sun.

Alexander Palace
10am–4:30pm Wed–Mon.

Alexander Pushkin's statue (1900), by Roman Bach

TSARSKOE SELO PARK

Admiralty ⑦
Agate Rooms ②
Alexander Palace ⑰
Cameron Gallery ③
Catherine Palace pp150–51 ①
Chesma Column ⑧
Church of the Sign ⑮
Creaking Pavilion ⑫
Girl with a Pitcher ⑪
Great Caprice ⑬
Grotto ⑥
Hermitage ⑤
Lower and Upper Baths ④
Lycée ⑭
Marble Bridge ⑩
Pushkin's Dacha ⑯
Turkish Bath ⑨

Imperial standard of the Romanovs flying at the Catherine Palace ▷

Pavlovsk ❻

Павловск

Pavlovsk

To CELEBRATE THE BIRTH of his heir, Catherine the Great presented her son, the Grand Duke Paul, with these lands in 1777. She also "gave" him her favourite architect, Charles Cameron, to design both palace and park. Work at Pavlovsk (from "Pavel" or Paul) began in 1780 and was continued by Paul's grieving widow, Maria Fyodorovna, long after his death. "English gardens" were at the height of fashion and inspired Cameron's design of a seemingly natural landscape dotted with pavilions (used for informal parties), romantic ruins and attractive vistas around the Slavyanka river.

Cold Baths
This austere pavilion was built by Cameron in 1799 as a summer swimming pool, complete with elegant vestibule, paintings, furniture and rich wall upholstery.

The Apollo Colonnade
Cameron's colonnade (1782–83) encircles a copy of the Apollo Belvedere, above a romantically dilapidated cascade.

Three Graces Pavilion

The Centaur Bridge by Voronikhin (1805) nestles on a bend of the Slavyanka river.

Aviary

Cameron's Dairy (1782) housed both a milking shed and a stylish salon.

★ **Pavlovsk Palace**
Cameron's elegant Palladian mansion (1782–6) forms the central block of today's palace (see pp158–9), with wings added in 1789 by Paul's favoured architect, Vincenzo Brenna.

★ **Temple of Friendship**
This Doric temple (1780) was the first use of Greek forms in Russia.

Green Woman Alley

Pavlovsk Railway Station

Visconti Bridge
*One of the most famous bridges
which cross the winding
Slavyanka, it was
designed by
Andrey
Voronikhin
in 1807.*

The Étoile
*The Étoile, the earliest
landscaped area in the
park, was laid out by
Cameron in 1780. The
circle of statues represents
the nine Muses, protectresses
of the arts and sciences.*

**The Beautiful
Valley** was the
favourite spot of
Elizabeth, wife
of Alexander I.

0 metres	200
0 yards	200

Paul's Mausoleum
(1808–9) bears the
inscription
"To my beneficient
consort".

The Rose Pavilion
was the favourite
haunt of Maria
Fyodorovna
from 1812. She
held many
concerts and
literary evenings
in this cottage.

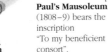

STAR FEATURES

★ Temple of
Friendship

★ Great Palace

Pil Tower and Bridge
*Brenna's tower (1795–97) contained a
spiral staircase, lounge and library. The
bridge was a later addition made in 1808.*

Exploring Pavlovsk Palace

CATHERINE COMMISSIONED Charles Cameron to build the Great Palace (1782–86) whilst Paul and his wife Maria Fyodorovna travelled around Europe incognito as the Comte and Comtesse du Nord. They, meanwhile, bought up everything they saw including French clocks,

Late 18th-century clock, Grecian Hall Sèvres porcelain, tapestries and furniture, to fill their new home. Once back in Russia, they brought in Brenna to add taller, more elaborate wings to Cameron's elegant Palladian mansion, turning it into a true palace.

West façade of the Palladian mansion

PLAN OF PAVLOVSK PALACE, FIRST FLOOR

KEY

☐ State rooms

☐ Southern wing

Stairs to private apartments and Egyptian Vestibule on the ground floor

1 Italian Hall
2 Paul's Study
3 Tapestry Room
4 Hall of War
5 Grecian Hall
6 Hall of Peace
7 Maria Fyodorovna's Library
8 Boudoir
9 State Bedroom
10 Dressing Room
11 Picture Gallery
12 Throne Room
13 Hall of Knights
14 Chapel

STATE ROOMS

The Italian Hall, originally by Cameron and Brenna, 1789

NEARLY ALL OF the palace apartments at Pavlovsk, including the official ones, are relatively modest in scale. They reflect Maria Fyodorovna's intensely feminine tastes which have given Pavlovsk a distinct charm rather than grandeur.

A fire in 1803 necessitated some remodelling of the palace interiors by Andrey Voronikhin. The entrance hall, or Egyptian Vestibule, gained its present appearance after he added the painted bronze figures and zodiac medallions. At the top of the stairs is Brenna's State Vestibule, where the bas-reliefs reflected Paul's passion for all things military. It leads onto the Italian Hall, situated beneath the central cupola, with lantern windows and heavy doors of rosewood and mahogany.

The northern row of rooms on this floor were for Paul, the southern ones for Maria. Paul's Study is dominated by Johann Lampi's fine portrait of Maria (1794), who holds a drawing of six of their children. Beneath it is a model temple of amber,

ivory and gilded bronze, made by Maria's herself. Next door, the Tapestry Room is named after the Don Quixote tapestries made by Gobelin and presented to Paul by Louis XVI. The mahogany writing table was actually made for the new Engineers' Castle *(see p101)* but, after Paul's murder there in 1801 *(see p22)*, Maria moved much of the specially-designed furniture to Pavlovsk Palace.

The corner rooms are a Hall of War for Paul and Maria's contrasting Hall of Peace, both richly adorned with bas-reliefs and heavy gilding. Between the two lies the magnificent Grecian Hall, Cameron's Neo-Classical masterpiece.

Maria Fyodorovna's rooms commence with a small, comfortable library. The chair at the desk was designed for her by Voronikhin; note the pots built into the spine for flowers. Her Boudoir has pilasters painted with motifs copied from the Raphael Loggias in the Vatican, and a porphyry fireplace. The State Bedroom was reputedly never slept in, but was part of court ceremony. Opposite the

Maria Fyodorovna's Boudoir, designed by Brenna, 1789

Brenna's Picture Gallery (1789), with chandeliers by Johann Zeck

bed is a 64-piece Sèvres toilet set, complete with a coffee cup and an eye bath, which was a gift from Marie Antoinette.

Another present dominates the Dressing Room, a superb set of steel furniture including dressing table, chair, vases and ink stand made by the renowned gun-makers of Tula (1789). This was presented to Maria by Catherine the Great.

SOUTHERN WING

FROM THE ELEGANTLY curved picture gallery, built in 1798, there are excellent views. Only a few of the paintings, mostly purchased during the young couple's trip to France, are worthy of special notice, as their taste was for applied arts.

The largest room in the palace is the Throne Room, designed by Brenna (1797) after Paul became tsar. Despite its name it was generally used for balls and state dinners. The tables are now laid with part of a 606-piece gilded dinner service. Vast blue Sèvres vases

stand on plinths, bought directly from the factory (Paul and Maria spent huge sums on porcelain there alone). The ceiling was painted during restoration after World War II *(see p26)*, and is taken from an original design which was never used.

The Knights of St John chose Paul as Grand Master when they fled Napoleon's occupation of Malta in 1798. This suited Paul's military taste and he commissioned vast lamps, thrones and decorative items (now in the Hermitage), as well as the Hall of Knights, for ceremonies of the Order. The pale green room is adorned with Classical statues, saved from the Germans in World War II by being buried in the grounds.

The suite of rooms ends with the Imperial Chapel of SS Peter and Paul, a very un-Orthodox church by Brenna (1797–98), decorated with copies of European paintings.

PRIVATE APARTMENTS

LOCATED ON THE ground floor are the private apartments. The Pilaster Room (1800), with its golden pilasters, is furnished with a dark mahogany suite. The Lantern Study, designed a few years later by Voronikhin, is named after its apsed bay window forming the "lantern".

Maria Fyodorovna's Dressing Room leads into the Bedroom (1805) she actually used (as opposed to the State Bedroom upstairs). Pieces of the original silk were saved in the war and used to edge the new curtains.

The small pink and blue Ballroom was for private parties and hung with paintings by the most fashionable artist of the day, Hubert Robert. The General Study, used as a family sitting room, is decorated with portraits of the family. The Raspberry Room, Paul's private study, contains paintings with views of Gatchina Palace, made for the Engineers' Castle.

The Lantern Study, one of Voronikhin's most successfully designed interiors, 1804

MARIA FYODOROVNA (1759–1828)

Paul's wife, Maria Fyodorovna, bore 10 children, and Pavlovsk was considered her 11th child. Paul himself preferred Gatchina *(see p145)* and in 1788 Maria was given Pavlovsk entirely. She devoted all her energy to adorning both palace and park, giving precise directions to designers and architects, who bemoaned their lack of independence. Born Sophia of Württemberg-Stuttgart, Maria had a practical German upbringing which she put to good use. Pieces of her own work, from furniture to family portraits, are throughout the palace.

Inkstand (1795) created from initial design by Maria Fyodorovna

Novgorod ❼

Detail of bronze door on Cathedral of St Sophia

THE ANCIENT TOWN of Novgorod (New Town) was founded in 859 by the Varangian (Viking) Prince Rurik *(see p17)*. The city's proud tradition of self-government began in the 11th century and lasted until 1478, when Ivan III subjugated the city. Favourably sited on the River Volkhov with convenient connections from Scandinavia to the Aegean, the city of Novgorod became a powerful trading community during this period. In 1570, Ivan the Terrible put Novgorod to the sword, torturing and massacring thousands of its inhabitants when the city plotted against him. It was, however, the rise of St Petersburg which finally set the seal on Novgorod's decline. Much of the city's splendid cultural heritage, damaged in World War II, is now being restored and can be appreciated in the many medieval churches and picturesque streets of the old town.

Bejewelled metal icon cover on display in the Chamber of Facets

The Kremlin

Situated on the left bank, or Sofiskaya Storona (Sophia side), of the River Volkhov, the formidable red-brick walls and cone-topped towers of the oval-shaped Detinets, or Kremlin, date from the 11th to the 17th centuries. According to the prevailing practice at the time, the first stone of the original walls was laid on the body of a living child.

Of the many towers, the 17th-century Kukui is the most remarkable, and also the tallest at 32m (105ft). The lower floors once contained a wine cellar and treasury chamber, while the octagonal room beneath the cupola was used, according to chronicles, "for surveying the whole town".

Kremlin walls, with the silver dome of St Sophia's Belfry (15th century)

At the heart of the fortress is Novgorod's oldest and largest church, the strongly Byzantine **Cathedral of St Sophia** (1045–62). It was modelled on the cathedral of the same name in Kiev, but the tendencies of the Novgorod school already appear in the lack of ornament and the scarcity of windows,

necessary because of the cold. On the north wall a section of whitewash has been removed to reveal the original mosaic effect of the grey-yellow stone and brick façade.

The exquisitely sculpted and extremely rare bronze doors adorning the west side were seized as booty in 1187 from the Swedish town of Sigtuna. In the lower left hand corner there are portraits of the craftsmen, named in the Latin inscription as Riquin and Weissmut. The interior is divided by piers into five aisles, three ending in altar apses. Fragments of early frescoes survive, but the iconostasis is one of the oldest in Russia and contains icons from the 11th–17th centuries.

East of the cathedral is **St Sophia's Belfry**, much altered since it was first built in 1439. The bells, now displayed below, were cast in the late 16th and early 17th centuries.

The northwest corner of the Kremlin is occupied by the **Archbishops' Court**, in its heyday a powerful body with its own treasury, police force and military guard. Beneath the 15th-century clock tower an attractive staircase leads to the **Library**, housing magnificent medieval religious manuscripts. Backing onto the cathedral, the **Chamber of Facets** is the most famous part of this ensemble. A superb star-vaulted reception hall dates from 1433 and displays treasures from the cathedral, including goblets, jewelled mitres and icon covers in precious metals.

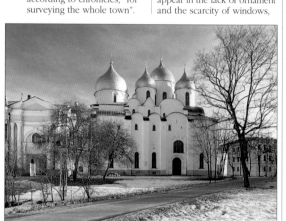

The 11th-century Cathedral of St Sophia, the landmark of Novgorod

Within the Kremlin is the **Museum of History, Architecture and Art**, which houses a magnificent collection of 12th–17th-century icons of the Novgorod school. One of the most remarkable is the 12th-century portable icon of the Virgin of the Sign, whose miraculous image is said to have saved Novgorod from the armies of Prince Andrey Bogolyubskiy of Suzdal in 1169. Scenes from the battle are depicted on a vibrant 15th-century icon *(see p163)*. There are also works by leading 18th- and 19th-century artists, including Dmitriy Levitskiy, Karl Bryullov and Vasiliy Serov *(see p106)*. The museum has a number of precious public documents and private letters written on birch bark, some of which date from the 11th century. These give details of ordinary, everyday life and are evidence of the unusually widespread literacy among the city's inhabitants.

In the Kremlin's central square, the huge, bell-shaped **Millennium Monument** was sculpted by Mikhail Mikeshin. The monument was unveiled in 1862, a thousand years after Rurik's arrival in Novgorod. The figure kneeling before the Orthodox cross personifies Mother Russia while, below, the decorative frieze depicts Rurik, Ivan III, Mikhail (the first Romanov tsar), Peter the Great and many others. The frieze around the base shows over 100 figures: heroes, statesmen, artists, composers, princes and chroniclers from different periods of Russian history.

The carved Royal Gates of an iconostasis in the Museum of History, Architecture and Art

🕆 Cathedral of St Sophia
📞 (81622) 73556. ⏰ 8am–1pm, 2–8pm daily. 📷

🏛 Chamber of Facets
📞 (81622) 73785. ⏰ 10am–6pm Thu–Tue. 📷 ✆ English by appt.

🏛 Museum of History, Architecture and Art
📞 (81622) 73770. ⏰ 10am–6pm Wed–Mon. 📷 ✆ English by appt.

VISITORS' CHECKLIST

190 km (118 miles) S of St Petersburg. 🚶 190,000. 🚆 from Moscow Station. 🚌 from Coach Station 2 (see p221). ℹ Intourist Hotel, ul Dmitrevskaya 16, (81622) 75089. ✆ by appt (tel: 73770).

commercial centre, once the site of the medieval market, part of whose wall still stands.

The oldest church on this side of the river, **St Nicholas' Cathedral** (1113–36), was built by Prince Mstislav. It dominates the area and once symbolized the prince's power.

Novgorod's merchants were keen to show their recognition of God's hand in their prosperity, and so funded many of the city's churches. **St Paraskeva Pyatnitsa**, erected in 1207 and then rebuilt in 1345, was dedicated to the patron saint of commerce. The more decorative **Church of the Holy Women** and **Church of St Procopius**, both 16th century, were financed by wealthy Moscow merchants. The fanciful tastes of the Muscovite patrons mark a departure from Novgorod's austere style.

Yaroslav's Court
Across the River Volkhov was the official seat of the princes, known as Yaroslav's Court. The palace of Yaroslav the Wise (1019–54) has since disappeared but several churches have survived. The area adjacent to the Court is Novgorod's

Millennium Monument, celebrating Novgorod's 1,000 years of history

Yuriev Monastery walls and bell tower with the silvery domes of the Cathedral of St George in the background

Beyond Yaroslav's Court

In the 12th century, Novgorod boasted over 200 churches, while there are only 30 today. Many of these are hidden away in the quiet hinterland of 19th-century streets to the east of Yaroslav's Court. On Ilyina ulitsa, the arrangement of windows, niches and inset crosses on the **Church of the Saviour of the Transfiguration** façade (1374) is almost whimsical. Inside, there are original frescoes by one of Russia's greatest medieval artists, Theophanes the Greek (1335–c.1410), who came from Constantinople and decorated 40 Russian churches. Andrey Rublev (1360–1430), Russia's most famous icon painter, worked under Theophanes at the beginning of his career.

On the same street, the five-domed **Znamenskiy Cathedral**, or Cathedral of the Sign (1682–8), has an attractive gateway and faded frescoes on the outer walls. The beautiful interior was decorated in 1702 by Ivan Bakhmatov.

The **Church of Theodore Stratilates** on Mstinskaya ulitsa to the north was built in 1360–61 by the widow of a wealthy Novgorod merchant. The delicate purple and pink frescoes contrast with the harsher colours found in most 14th-century Novgorod frescoes. *The Annunciation*, for example, combines sensitivity and charm with religious intensity.

Fresco inside Znamenskiy Cathedral

Further Afield

A pleasant stroll 3 km (2 miles) south along the river bank leads to the **Yuriev Monastery**. This is the largest and most important monastery in the area, founded in 1030 and built on the orders of Prince Vsevolod. Its imposing Cathedral of St George was built in 1119–30 by "Master Peter", the first named architect in Russian chronicles. This beautifully proportioned church with its three asymmetrical cupolas was restored in the 19th century, and unfortunately most of the interior murals were lost. There were once 20 monastic buildings in the complex, dating mainly from the 19th century.

In the woods across the road lies the fascinating open-air **Museum of Wooden Architecture**, which displays churches and peasant huts moved from local villages. Of particular interest are the 17th-century two-tiered Kuritsko Church of the Dormition and the tiny wooden church of St Nicholas from Tukhel village.

🎟 **Yuriev Monastery**
Yurevskaya nab. 🄲 (81622) 73020.
🕐 7am–8pm daily.
🏛 **Museum of Wooden Architecture**
Yurevo. 🄲 (81622) 78160.
🕐 10am–6pm (mid-Oct–mid-Apr: 10am–4pm) daily. 📷 🎫

Rebuilt 19th-century peasant hut (*izba*), Museum of Wooden Architecture

Russian Icon Painting

THE RUSSIAN ORTHODOX Church uses icons for both worship and teaching, but never for mere ornament, and there are strict rules for the creation of each image. Icons were believed to be imbued with the force of the saint depicted, and were therefore invoked for protection during wars. Because the content was considered more important than the style, old, revered icons were often repainted again and again.

Early stone icon found in Novgorod

The first icons were brought to Russia from Byzantium. Greek masters came too, to train local painters. The northern schools which developed during the 13th–15th centuries were less restricted by Byzantine canons and have an earthy style linked to Russian peasant life. Novgorod, never under the Mongol yoke and with a thriving economy, was the source of many of the finest icons made for the northern monasteries.

Virgin of Vladimir
The most venerated icon in Russia, this 12th-century work was made in Constantinople. Its huge influence on Russian icon painting cannot be overstated.

Battle of Novgorod and Suzdal
This mid-15th-century work of the Novgorod School is thought to be Russia's earliest historical painting. Icons could have a political purpose – in this case to use Novgorod's great past as a justification for its independence from Moscow. Note the multiple touches of red – a colour central to everyday Russian life and typical for icons of the Novgorod School.

THE ICONOSTASIS

The iconostasis screens off the sanctuary from the main part of the church, as if it were a boundary between heaven and earth. In Russian practice it is covered with icons strictly arranged in up to six tiers, each with its own dogmatic purpose.

The Festival Tier shows the 12 major church festivals, such as the Entry into Jerusalem and the Crucifixion. Such pictorial representation aided the faith of the illiterate.

The Royal Gates represent the entrance from the temporal world to the spiritual, between which the priests pass during the service.

Christ Enthroned

The Deesis Tier, above the Royal Gates, contains Christ Enthroned, flanked by the Virgin and St John interceding on behalf of mortal sinners.

The Local Tier is for local saints, those the church is dedicated to and patron saints of major donors.

Old Testament Trinity by Rublev
Andrey Rublev was one of the greatest artists of the Moscow School. He was strongly influenced by recent developments in Byzantine painting, brought to Russia by Greek masters in the late 14th century. His Trinity icon dates from the early 15th century.

TRAVELLERS' NEEDS

WHERE TO STAY

THERE IS A SERIOUS dearth of good accommodation in St Petersburg, particularly in the city centre and in the lower price bracket. The majority of tourists visiting St Petersburg arrive with a package tour and are housed in one of the large, modern hotels formerly managed by the State Tourist Agency, Intourist. These are anonymous and rarely central but, on the whole, provide a reasonably good service with many amenities such as restaurants, bars and sports facilities. The would-be individual tourist is no longer compelled to travel on a package tour,

Doorman at Hotel Europe

as was the case during the Soviet era. Nowadays visas and hotel bookings can be made independently and hotels can be reserved directly or through a booking agency. For the summer months, particularly during the White Nights, it is recommended to make bookings well in advance for the city's most prestigious and centrally located hotels.

Those on a tight budget with no knowledge of Russian are advised to make arrangements in advance. Rooms are limited and visitors with no reservations may be refused. There is a selection of hotels on *pp172–73*.

Pribaltiyskaya, a popular hotel for package tours

WHERE TO LOOK

VERY FEW hotels are located in central St Petersburg and the hotels listed in this chapter are scattered around the city, often at a distance from the centre. Visitors on a package tour usually find they are staying in a former Intourist hotel such as the Pribaltiyskaya or Pulkovskaya situated in modern high-rise areas on the city's outskirts. It is important for the independent traveller to decide at the start what your priorities are going to be: location, price or service.

HOW TO BOOK

HOTEL RESERVATIONS for the White Nights *(see p51)* should be made up to six months in advance. The best way to book independently is by fax. The larger hotels will require a credit card number and money will be debited if a cancellation is made less

than 24 hours in advance. Most hotels will confirm your reservation, and this confirmation can be used when applying for a visa *(see p202)*.

The **St Petersburg International Youth Hostel** can now take bookings by e-mail, which is increasingly being used by other hotels. For a choice of accommodation, the most reliable booking organization in St Petersburg is **Ost-West Kontaktservice** which also offers guide and transport bookings *(see p200)*.

FACILITIES

ALL THE HOTELS listed include at least a shower and a television and usually an individual telephone. Most hotels have a luggage room for storing baggage after the midday check-out time.

Ex-Intourist hotels are all very similar, with a vast lobby, several restaurants and cafés, bars, discos and usually a

sauna. These were built at the height of the Soviet tourist boom with the aim of keeping foreign tourists in restricted areas, generally situated away from the centre. As foreigners were bussed to and from the sights and were rarely allowed to wander on their own, the hotels tend to be far removed from public transport facilities. While greater freedom is now the norm, limited public transport from these hotels is often a problem for those wanting some independence.

PRICE

LACK OF sufficient competition is the main reason for prices still being relatively high for hotel accommodation in St Petersburg. Middle range hotels ($70–90 per person) are all located outside the centre with encumbent public

Fitness Centre, one of many facilities at the Grand Hotel Europe

transport problems. To stay in the city centre with all facilities your only choice is to opt for top range hotels, such as the Grand Hotel Europe, which can offer anything from an exclusive single room to imperial suites worth several thousand dollars a day.

Prices are rarely on display, and, in most hotels, rates increase during the high season, late May until late September.

Entrance to the luxurious, modern Nevskij Palace Hotel

HIDDEN EXTRAS

MOST HOTELS include local taxes in their prices, with the notable exception of the exclusive Grand Hotel Europe. Breakfast is generally included in the room rate. If it is not, it can be a significant addition to your final bill in the larger hotels. The biggest shock, however, is likely to be the cost of international or even local phone calls from your hotel room. The larger hotels have their own satellite lines which make all calls easy but very expensive. Bear in mind that calls which use the local network are relatively cheap and phonecards can be purchased to make international calls from street booths *(see p208)*. Even BCL satellite lines in hotel and restaurant lobbies are cheaper than calling through the hotel operator.

The Pribaltiyskaya adds a hefty booking charge for an individual booking, which can radically affect the cost of a short stay. Some hotels charge a small extra sum for registering your passport which is in any case obligatory *(see p202)*.

SECURITY

SECURITY IN HOTELS has become stricter in recent years, with the top range establishments using metal-detectors and selective bag searches at entrances. Smaller hotels have a doorman, who may ask to see a visitor's card or identification. Since this is simply a precaution for your protection, there is no reason to object.

Many hotels have safes in the rooms, and security deposit boxes at the front desk. Large sums of money and valuables should always be left in one of these places.

DISABLED TRAVELLERS

DUE TO THE thick snow in winter, most buildings in St Petersburg have steps up to their entrances, making access extremely difficult for disabled visitors. The Grand Hotel Europe and Nevskij Palace, St Petersburg's two most elite hotels, are the only places which are fully wheelchair accessible and where the staff have been trained to be

Room in the Grand Hotel Europe

of assistance. However, more and more hotels are adding ramps, widening doors and trying to adapt to meet the needs of disabled travellers.

CHILDREN

ST PETERSBURG has never been vaunted as a great children's destination and very few of the hotels cater specifically for them. It is possible to arrange babysitters in the Grand Hotel Europe or the Nevskij Palace, if required, but it is best avoided in other hotels.

The elegant Winter Garden restaurant in the Astoria Hotel

BUDGET HOTELS

ACCOMMODATION in St Petersburg is not cheap by any means and anyone on a low budget should be prepared for prices corresponding to around $30 or more per person per night for one of the cheaper hotels. The lower-price hotels such as Oktyabrskaya and Rus offer some of the best locations, but also tend to be rather run down. Mir, further from the centre, offers more pleasant surroundings, while Matisov Domik, which is undoubtedly the best of the few hotels in the lower price bracket, combines personal service and attractive location.

Efficient and helpful travel bureau service at the St Petersburg International Youth Hostel

often booked up well in advance, provides a travel bureau, English-language videos every evening and excellent advice on St Petersburg. They also issue invitations for visa applications (see p202).

The slightly larger and less polished **Holiday Hostel**, just behind Finland Station (see p126), tends to be a popular choice with Russian visitors,

making it ideal for those wishing to get into the swing of local life. The most centrally located hostel, right behind the Kazan Cathedral (see p111), is **Hertzen University Hostel** which is run by the university. While you cannot book with them direct, visa support and bookings are available through **Ost-West Kontaktservice**.

An excellent alternative for those seeking a novel experience is to stay at the quaint **Petrodvorets Sanatorium**, housed in the former stables of Peterhof's magnificent palace (see pp146–9). At very low prices for a double room, and with the hydrofoil (see p221) running from the palace

Lobby of the small, family-run Matisov Domik

HOSTELS

FOR THE BUDGET traveller seeking comfortable accommodation in a reasonably central location, the functional **St Petersburg International Youth Hostel** is the cream of the crop. The hostel, which is

Petrodvorets Sanatorium, occupying the stables at Peterhof

Impressive façade of the Oktyabrskaya Hotel, dating from 1847

to the city centre during the summer, this offers a marvellous opportunity to stay in a leafy country setting within easy access of St Petersburg. The food is poor at the sanatorium, but Peterhof has a number of pleasant cafés.

STAYING WITH FAMILIES

FOR A REALLY good insight into Russian life, staying with a family can be an interesting and cheap option. The system works very much like any bed and breakfast in Europe with prices including breakfast but no other meals, although extra meals can usually be provided at a cost.

Ost-West Kontaktservice has a wide range of families while **St Petersburg Bed and Breakfast** offers a more limited selection. All families are checked out personally by the organizations who will then do their best to suit the accommodation to your needs.

Canongate Books Limited publishes *Russia* in their *People to People* series, with introductions to over 1,000 Russians willing to offer hospitality and assistance to visitors. You will, of course, be expected to cover your own expenses.

Dacha in pine forest near Repino and the Gulf of Finland *(see p144)*

CAMPING

ST PETERSBURG'S weather does not make it ideal for camping. Visitors are restricted to **Olgino Motel-Camping** which is situated in woods on the Gulf of Finland, to the northwest of St Petersburg. The camp site is about 35 minutes' drive from the city and has poor public transport facilities.

RENTING A DACHA

FOR THOSE spending some time in and around St Petersburg, renting a *dacha* or country house can be an attractive and much more tranquil alternative to staying in the city. One of the most pleasant times of the year to do this is after the snows have thawed and spring has fully set in. For further information contact **Ost-West Kontaktservice** or **RIK**.

USING THE LISTINGS

The hotels on pages 172–3 are listed according to area and price category. The symbols summarize the facilities at each hotel.

⚏ all rooms have bath and/or shower unless otherwise indicated
1 single-rate rooms available
⚏ rooms for more than two people available, or an extra bed can be put in a double room
24 24-hour room service
TV television in all rooms
Y mini-bar in all rooms
▤ air conditioning in all rooms
⛨ gym/fitness facilities
⛱ swimming pool
⛉ business facilities: message-taking service, fax service, meeting room
⚇ babysitting service
♿ wheelchair access
⬆ lift
P car parking available
Y bar
⫸ restaurant
⬚ credit and charge cards accepted:
AE American Express
DC Diners Club
MC Mastercard
V VISA
JCB Japanese Credit Bureau

Price categories are based on a standard double room in high season, including breakfast, tax and service.
$ under US$100
$$ US$100–150
$$$ US$150–200
$$$$ US$200–300
$$$$$ over US$300

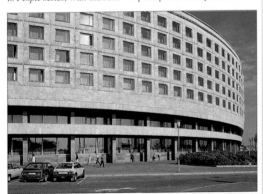
Imposing sweep of the 1970s Moskva Hotel façade

Popular Hotels in St Petersburg

ACCOMMODATION IN ST PETERSBURG has improved in
recent years, but there is still really only a
handful of hotels from which to choose.
Unfortunately few of these are conveniently situated for the city centre and it
is important to decide on your priorities,
be it location, price, character, service
or amenities. This selection represents
the city's most popular hotels.

Hotelship Peterhof
Staying on board a ship is an
appropriately novel way to spend
your nights in a city characterized
by its waterways and islands.

Pribaltiyskaya
The dark, sedate interiors of
this popular package-tour
hotel contrast with the
stunning views over the
Gulf of Finland.

Matisov Domik
The intimate, friendly ambi-
ence of this small hotel makes it
one of St Petersburg's most wel-
coming and pleasant retreats.

Sovietskaya
This 1970s hotel offers wonderful views of the city
centre from its rotunda bar. At sunset or during
White Nights the vista is particularly magical.

Astoria Hotel
One of the city's most luxurious
and centrally located hotels, the
Astoria is perfect for exploring
St Petersburg on foot. The
attractive building overlooks
St Isaac's Square and Cathedral.

St Petersburg
The package-holiday tourists usually housed in the St Petersburg get one of the city's most beautiful views over the Neva and Palace Embankment from the Bel-Etage café.

Grand Hotel Europe
Situated in the heart of the city, this historic hotel is the finest place to stay in St Petersburg. Elegant decor and refined service are complemented by many facilities.

Nevskij Palace
This spotless, well-run and efficient hotel is characterized by sparse, bright, modern interiors. It is well-located on Nevskiy prospekt and has excellent restaurants and business facilities.

Moskva
Of all St Petersburg's large tourist hotels, the Moskva enjoys the best location, with good transport amenities, and bars and cafés both in the hotel and nearby.

Pulkovskaya
Comfortable and clean, this vast modern hotel has many business facilities, including an auditorium. The hotel's main advantage is its proximity to the airport.

| 0 kilometres | 2 |
| 0 miles | 2 |

St Petersburg

Matisov Domik
Матисов домик

Nab reki Pryazhki 3/1, 190121. **Map** 5 A3. **C** 219 5445. **FAX** 219 7419. **Rooms:** 23. 🛏 1️⃣ 🟩 24 📺 📶 🟧 🟥 🟦 **P** 📶 ★ 🟩 *MC, V.* $

The foreign diplomatic and business community soon discovered the rare charm of this small family establishment when it opened in 1993, on a small island by the Pryazhka river. With just 23 rooms in a compact modern building overlooking a tree-lined waterway, this is a real getaway location offering very friendly service. For business purposes it has a conference hall and basic fax and photocopier facilities. Transport to the centre is by tram only, and it can be difficult to catch a taxi, but from the hotel it is only 15 minutes' walk through attractive streets to the Mariinskiy Theatre *(see p119)*.

Mir
Мир

Ul Gastello 17, 196135. **C** 108 5166. **FAX** 108 5165. **Rooms:** 120. 1️⃣ 🟩 24 🟥 🟦 **P** 📶 🟦 $

Situated opposite the marvellous 18th-century Chesma Church *(see p130)*, this 1970s building is gradually being done up to meet foreign standards. The hotel is becoming more popular and, in the high season, it can be difficult to get a room here. With Moskovskaya metro station and some wonderful examples of Stalinist architecture reasonably close by, Mir enjoys a modest but well-deserved reputation among budget travellers and businesspeople.

Moskva
Москва

Pl Aleksandra Nevskovo 2, 193317. **Map** 8 E3. **C** 274 0022. **FAX** 274 2130. **Rooms:** 770. 🛏 1️⃣ 🟩 24 📺 🟥 🟦 **P** 📶 🟦 🟩 *AE, DC, MC, V.* $

Of all the old Intourist hotels, this is the best situated, right opposite the Alexander Nevsky Monastery *(see pp130–31)*, with the metro station nearby as well as many buses, trams and trolleybuses.

The Moskva once had a bad reputation for attracting second-rate criminals, but now it is just a plain package-tour hotel. The enormous, curving 1970s block is dark inside, and on a scale intended to cater for large groups. It has more personal touches than other Intourist hotels, such as the traditional Soviet-style

key lady sitting by the lifts on each floor, available to help with anything from ironing and emergency clothing repairs to making tea.

Okhtinskaya
Охтинская

Bolsheokhtinskiy pr 4, 195027. **C** 227 4438. **FAX** 227 2618. **Rooms:** 300. 🛏 1️⃣ 🟩 24 📺 🟥 🟦 **P** 📶 🟦 🟩 *AE, DC, MC, V, JCB.* $

With views of the Smolnyy Convent just across the Neva, this 1970s hotel offers clean, bright rooms at reasonable prices. The surrounding area is mainly high-rise, but is pleasant enough. It is a short walk from various bus, tram and trolleybus routes, which take just under half an hour to reach the centre. The Nevsky Melody *(see p196)* entertainment complex just round the corner attracts a noisy crowd in the evenings, but the hotel itself is generally quiet.

Oktyabrskaya
Октябрьская

Ligovskiy pr 10, 193172. **Map** 7 C2. **C** 277 6330. **FAX** 315 7501. **Rooms:** 672. 🛏 1️⃣ 🟩 📺 🟥 🟦 🟩 *MC, V.* $

This hotel's fascinating history can be appreciated despite the fact that it is now very run down. Built in 1847, it became a hospital for the starving during World War II, and in 1944 housed the Estonian government forced into exile by the Nazis.

Although room security is poor, the hotel is very conveniently located and is favoured by regular visitors to the city, who feel that they are staying in a truly Russian hotel. Its dark, brooding corridors, traditional Russian cakes in the café and remnants of former glory, such as the bronze statues at the foot of the stairs, add to its character. At peak periods, guests may also be housed in the extension, located opposite Moscow Station, but this should be avoided.

Rus
Русь

Artilleriyskaya ul 1, 191104. **Map** 3 B5. **C** 273 4683. **FAX** 279 3600. **Rooms:** 163. 🛏 1️⃣ 🟩 24 📺 🟥 🟦 🟩 *AE, MC, V, JCB.* $

Conveniently located just 15 minutes' walk from Nevskiy prospekt, this modern hotel now lets out many of its rooms as office space. It is the cheapest hotel in the centre, but the service and small rooms leave something to be desired. The lack of restaurant is no hardship, with a variety of good cafés and restaurants only a

short walk away. For those with few demands it offers a superb deal. The sauna is to be recommended, but is so popular that it can be difficult to book.

Hotel Deson-Ladoga
Отель Десон-Ладога

Ul Shaumiana 26, 195213. **C** 528 5628. **FAX** 528 5448. **Rooms:** 96. 🛏 1️⃣ 🟩 24 📺 🟥 🟦 **P** 📶 🟦 🟩 *DC, MC, V.* $$

This Russo-Hong Kong joint venture hotel is set in an area of 1960s apartment blocks, accessible by direct metro and trolleybus routes from Nevskiy prospekt. Clean and efficient, if somewhat impersonal, it is ideal for those looking for a high standard of service at a moderate price. All staff speak excellent English, while the rooms are bright and spacious and the bathrooms immaculate. The room price includes breakfast and a morning sauna. The restaurant offers both European and Chinese cuisine.

Neptune
Нептун

Nab Obvodnovo kanala 93-a, 191126. **Map** 6 F5. **C** 315 4965. **FAX** 113 3160. **Rooms:** 70. 🛏 1️⃣ 🟩 24 📺 🟥 🟦 🟦 🟩 *AE, DC, MC, V.* $$

Neptune is one of the few small hotels in town, offering Austrian efficiency and immaculate cleanliness as well as freedom from large package-tour groups. This makes it very popular with business travellers. Just five minutes' walk from Ligovskiy prospekt and plenty of public transport, or ten minutes from Pushkinskaya metro, this modern building is located in a more industrial part of the centre, on the Obvodnyy Canal.

Pulkovskaya
Пулковская

Pl Pobedy 1, 196240. **C** 123 5122. **FAX** 123 5856. **Rooms:** 840. 🛏 1️⃣ 🟩 📺 🟥 🟧 🟥 🟦 🟦 **P** 📶 🟦 🟩 *AE, DC, MC, V.* $$

The road from the airport emerges into the city at Victory Square, with its vast monument to the Siege of Leningrad *(see p27)*, and the Pulkovskaya hotel to your left.

Built by Finnish architects in 1978, this is another large, anonymous tourist hotel, much used by package tours. It does have a distinguished ambience, however, which sets it slightly apart from other Intourist hotels. Its restaurants have been revamped (with the addition of Oriental cuisine), and the small cafés are pleasant, but the food is not generally very exciting.

Sovietskaya
Советская

Lermontovskiy pr 43/1, 198103.
Map 5 B5. 🕿 329 0186. 📠 251
8890. *Rooms: 1000.* 🛏 ① ♨ 24
📺 📻 🎿 🅿 🍴 🍽 🖛 *AE,*
MC, V. $$

Visitors staying here should be sure
to book into the Riga Building
(12th and 14th floors reserved for
foreigners) or Fontanka Building,
which have superb views of the
Fontanka river and the city centre.

The circular café in the tower
offers coffee, wine and spirits and
a vast expanse of glass through
which to watch St Petersburg's
famous skyline. During White
Nights *(see p51)*, the passage from
piercing blue to red, orange and
violet can be awe-inspiring. The
rooms are modern and sparse, but
the service is pleasant, and several
trams run from nearby to the
centre or to the metro.

Hotelship Peterhof
Отель Петергоф

Nab Makarova, near the Tuchkov
Bridge, 199053. **Map** 1 A4. 🕿 325
8888. 📠 325 8889. *Rooms: 105.*
🛏 ① 📻 📺 🎿 🅿 🍴 🍽 ★
🖛 *AE, DC, MC, V.* $$

Since St Petersburg is a city of
islands and waterways, staying on
a ship seems very apt. This highly
modern boat offers a standard of
service which compensates for its
inconvenient location – on the
north side of Vasilevskiy Island.
Transport is somewhat scarce here,
but the hotel runs a fair-priced car
service to and from the centre.

There are small cabins on the
Main and Upper decks, and more
luxurious quarters on the Boat
Deck, from where the best views
are to be had. The Main Deck,
where the reception and shops are
located, can get busy, so try and get
a room higher up. The excellent
Svir Restaurant *(see p182)* and
Panorama Bar allow you to look
out along the Neva as you begin
the evening with a cocktail.

Pribaltiyskaya
Прибалтийская

Korablestroiteley ul 14, 199226.
🕿 356 0263. 📠 356 0094.
Rooms: 1200. 🛏 ① 24 📺 📻 ▤
📻 🎿 🅿 🍴 🍽
🖛 *AE, DC, MC, V, JCB.* $$

Situated on the western edge of
Vasilevskiy Island, the Pribaltiyskaya
offers stunning views over the Gulf
of Finland. In summer, families
enjoy the beach while the sun dips
onto the horizon but never sets,
and in winter the bleakness of the
iced-over Gulf is breathtaking.

The hotel itself, a vast, 1980s rabbit
warren with five restaurants, and a
small café on every floor, is charac-
terized by dark wood furniture and
dim lighting. There is no shortage
of rooms, all spacious and clean.
Pribaltiyskaya metro is a bus ride
or 20-minute walk away.

St Petersburg
Санкт-Петербург

Pirogovskaya nab 5/2, 194175.
Map 3 A2. 🕿 542 8149. 📠 248
8002. *Rooms: 410.* 🛏 ① ♨ 24
📺 📻 🎿 🅿 🍴 🍽 🖛 *AE,*
DC, MC, V. $$$

This hotel changed its name in
1991, when the city of Leningrad
became St Petersburg once more.
Still very much a 1960s hotel, it is
the first and smallest of the large
Intourist structures. The atmosphere
is provincial, from the foyer with its
potted plants to the little tea rooms
on each floor. The rooms are typical
tourist hotel fare, but those at the
front have magnificent views of the
broadest part of the Neva. However,
they also face southwest, which
means that during White Nights
(see p51) the sun shines into the
rooms for most of the night. The
Bel-Etage, where you can take tea
or beer, affords the same views.

Astoria Hotel
Гостинца Астория

Bolshaya Morskaya ul 39, 190000.
Map 6 D2. 🕿 210 5757. 📠 210
5133. *Rooms: 436.* 🛏 ① ♨ 24
📺 📻 🎿 📻 🍴 🅿 🍴 🍽 ▤
🍴 🍽 ★ 🖛 *AE, DC, MC, V, JCB.*
$$$

It's hard to beat the Astoria's front
room views, which look out over
St Isaac's Cathedral. This is the per-
fect place to stay if you want to see
St Petersburg on foot. One of the
city's top hotels, the building dates
from 1911–12 *(see p79)*, although it
has undergone renovation. The two
parts of the hotel, the Astoria and
the former Angleterre, have separate
entrances but are connected on
upper floors. The Astoria has the
most attractive interiors, and the
lobby is an elegant place to take
afternoon tea, accompanied by harp
or piano music. The Angleterre is
more modern, with a nightclub and
casino *(see p197)*. There are two
restaurants, the most famous being
the Winter Garden *(see p180)*.

Grand Hotel Europe
Гранд Отель Европа

Mikhaylovskaya ul 1/7, 191011.
Map 6 F1. 🕿 329 6000. 📠 329
6001. *Rooms: 301.* 🛏 ① ♨ 24 📺
📻 ▤ 🎿 📻 🍴 🅿 🍴 🍽
★ 🖛 *AE, DC, MC, V.* $$$$$

The most luxurious and expensive
hotel in the city, the Grand Hotel
Europe is a superbly restored Style-
Moderne monument *(see p101)*.
The historic interiors offer a range
of suites, including the Imperial
Suite costing around $2,500 a night.

The Grand Hotel Europe set the
standard for all St Petersburg hotels
to strive for when it reopened after
renovation in 1991. The impeccable
service combines old-fashioned
discretion with up-to-date quality,
while its restaurants, including the
famous Europe *(see p181)*, are
among the best. The internal yard
is now a light and airy atrium where
coffee and cakes are served all day.
Located just off Arts Square, it is
the most central of the city's hotels.

Nevskij Palace Hotel
Невский палас отель

Nevskiy pr 57, 191025. **Map** 7 B2.
🕿 275 2001. 📠 301 7323.
Rooms: 285. 🛏 ① ♨ 24 📺 📻 ▤
📻 🎿 📻 🍴 🅿 🍴 🍽 ★
🖛 *AE, DC, MC, V, JCB.* $$$$$

This top-class modern hotel prides
itself on being the base for celeb-
rities and film crews. It may seem a
little characterless, but it copes well
with both groups and individuals.
It has fine restaurants and a great
patisserie, the Vienna Café, patron-
ized by expatriates and locals alike.

The hotel's convenient location
and good conference and business
facilities make it popular with busi-
nesspeople. Two of the floors are
set aside for non-smokers, and the
ground floor has a range of art
galleries, banks and airline offices,
plus a good newspaper stand.

BEYOND
ST PETERSBURG

Beresta Palace Hotel
Береста палас отель

Studencheskaya ul 4A, 173014,
Novgorod. 🕿 (81622) 333 15.
📠 317 07. *Rooms: 226.* 🛏 24 📺
📻 🎿 📻 🍴 🅿 🍴 🍽 ★ 🖛 *AE,*
DC, MC, V. $$$

This is the only truly Western standard hotel in Novgorod, run by the
company that manages the Nevskij
Palace Hotel. Attractions include
great river views from some rooms,
good food and efficient service.
Novgorod's water has a yellowish
tinge, so the hotel's filter makes
bathing, not to mention drinking it,
all the more pleasant. Since the city
is much visited by businesspeople
during the week, the hotel offers
cheap weekend deals, often with
transport from St Petersburg. Book
these by fax or through the Nevskij
Palace Hotel in St Petersburg.

For key to symbols *see p169*

RESTAURANTS AND CAFÉS

THE RESTAURANT SCENE is changing rapidly in St Petersburg, as specialist eateries, cafés and bars spring up all over town. Eating out may still not be as exciting as in many European cities, but the options are increasing.

The big hotel restaurants lead the way in the top range and, in recent years, the concept of the "business lunch", with an inexpensive fixed price menu, has made its appearance. Since the hotel restaurants are also catering for the local community, they liven things up with regular special events, such as festivals of foreign

Sign for Tbilisi

cuisine or traditional Russian fare. These are advertised in the English-language press *(see p209)*. Ethnic food, from the former Soviet republics as well as from abroad, is a growing trend which provides more variety and a wider selection of vegetarian dishes. Small cafés offer reasonable food and are the most convenient place to eat away from Nevskiy prospekt *(see p108)*. Getting a plain green salad is usually the biggest problem for visitors, but there are a few American and French cafés and bars specially designed to satisfy such cravings for simple fresh food.

Interior of the family-run Staraya Derevnya restaurant

WHERE TO EAT

RESTAURANTS and cafés are scattered all over town, but it is possible to find good food without straying far from Nevskiy prospekt *(see pp46–9)*. Since restaurants in this area cater mainly for foreigners, they tend to be more expensive and accept credit cards. Cheaper eateries, such as Pirosmani *(see p181)*, Staraya Derevnya *(see p182)* and Staroe Kafe *(see p185)*, which have an enjoyable atmosphere and reasonable food, are often in more inconvenient locations. The moderate outlay on food usually allows for the taxi fare.

TYPES OF RESTAURANT

THE TOP RANGE restaurants largely serve European food with a few select Russian dishes. Smaller, more intimate

venues like 1913 Goda *(see p180)* and Staraya Derevnya pride themselves on serving specifically Russian cuisine. This is generally uncomplicated food such as fried meat or fish with a selection of vegetables and pickles. The increasing

Outdoor café in the arcade of Gostinyy dvor *(see p108)*

number of ethnic and regional restaurants provides a touch of variety. The former Soviet republics, Georgia and Armenia, have both left their mark on Russian cuisine with *lobio* (spicy beans), *shashlyk (see p176)* and *tolma* (stuffed vine leaves). A full range of these can be found at the Georgian Pirosmani *(see p181)* and Armenian Krunk *(see p183)*.

Indian, Chinese and, more recently, "traditional American" eateries are also popular.

All restaurants require smart dress, although a suit and tie are rarely obligatory.

READING THE MENU

MOST RESTAURANTS, as well as some cafés, have a summary of their menu in English. The disadvantage of this is that in smaller places the menu may change daily, but only in its Russian version. Thus the English menus are often misleading. Most waiters will make some effort to overcome language difficulties. In restaurants accepting credit cards there is usually at least one English-speaking waiter.

PAYMENT AND TIPPING

MAJOR RESTAURANTS are likely to accept some credit cards, but check beforehand. This guide gives an indication of price range in dollars, but restaurants will not accept foreign currency in payment for a meal, although some may have their own exchange office. Tips are 10–15 per cent unless service is already included. To ensure the waiter receives the tip, it is best to give it in cash, rather than including it on a credit card.

OPENING TIMES

ALTHOUGH lunching out is not such an accepted habit among Russians, most restaurants open at midday and stay open until around 11pm or midnight. In rare cases, when for example there is an adjoining casino or nightclub, they may stay open until 1am.

Cafés close early, around 10pm at the latest, while bars, particularly those with live music *(see p196)*, usually stay open until around 2 or 3am.

Last food orders are rarely taken after 11pm, even in bars, and many places stop serving an hour before closing time, so check last order times.

Street sign for Pirosmani

MAKING A RESERVATION

NEARLY ALL restaurants require reservations to be made. Some establishments, notably Pirosmani, refuse to accept casual guests without a reservation, even if they are not fully booked. Some English will be spoken in all major restaurants, but your hotel concierge will be able to make bookings for you.

Apart from in the hotel restaurants, it is usually only possible to reserve a table a few days in advance. The majority of upmarket restaurants, however, start taking bookings earlier during the

The beautifully decorated interior of the Russian Room in the Ambassador *(see p182)*

White Nights *(see p51)*. The city's most popular eateries can then be fully booked up to two weeks in advance so it is wise to plan ahead.

Cafés do not generally require reservations. Since they rely heavily on special events, they may sometimes be unexpectedly closed to the public.

CHILDREN

ALTHOUGH few restaurants or cafés cater directly for children, establishments will rarely refuse entry to them. The only places likely to turn children away are those more geared towards entertainment.

Russians are slowly acquiring the habit of taking their children out to dine with them. The fast food outlets are obviously a good option and Bistro Sadko's *(see p183)* can also be accommodating.

On the whole Russians love children and staff can often be persuaded to adjust a dish to suit a child's special requests.

VEGETARIANS

SINCE RUSSIAN food is very much meat oriented, vegetarian food is limited. The main hotel restaurants all offer several vegetarian dishes while ethnic food, particularly Georgian and Armenian, Indian and Mexican, may also have a higher proportion of vegetarian cuisine. Those

who eat seafood will find the choice considerably broader, but in general finding vegetarian food in Russia may be a somewhat unrewarding task.

SMOKING

NEARLY ALL restaurants will allow smoking, and smoking during meals is considered acceptable. Few places except the hotel restaurants have separate non-smoking areas. In smaller cafés serving food, smoking is often prohibited and desperate smokers may be forced outside.

DISABLED ACCESS

WAITERS and doormen in most restaurants are helpful to those in wheelchairs but cafés and bars prove more problematic. Not only are there usually stairs either up or down, but the doorways are narrow. The disabled are on the whole limited to the most expensive eateries and bars in the Nevskij Palace Hotel *(see p173)* and Grand Hotel Europe *(see p173)*.

USING THE LISTINGS

Key to symbols in the listings on pages 180–82.

¦@¦ fixed price lunch
V vegetarian dishes
ⱨ suitable for children
ⱡ wheelchair access
⊤ formal dress
▤ air conditioning
▦ outdoor eating
♬ live entertainment
♀ recommended wine list
★ highly recommended
⊘ credit cards accepted:
AE American Express
DC Diners Club
MC Mastercard
V VISA
JCB Japanese Credit Bureau

Price categories for a three-course meal for one, including service and tax (excluding wine):
⑤ US$20–30
⑤⑤ US$30–40
⑤⑤⑤ US$40–50
⑤⑤⑤⑤ US$50–60
⑤⑤⑤⑤⑤ over US$60

What to Eat in St Petersburg

RUSSIA'S VAST RANGE of climates and cultures has produced a diverse culinary repertoire. Traditionally each region has its own cuisine, but dishes such as *shashlyk*, from Georgia, are now popular throughout Russia. Influences from Europe and the Middle East have also added specialities to the Russian table. Despite this diversity, some ingredients, such as sour cream (*smetana*), curd cheese (*tvorog*), cucumbers, beetroot and dill, are still fundamental to the Russian taste.

Sprig of dill

Khachapuri
Originally from Georgia, these cheese-filled breads come in various shapes and sizes. The traditional filling is sulguni, *a cheese made from sheep's milk.*

Sliced apple
Sour cream
Pickled mushrooms
Rye bread
Herring fillets
Pickled cucumber

ZAKUSKI
Comprising a variety of hors d'oeuvres, *zakuski* are served as starters for lunch or dinner. The robust spicy and salty flavours stimulate the appetite. Caviar, *kolbasa* (smoked sausages), pickles and cheese are also typical.

Rassolnik
There are many versions of this classic soup, including recipes using chicken, fish or kidney. Pickled cucumbers are a vital ingredient in all of them.

Solyanka
Made from either meat or fish, this soup has a distinctive rich, spicy taste. The meat version has a strong tomato flavour.

Borshch
Borshch gets its colour from beetroot and tastes sour and sweet. It is served hot in winter and chilled in summer.

Shashlyk
This version of a kebab is made from marinated mutton or lamb. The pieces of meat may be interspersed with vegetables such as onions and peppers.

RUSSIAN CAVIAR

Black caviar (*ikra*) is sturgeon roe. It is produced by three species of sturgeon, all found in the Caspian sea. Beluga caviar is the rarest and has a distinctive nutty taste. Osetra has a creamy flavour, often compared to brie, while sevruga tastes of sea salt. Red caviar (*keta*) is salmon roe. Caviar is often served with buckwheat pancakes (*blini*) and sour cream (*smetana*).

Red caviar
Red caviar jar
Sour cream
Blini
Black caviar
Black caviar jar

Osetrina
The sturgeon is renowned for its roe (caviar), but the fish itself is also eaten in a variety of ways, such as salted or smoked.

Savoury Pirozhki
Pirozhki can be stuffed with a variety of fillings such as meat and rice, fried cabbage, curd cheese or mushrooms.

Kotlety po-Kievskiy
Chicken breasts are filled with garlic butter, coated in breadcrumbs and deep fried. This is called Chicken Kiev in English.

Pelmeny
Originally a Siberian dish, these meat or fish dumplings are typically served in broth or with sour cream, butter or vinegar.

Kulebiaka
Puff or yeast pastry encloses a filling of salmon, rice, hard-boiled eggs and mushrooms. The pie is sliced and served cold.

Golubtsy
Minced meat and rice rolled in cabbage leaves, golubtsy are boiled or baked and are often served with a tomato sauce.

DESSERTS

An important part of any Russian meal, most desserts are uncompromisingly rich. Russian cuisine has a wide variety of cakes, pies, tarts, pastries and ice cream.

Bef Stroganov and Kasha
This dish of sautéed strips of beef in a sour cream, onion and mushroom sauce is often served with boiled buckwheat (grechnevaya kasha).

Vatrushki are sweet cheese-filled tartlets.

Vareniki are boiled sweet dumplings, with various fruit fillings.

Khvorost are deep-fried biscuits, with honey and sugar.

Sweet Pirozhki
Made with yeast dough, sweet pirozhki can have a variety of fillings, including fruit or jam, and may be served with cream.

Sharlotka
Devised for Tsar Alexander I by French chef Antoine Carême, this sponge cake is filled with custard and fruit purée.

Morozhenoe
Ice cream is traditionally a favourite dessert in Russia. It is often served with fresh fruit.

What to Drink in St Petersburg

Shot of Starka

Rᴜssɪᴀɴ ᴠᴏᴅᴋᴀ is famous throughout the world and the Liviz distillery in St Petersburg is Russia's second largest distillery, the largest being in Moscow. Vodka is thought to have been invented by Muscovite monks in the 14th or 15th century. Peter the Great *(see p18)* was particularly fond of anise- or pepper-flavoured vodkas and devised modifications to the distillation process which greatly improved the quality of the finished drink.

Tea is Russia's other national drink. Traditionally made using a samovar and served black, tea has been popular in Russia since the end of the 18th century, when it was first imported from China.

A 19th-century Russian peasant family drinking vodka and tea

Smirnov   **Sinopskaya**   **Sankt-Peterburg**

Cʟᴇᴀʀ Vᴏᴅᴋᴀ

Vᴏᴅᴋᴀ ɪs ᴘʀᴏᴅᴜᴄᴇᴅ from grain, usually wheat, although some rye is also used in Russia. St Petersburg's Liviz distillery produces some excellent vodkas using the renowned pure waters from Lake Ladoga. From the cheaper Sankt Peterburg to the top quality, smooth-tasting Sinopskaya and Diplomat, Liviz dominates the vodka market in northern Russia. They also make Russia's most famous vodka, Stolichnaya (meaning "from the capital city") under licence, but mainly for export. A recent and excellent arrival on the market is the Russian Smirnov, made just outside Novgorod *(see pp160–63)* and not to be confused with the Western Smirnoff.

Kubanskaya

Vodka is always served with food in Russia, often with a traditional range of richly-flavoured accompaniments called *zakuski (see p176)*.

Fʟᴀᴠᴏᴜʀᴇᴅ Vᴏᴅᴋᴀ

Tʜᴇ ᴘʀᴀᴄᴛɪᴄᴇ ᴏғ flavouring vodka has entirely practical origins. When vodka was first produced commercially in the Middle Ages, the techniques and equipment were so primitive that it was impossible to remove all the impurities. This left unpleasant aromas and flavours, which were disguised by adding honey together with aromatic oils and spices. As distillation techniques improved, flavoured vodkas became a speciality in their own right. Limonnaya, its taste deriving from lemon zest, is one of the most traditional, as is Pertsovka, flavoured with red chilli pepper pods. Okhotnichya (hunter's vodka) has a wider range of flavourings including juniper, ginger and cloves. Starka (old vodka) is a mixture of vodka, brandy, port and an infusion of apple and pear leaves, aged in oak barrels.

Pepper vodka

Limonnaya   **Okhotnichya**   **Starka**

Major Wine Regions

■ Wine growing region	■ Russia
■ Moldova	■ Georgia
■ Ukraine	■ Armenia
	■ Azerbaijan
	— International boundaries

White and red Georgian wine   **Shampanskoe**

Wine

THE SOVIET UNION was one of the world's largest producers of wine (*vino*), but many of the major wine regions are now republics in their own right. Several indigenous types of grape are cultivated in the different regions, along with many of the more familiar international varieties.

Georgia is considered the best wine-making area. Its wines include those made from the Rkatsiteli grape, characterized by a floral aroma and subtle, fruity flavour, and the Gurdzhaani which gives a unique, slightly bitter touch. Among its best red wines is the smooth Mukuzani. Moldova produces white, sparkling wines in the south and central regions, while the south is also known for its red wines. Since 1799, Moldova also produces a sweet, champagne-like wine called Shampanskoe.

Other Alcoholic Drinks

BRANDY (KONYAK) WAS ORIGINALLY a by-product of wine-making and commercial production only began in Russia in the 19th century. Armenian brandy is one of the finest with a distinctive vanilla fragrance, resulting from its ageing in 70–100-year-old oak barrels. Georgia and Daghestan also produce good brandies. St Petersburg beer (*pivo*) is amongst the best in Russia. Baltika, Vena and Stepan Razin make a full range of beers in bottles and on draught. Since few preservatives are used, the true taste is preserved. Various imported beers are also available.

Baltika Beer   **Armenian brandy**

Other Drinks

KVAS IS A MILDLY ALCOHOLIC DRINK made from rye and barley, consumed by adults and children alike. Russia's vast range of mineral waters (*mineralnaya voda*) includes many with unusually high mineral contents. Mineral waters from the Caucasus, Siberia and Georgia are particularly prized. Also widely available are fruit juices (*sok, mors* or *kompot*), including apple, tomato and cranberry (*klyukva*), a traditional Russian favourite.

Mineral water   **Kvas**   **Cranberry juice**

Tea

RUSSIAN TEA IS SERVED BLACK with a slice of lemon and is usually drunk from tall glasses rather than cups. Sweetened with jam instead of sugar, tea (*chay*) is an ideal accompaniment to rich cakes and pastries. The boiling water for tea traditionally comes from a samovar. The water is used to brew a pot of tea, from which a little is poured into the glasses. This is then diluted with more hot water.

A glass of tea, with jam (varenye) to sweeten it

The Samovar

Made from brass or copper, samovars traditionally provided boiling water for a whole variety of domestic purposes and used to be an obligatory wedding gift. Modern ones are made of stainless steel and used mainly for boiling water to make tea. Sometimes eggs are put in the top to cook in the boiling water. The word samovar comes from *samo* meaning "itself" and *varit* meaning "to boil".

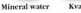

CENTRAL ST PETERSBURG

Demyanova Ukha
Демьянова уха

Kronverkskiy prospekt 53. **Map** 1 C3.
📞 232 8090. ⏲ noon–11pm daily.
🍴⑤ 👥 🎵 ★ ⑤

Demyanova ukha literally means Demyan's fish soup, but in Russian folklore it stands for hospitality and over-eating home-cooked dishes. Everything is done to make this homely restaurant live up to its name. Only fish dishes are served, from the famous *ukha* (clear soup with fish dumplings) to sturgeon, salmon, pike and trout, plus local delicacies such as *vobhya*, which is caught locally in May and smells like fresh cucumbers. The interior is decorated like the inside of an *izba*, or peasant's hut, and booking is advised as this is one of the few good restaurants near the Peter and Paul Fortress *(see pp66–7)*.

Literary Café
Литературное кафе

Nevskiy prospekt 18. **Map** 6 E1.
📞 312 6057. ⏲ noon–11pm daily.
🍴⑤ 👥 🎵 ⑤ DC, MC. ⑤

Located in the former Wolf and Beranger coffee house, from where Pushkin departed for his fatal duel in 1837 *(see p83)*, the Literary Café *(Literaturnoye cafe)* seeks to echo the best of early 19th-century culture. String quartets and poetry readings set in the vaulted rooms have made the restaurant very popular, albeit largely with tourists. Its mainly Russian menu offers reasonably good food, but dining here is really more of an historical than a gourmet experience.

Nikolay
Николай

Bolshaya Morskaya ul 52. **Map** 5 C2.
📞 311 1402. ⏲ noon–midnight (bar: 7pm–last customer) daily. 🅥 👥 🎵 ⑤ MC, V. ⑤

Housed in the elegant mid-19th-century Polovtsov Mansion on leafy Bolshaya Morskaya ulitsa *(see p122)*, this restaurant, which also comprises the "Matador" bar, was, in Soviet days, the formal dining room of the Union of Architects. The walls have retained the original walnut panelling, embossed leather and painted scenes of chivalry, making this one of the most truly historic restaurant interiors. Booking is advised, although the quality of food and service do not match the impressive ambience. The menu consists of standard Russian dishes and the clientele is mostly foreign.

Tandoor
Тандор

Voznesenskiy prospekt 2. **Map** 6 D1.
📞 312 3886. ⏲ noon–11pm daily .
🍴⑤ 🅥 👥 🎵 ★ ⑤ AE, DC, MC, V, JCB. ⑤

The best Indian restaurant in town, Tandoor is a popular choice with Indian businessmen. The menu offers no Russian or European food at all. Most dishes are moderately spiced, but the more adventurous may like to try the hotter varieties. There are home-made breads, three kinds of lassi and a variety of vegetarian dishes. With its cool, pleasant interior, oil paintings of the Raj and a carved wooden elephant, plus its central location opposite the Admiralty *(see p78)*, Tandoor gets very overbooked throughout the year, so reservations are advised.

1913 God
1913 год

Voznesenskiy prospekt 13. **Map** 5 C3.
📞 315 5148. ⏲ noon–1am daily.
🍴⑤ 🅥 👥 🎵 ★ ⑤ DC, MC, V. ⑤⑤

Conveniently placed for visits to the Mariinskiy Theatre *(see p119)*, this small restaurant provides the best of Russian food and service at a modest price. The name recalls Russia's so-called "best year", when the country celebrated three centuries of Romanov rule. Portions are generous and the restaurant takes pride in rural Russian dishes such as *draniki*, or potato pancakes, with bacon and sour cream, as well as in more international dishes such as lobster fricassee. The restaurant is popular with the city's artists and critics. Booking is advised.

Bistro le Français
Бистро ле Франсес

Galernaya ulitsa 20. **Map** 5 B2.
📞 315 2465. ⏲ 11am–3am (bar: 9pm–3am) daily. 🍴⑤ 🅥 👥 🎵 ⑤ AE, DC, MC, V. ⑤⑤

The local French community flocks to this delightful, bustling bistro situated just behind the Senate and Synod by St Isaac's Square *(see p79)*. With its checked tablecloths, home-made bread and regularly changing menu, this is one of St Petersburg's few "national" restaurants to successfully recreate the atmosphere of a traditional French bistro. It has no token Russian dishes. Instead it serves specialities such as *foie gras, pavé de boeuf* in a red wine sauce and the chef's own mouth-watering crème brûlée. English and French are spoken and it is advisable to book ahead.

Milano
Милано

Karavannaya ulitsa 8. **Map** 7 A1.
📞 314 7348. ⏲ noon–midnight daily. 🍴⑤ 👥 🎵 ⑤ AE, DC, MC, V, JCB. ⑤⑤

Clean-cut lines and simplicity give the Milano a very north-Italian feel. In summer, it is a delight to leave the heat and bustle of Nevskiy prospekt for this cool trattoria, while in winter the restaurant is warm and inviting. Mediterranean seafood is the house speciality, the unusual scampi with cognac being the most expensive dish on the menu. Little is available for the true vegetarian. Three-course business lunches are served before 5pm, children are not allowed in after 6pm and there is live music on Fridays and Saturdays.

Staraya Tamozhnya
Старая таможня

Tamozhennyy pereulok 1. **Map** 1 C5.
📞 327 8980. ⏲ 9pm–3am daily.
🍴⑤ 🅥 👥 🎵 ⑤ MC, V. ⑤⑤

Specializing in Russian food and hospitality, Staraya Tamozhnya (The Old Customs House) is almost the only restaurant on the Strelka *(see pp58–9)* of Vasilevskiy Island. It is a perfect place for snacks or lunch, and offers an appetizing dinner menu including steaks in a variety of marinades and sauces, and tender rabbit cooked in sour cream. The extensive wine list caters for all price ranges. Live jazz and Russian folk music in the evenings inspire dancing on the small dance floor.

Vienna
Вена

Malaya Morskaya ul 13/8. **Map** 6 D1.
📞 311 3227. ⏲ noon–midnight daily. 👥 🅣 🎵 ⑤ AE, MC. ⑤⑤

Very popular with wealthy locals, Vienna is situated close to the Hermitage *(see pp84–93)*. White and pink decor, with trellis-work and mirrors, makes the interior very light and airy. The menu is written in English, as the restaurant is often used by tourist groups. The otherwise European selection of dishes also includes a wide range of different blini and caviar. Reservations and formal dress are recommended.

Winter Garden
Зимний сад

Hotel Astoria, Bolshaya Morskaya ul 39. **Map** 6 D2. 📞 210 5815. ⏲ noon–11:30pm daily. 🍴⑤ 🅥 👥 🎵 🎵 ⑤ AE, MC, V. ⑤⑤

With its string quartet, conservatory feel and echoes of 1950s seaside resorts, the Winter Garden (*Zimniy sad*) of the Astoria Hotel (*see p173*), retains its old world charm.

During World War II, Hitler planned to hold his victory party here once he had taken Leningrad (*see p27*), but he never succeeded in entering the city. The Winter Garden may have relied too heavily on that kind of fame in the past, but the food is improving. The blini, caviar and sturgeon *shashlyk* (kebab) are excellent. Booking is recommended for evening meals.

Adamant
Адамант

Nab reki Moyki 72. **Map** 5 C2.
311 5575. noon–midnight daily. V AE, DC, MC, V. $$$

Situated just off St Isaac's Square (*see p79*) on the Moyka canal, the elegant Adamant is a top-quality restaurant and booking is advised. Like many of the city's restaurants catering largely for rich Russians, there is a great emphasis on seafood, but one of Adamant's real delights is the rarely found mature *shchi* (traditional cabbage soup) which is left to bake for a whole day. The menu's poor translation, however, may prevent you from choosing the best dishes.

Bella Leone
Белла Леоне

Vladimirskiy prospekt 9. **Map** 7 A2.
113 1670. noon–midnight daily. V AE, MC, V. $$$

In keeping with the fashions of its wealthy clientele, Bella Leone has noticeably altered its character in recent years. Once specializing in Italian dishes, the restaurant has since introduced seafood delicacies and Russian dishes to its menu.

With an autographed wall bearing signatures of famous visitors, such as Liza Minelli and Michael Caine, the restaurant puts an emphasis on fashion and fame, as well as cuisine. Lobster fricassee or crab-stuffed chicken are highly recommended, and the service and atmosphere add to the pleasure of eating here. Booking is advised after 7pm. The bill includes a service charge.

Chopsticks
Чопстикс

Grand Hotel Europe, Mikhaylovskaya ulitsa 1/7. **Map** 6 F1. 329 6000.
noon–11pm daily. V ★ AE, DC, MC, V, JCB. $$$

In some respects, this is an ordinary Chinese restaurant, with an average range of Chinese dishes in a rather typical interior. In the context of St Petersburg, however, Chopsticks offers a welcome alternative to the standard Russo-European fare.

You are advised to book, especially for dining in the evening, to savour this oasis of calm in the heart of St Petersburg. With its superb service and serene ambience, it offers a reasonably priced, hassle-free evening out.

Rossi's
Росси

Grand Hotel Europe, Mikhaylovskaya ulitsa 1/7. **Map** 6 F1. 329 6000.
noon–11pm daily. V ★ AE, DC, MC, V. $$$$

Excellent freshly prepared antipasti and home-made pasta are served at this elegant, modern Italian restaurant, which maintains a great reputation. If you are willing to pay the price, and don't want the pomp and display of the Europe, Rossi's is unbeatable. Small stylish touches, such as the balance and contrast of colour when serving a yellow buttery sauce and black tagliatelle, set this place apart.

Senat-Bar
Сенат Бар

Galernaya ulitsa 1. **Map** 5 C1.
314 9253. 11am–5am daily. V AE, DC, MC, V, JCB. $$$

The vast selection of wines and beers on offer at this Dutch-owned bar and restaurant give it an edge over other establishments in town. Well used to serving foreigners of all nationalities, the staff speak good English and offer sound advice on the menu. Vegetarian dishes are few, but can be specially prepared. Otherwise, pork chops with plums, banana and bacon, or carpaccio made from tender veal in a basil dressing with Parmesan cheese and spices are a carnivore's delight. Desserts are varied and delicious. The Senat-Bar gets very full during the summer months and late diners are advised to book, since it gets busier after 9pm.

Dvoryanskoe Gnezdo
Дворянское гнездо

Ulitsa Dekabristov 21. **Map** 5 C3.
312 3205. noon–1am daily. ★ AE, DC, MC, V, JCB. $$$$$

The city's most distinguished restaurant, Dvoryanskoe Gnezdo (The Noble Nest) is small, intimate and wholly luxurious, with unintrusive service. Housed in the former summer house of the Yusupov Palace (*see p120*), just round the corner from the Mariinskiy Theatre (*see p119*), it is one of the few places to do pre- and post-theatre suppers.

Pre-dinner drinks are served in the small bar upstairs, before you are brought down to the candle-lit dining room, where the menu is a gourmet's delight. Dishes such as lamb fillets with poppy seed and sage crust or poached monkfish on a bed of green olives are made with care and attention and invariably fresh ingredients. Seriously smart (if not officially formal) dress and booking are recommended.

Europe
Европа

Grand Hotel Europe, Mikhaylovskaya ulitsa 1/7. **Map** 6 F1. 329 6000.
7–10.30am (breakfast), 7–11pm daily; noon–3pm Sun (brunch). ★ AE, DC, MC, V. $$$$$

The exclusive and lavish Europe, with its magnificent Style-Moderne interior, has been one of the city's top restaurants since it opened at the beginning of the 20th century. With excellent restoration, superb food, silver service and inventive menu, this elegant restaurant is hard to fault. The cost, however, is high, with wine list prices ranging from $50 to $1,500. Sunday brunch is an alternative way of enjoying the Europe for those not wishing to be quite so extravagant. Reservations are recommended at any time.

FURTHER AFIELD

Pirosmani
Пиросмани

Bolshoy prospekt 14, Petrogradskaya. **Map** 1 B3. 235 6456. noon–11pm daily. V ★ $

Booking is absolutely imperative at this restaurant, where wholesome Georgian food is served in a marvellously kitsch recreation of a Georgian hill village, complete with a stream, and with two of the tables on "rafts". The restaurant takes its name from Georgia's most famous painter, a self-taught artist who influenced the Russian avant-garde. Try not to sit too close to the singer, as it can become difficult to talk.

Vegetarians and carnivores alike will enjoy aubergines stuffed with walnuts or *lobio* (spicy beans), while fried *suluguni* (salty cheese) is a rich delicacy. There are hearty meat soups and main courses such as *shashlyk* of pork, chicken or fish served in spicy and garlic sauces.

For key to symbols *see p175*

Staraya Derevnya
Старая деревня

Savushkina ul 72. 【 431 0000.
◯ 1–10pm daily. V ⚹ 🎫 🎵 ♀
★ ⑤

In this family-run restaurant the owners seek to create an early 20th-century feel with Viennese chairs, intimate tables with fresh flowers, antique sideboards and exhibitions of work by local artists. The menu is mainly traditional Russian, with some European dishes. In the evenings there is live music, such as traditional gypsy music and Russian ballads. Prince Charles ate here during a visit to the city, and the restaurant continues to enjoy a good reputation with the foreign community and visitors. Located in a leafy suburb of St Petersburg, out towards the Gulf of Finland, it is best reached by taxi.

Ambassador
Амбассадор

Nab reki Fontanki 14. **Map** 3 A5.
【 272 9181. ◯ 1pm–midnight daily. V ⚹ 🎫 ♀ ♀ 🍴 AE, DC, MC, V, JCB. ⑤⑤

Take your pick of the European Room, decorated in early 19th-century Neo-Classical style, or the Russian Room, with traditional low vaults and a painted ceiling. A pleasure to walk to, particularly during the White Nights (see p51), this intimate restaurant is opposite the Engineers' Castle (see p101), just across the Fontanka river. The fare is a mixture of Russian and European, including all the old favourites such as caviar, borshch and steak, accompanied by bala-laika music, or jazz on Mondays.

Le Café Bahlsen
Nevskiy pr 142. **Map** 7 C2. 【 271 2811. ◯ 1pm–1am (Oct–Apr: noon–midnight) daily. V ⚹ 🎫 🎫 🎵 ♀ 🍴 AE, DC, MC, V. ⑤⑤

The only German restaurant and café in St Petersburg that is not a bierstube, Le Café Bahlsen is small and modern with views onto Nevskiy prospekt. It is very popular with those who like to eat out somewhere good but with no pretensions. For the truly hungry, they do a massive grill platter, cooked on a hot stone at your table, with spices you add yourself, and a double vodka to chase it.

Admiralty
Адмиралтейство

Nevskiy Palace Hotel, Nevskiy pr 57.
Map 7 B2. 【 275 2001. ◯ 5–11pm daily. ❶❶ V ⚹ ⚹ 🎵 🍴 AE, DC, MC, V, JCB. ⑤⑤⑤

A nautical theme prevails in this restaurant. Model ships and copies of the angels on the façade of the Admiralty building (see p78) are scattered around. The Russian menu includes many Georgian dishes such as lobio (spiced beans) and satsivi (chicken in a spicy walnut sauce), as well as khachapuri (cheese breads). Those who want good, reasonably priced food in the comfort of a hotel will find it here, albeit without too much excitement.

Afrodite
Афродита

Nevskiy pr 86. **Map** 7 B2. 【 275 7620. ◯ noon–1am daily. ❶❶ V ⚹ 🎫 ♀ 🎵 ♀ ★ 🍴 AE, DC, MC, V, JCB. ⑤⑤⑤

Afrodite started a fashion which quickly spread to other up-market places – it was the the city's first Western-style seafood restaurant. It also serves the widest selection of delicacies, including alligator with red paprika sauce or barracuda steak. Traditional Russian dishes, such as home-made pelmeny (beef dumplings), and delicious salads are also on the menu. However, with its unobtrusive service and pastel-coloured walls, the Afrodite may seem lacking in atmosphere.

Imperial
Империал

Nevskij Palace Hotel, Nevskiy pr 57.
Map 7 B2. 【 275 2001. ◯ 7–10:30am (breakfast), 7–11pm daily; noon–4pm Sun (brunch). V ⚹ ⚹ 🎫 ♀ 🍴 AE, DC, MC, V. ⑤⑤⑤

Situated on the first floor of the Nevskij Palace Hotel, the Imperial has a glazed façade offering excellent views over Nevskiy prospekt. This is actually the hotel's breakfast room, but for dinner they offer a straightforward international haute cuisine menu, well cooked and well presented. The main drawback is the rather too hotel-like neutrality of the interior, but the desserts are heavenly, the wine is good and, if you like watching the world go by, no other restaurant matches it.

Svir
Свирь

Hotelship Peterhof, nr Tuchkov Bridge.
Map 1 A4. 【 325 8888. ◯ noon–11pm daily. 🎫 V ⚹ 🎫 ♀ ♀ ★ 🍴 AE, DC, MC, V. ⑤⑤⑤

The Svir has made a name for itself with its monthly food festivals, which compensate for the relative lack of variety in the city's other restaurants. Whether the food is Mexican, Italian or Turkish, they fly in skilled chefs to bring a bit of sunshine to the winter months.

In the summer cooling fruit and cocktails are added to the menu. It can be fun dining on the river, but getting to the hotelship is a chore. A taxi (10 minutes from Nevskiy prospekt) is more or less obligatory.

Landskrona
Ландскрона

Nevskij Palace Hotel, Nevskiy pr 57.
Map 7 B2. 【 275 2001 ext 201.
◯ 12:30pm–1am daily. ❶❶ V ⚹ ⚹ 🎫 ♀ 🎵 ♀ ★ 🍴 AE, DC, MC, V, JCB. ⑤⑤⑤⑤⑤

The best of European cuisine and a high standard of service are offered here in a modern interior. A jazz duo, rather than the classical music heard in other leading restaurants around the city, adds an unusual touch. The food, however, is as classical as the silver service, with complimentary hors d'oeuvres, obligatory white wine sorbet between courses and dishes such as the divine beef fillet in a blue cheese sauce, or terrine of rabbit in a cider jelly, which comes in vast portions.

NOVGOROD

Detinets
Детинец

Intercession Tower, Detinets (the kremlin). 【 (81622) 746 24.
◯ 11am–6pm, 7–11pm daily. V ⚹ 🎫 ♀ ⑤

In a useful position for visitors, the Detinets is located right inside the kremlin, and offers good traditional Russian cuisine. The attractive medieval interior of the 16th-century Intercession Tower, with its vaulted ceiling, makes an excellent setting for hearty Russian potato salads and meat-based dishes. The stews are tasty and filling; the pelmeny are home-made. The Detinets is a perfect lunch stop on a visit to this wholeheartedly medieval city. There is live music in the restaurant every evening except Monday.

Beresta
Береста

Studencheskaya ul 3. 【 (81622) 304 01. ◯ 6:30–11am, noon–5pm, 6–11pm daily. 🎫❶ V ⚹ ⚹ 🎫 🎵 ♀ 🍴 AE, DC, MC, V. ⑤⑤⑤

For those wanting a little more than Russian simplicity, the Beresta is a good choice, found within the Beresta Palace Hotel (see p173). It has a changing, international menu and a range of Russian dishes. Just 15 minutes' walk from the kremlin, it is a convenient dinner venue before the return to St Petersburg.

Light Meals and Snacks

THE EXTERIOR, and sometimes even the interior, of a café usually gives little indication of what is on offer, making it difficult to differentiate between a good and a bad establishment at first glance. Many of the newer places have Western-style names and decor and offer foreign cuisine, but are often quite expensive. Russian and ethnic cafés, however, can serve tasty food ranging from a simple sandwich to a reasonably priced three-course meal. These cafés are scattered all over the city, and some are worth making a special trip to, but you can generally rely on most of them for a good unpretentious meal or snack. In most places, meat dominates the menu, so vegetarians might have a difficult time.

The distinction between bars, such as the "pubs" and German cafés, and other establishments is often blurred. Even small cafés and cake shops offer beer and spirits at any time of the day, and many are open past midnight.

RUSSIAN

THE LOCAL foreign community often sticks to familiar fast food and steaks, but traditional Russian dishes such as *borshch*, *pelmeny* (dumplings filled with meat), beef wrapped in cheese and *draniki* (potato pancakes, a traditional rural dish) are widely offered.

Priboy is well located just behind the Hermitage (*see pp84–93*), while **Diana**, **Nik** and **Aprel-Palmira** are also close to Nevskiy prospekt (*see p108*). The cellar-like **Krokodil** is popular with the bohemian crowd and tends to host special events as well as offering a sound traditional menu. **Kafe Ambassador** has the advantage of late opening hours – until 5am – as well as excellent views across the Fontanka to the Engineers' Castle (*see p101*). Also on the Fontanka is **Staroe kafe**. Just off St Isaac's Square (*see p79*) is the **Idiot**, named after the Dostoevsky novel, which has both literary and culinary pretensions, offering books for sale and poetry readings as well as local beer and food. Although it ostensibly stays open until 11pm, it actually closes when the last customer leaves, often around 4am.

For those wanting to try the famous Russian *blini* (pancakes), a number of places serve them in both savoury and sweet varieties, stuffed with caviar, cottage cheese, salty *brinza* cheese or apricots.

Russkiye bliny and **Skazka** have a wide selection of inexpensive pancakes and *blinchiki* (folded pancakes), while **La Chandeleur** offers a broader, more Gallic menu, which includes alcohol.

GEORGIAN AND ARMENIAN

GEORGIAN AND Armenian food is much loved by locals, despite the independence of these former states. **Metekhi** and **Tbilisi** offer a selection of *lobio* (spicy beans), *satsivi* (chicken in a spicy walnut sauce), *kharcho* (heavy meat soup) and the ubiquitous *shashlyk* (kebab). **Baghdad**'s speciality is *manty*, an Uzbek version of *pelmeny*, and noodle soups, while they also do a delicious *koreyskiy salat* (spicy Oriental carrot salad). The decoration in this tiny basement café is also impressive. **Shakherezade** makes excellent, if rather oily, hummus and falafel. **Krunk** describes itself as an Armenian café. Despite this, the menu is largely made up of international dishes, except for *dolma* (their Armenian version of stuffed vine leaves).

PIZZA AND PASTA

PIZZA AND PASTA houses are highly popular with locals, particularly wealthy couples. For visitors, especially non-Russian-speaking visitors, these places pose fewer language

problems and provide familiar, easy meals. Pizza places are most common, and there are well-known Western names such as **Pizza Hut**. **Pizza House** is the oldest takeaway in St Petersburg and serves some of the thinnest pizzas ever seen. **La Strada** is a model example of how to convert a gloomy yard into a flashy two-storey interior. At the lower end of the market, **Pizza Pronto** is a cheap and cheerful alternative.

GERMAN

THE FIRST GERMAN (and non-state-owned) bar to open in St Petersburg was **Chayka**, which is still a noisy and busy bar offering generous portions of wurst and chips or Baltic herring. While similar establishments such as **Antwerpen** and **Nevskij 40** are more important for their location than the quality of their food (which is not bad), places like **Le Café Bahlsen** and **Schwabskiy domik** offer a more traditional menu and are popular with the many German businesspeople and tourists who flood the city. Nevskij Palace's **Bierstube** probably has the greatest variety of both German and Austrian dishes but at a higher price. As in the majority of Russian restaurants, most meals are meat-based.

NORTH AMERICAN

FOR THOSE craving big juicy steaks, salvation lies in **Daddy's Steak Room** and **Montreal Steak**. Despite its more distant location, Daddy's is popular all year round and, with the opening of Montreal Steak in the centre of town, carnivores are assured of a good reliable meal. **California Grill** is slightly less expensive and oriented towards a student clientèle, while **Bistro Sadko** is a St Petersburg institution – an American bar offering hamburgers, chips and tempting desserts, as well as salads, vegetarian options and a Russian menu. It also provides one of the best places to stop and people-watch on busy Nevskiy prospekt.

For key to symbols *see p291*

MEXICAN AND SPANISH

ST PETERSBURG WAS overcome when **La Cucaracha** opened its doors in 1995 and tequila mania hit the city. Cocktails, tortilla chips and dips, or delicious full meals served mostly by Mexican waiters and with live Mexican music, mean continued popularity for this comfortable bar. Just a few hundred yards up the Fontanka, **Snack Bar Casa de Don Quixote** has good music and the café is open all night. It is never particularly lively but is highly recommended for a snack, drink or cup of coffee in the early hours of the morning.

FAST FOOD

THE LAST FEW YEARS have seen an increase in the number of fast food outlets, led by **Grill Master**, **Carrol's** and **McDonalds**. In addition to the standard international chains, however, St Petersburg has three excellent local options right in the centre. **Green Crest** offers salads, rarely found elsewhere, with plenty of mayonnaise, while **Minutka** has a selection of both salads and sandwiches. Popular with ravers and clubgoers, as well as those who have been out watching the bridges go up during White Nights (see p51), is **Layma**, which is open 24 hours. It serves steak and chops with chips, plus soups, *pirozhki*, salads, beer and genuine freshly-squeezed orange juice.

Hamburger stands are making an appearance on the streets of St Petersburg, but the Russian idea of fast food is a small open sandwich with fish, cheese or salami, or alternatively *pirozhki*, small doughy patties filled with cabbage, rice and egg, or with something sweet like apple. It is best to avoid the fried *pirozhki* with meat and sausages which are sold up and down Nevskiy prospekt.

Arab foodstalls all over town have made *shawerma* and kebabs a popular and cheap alternative to hamburgers. If tempted, you are advised to buy from an Arab seller, rather than Russian, as the difference between *shawerma* and hamburger can become blurred.

PASTRIES AND SWEETS

RUSSIANS ARE notoriously sweet-toothed and tea is never offered without biscuits or cakes in private homes. Cakes and pastries are sold in most of the city's cafés, and ice cream is eaten on the street in both winter and summer. The Oriental delights of **Shakherezade**, offering a variety of honey and almond sweets such as *paklava*, are highly popular with locals and, as with most Russian cafés, they usually offer mounds of whipped cream piled with fresh and dried fruits and nuts. **Sladkoezhka** (literally sweet-eater) has almost entirely fresh cream desserts. Sweet pastries galore can be taken out at the bakery **Nevskiy 27**, or eaten in at the canalside **Kafe Sankt-Peterburg**, which has tables on an outdoor terrace in summer. More luxurious European-style cheesecakes and pastries are the fare at **Nik**, or can be tried at a higher price in the **Vienna Café** of the Nevskij Palace Hotel (see p173). Traditional English and Continental afternoon tea are offered on the mezzanine of the **Grand Hotel Europe** (see p173) and in the lounge of the **Astoria Hotel** (see p173), usually accompanied by live classical music.

PUBS

A COMBINATION OF English and Irish pubs and German bars, the city's "pubs" are often run by foreigners. Although the interiors and the food tend to be a little unadventurous, the beer is generally good. Draught Guinness is available at two Irish bars, **Mollie's Irish Bar** and **Shamrock**, the latter conveniently located opposite the Mariinskiy Theatre (see p119). **Korsar** and **Rose Pub** both provide a varied and highly energetic programme of live music and themed entertainment, but probably the liveliest place of all is **Tribunal**. A total contrast is the strangely named **Wooden Pub**, which looks more like a small barn than anything else, and is very quiet. Here they serve huge portions of filling and wholesome food at moderate prices. The **Maltiyskiy orden**, also known as The Mermaid, has a summer terrace on the Moyka.

EATING OUT ON DAY TRIPS

FINDING A PLACE to have lunch outside the city can seem difficult. Pavlovsk (see pp156–9) and Peterhof (see pp146–9) now have reasonable restaurants in the palaces themselves, although space is limited at Peterhof during the summer. Pavlovsk also has the kitsch **Podvorye** just beside the station, a fun experience with folk songs and traditional Russian meals in a pseudo-traditional mansion. In Peterhof there is also the tiny and inexpensive **Trapeza** café just along from the east entrance to the park.

Tsarskoe Selo does not have a decent café in the palace itself (see pp150–55), but the town is well supplied with small cafés along the central Oranzhereynaya ulitsa in addition to the adequate **Tsarskoe Selo** restaurant at the station.

Oranienbaum (see p144) and Gatchina (see p145), further removed from the tourist trail, are a gastronomic desert, and it is best to take a picnic with you. For those travelling to Ilya Repin's house at Repino (see p144), the only alternative to a picnic is barbecued *shashlyk* at the roadside, or the restaurant at the Repino sanatorium, which should be avoided. Most hotels and a few cafés in the centre of St Petersburg, such as **La Chandeleur**, can provide packed meals.

Novgorod (see pp160–63) has more to offer in terms of luncheon venues. Try the **Detinets** café in the kremlin, or the **Beresta**, which offers excellent European cuisine. The **Aziya** restaurant serves good Korean food in an intimate setting, and a quick pizza can be snatched at **Kafe Charodeyka**, situated just opposite the entrance to Novgorod's historic kremlin.

DIRECTORY

RUSSIAN

Aprel-Palmira
Апрель-Пальмира
Pushkinskaya ul 16.
Map 7 B3. ☎ *164 6303.*

Diana
Диана
Sadovaya ul 56.
Map 6 D3. ☎ *310 9355.*

Idiot
Идиот
Nab reki Moyki 82.
Map 5 C2. ☎ *315 1675.*

Kafe Ambassador
Кафе Амбассадор
Nab reki Fontanki 14.
Map 3 A5. ☎ *275 9522.*

Krokodil
Крокодил
Galernaya ul 18.
Map 5 C1. ☎ *314 9437.*

La Chandeleur
Bolshaya Konyushennaya
ulitsa 1. **Map** 2 E5.
☎ *314 8380.*

Nik
Ник
Vladimirskiy pr 1.
Map 7 A2. ☎ *311 7693.*

Priboy
Прибой
Nab reki Moyki 19.
Map 2 E5. ☎ *311 8285.*

Russkiye bliny
Русские блины
Ul Furmanova 13.
Map 3 A4. ☎ *279 0559.*

Skazka
Сказка
Nevskiy pr 27.
Map 6 E1. ☎ *315 9490.*

Staroe kafe
Старое кафе
Nab reki Fontanki 108.
Map 6 E4. ☎ *316 5111.*

GEORGIAN AND ARMENIAN

Baghdad
Багдад
Furshtatskaya ul 35.
Map 3 C4. ☎ *272 2355.*

Krunk
Крунк
Solyanoy per 14.
Map 3 A5. ☎ *273 4523.*

Metekhi
Метехи
Ul Belinskovo 3.
Map 7 A1. ☎ *272 3361.*

Shakherezade
Шахерезада
Razyezhaya ul 3.
Map 7 A3. ☎ *112 4271.*

Tbilisi
Тбилиси
Sytnynskaya ul 10.
Map 2 D2. ☎ *232 9391.*

PIZZA AND PASTA

La Strada
Страда
Bolshaya Konyushennaya
ulitsa 27. **Map** 6 E1.
☎ *312 4700.*

Pizza House
Пицца-Хаус
Podolskaya ul 23.
Map 6 E5. ☎ *316 2666.*

Pizza Hut
Пицца-хат
Nab reki Moyki 71/16.
Map 5 C2. ☎ *315 7705.*

Pizza Pronto
Пицца-пронто
Zagorodnyy pr 8.
Map 7 A3. ☎ *315 8948.*

GERMAN

Antwerpen
Антверпен
Kronverkskiy pr 13/2.
Map 2 E2. ☎ *233 9746.*

Bierstube
Бирштубе
Nevskij Palace Hotel,
Nevskiy pr 57. **Map** 7 B2.
☎ *275 2001.*

Chayka
Чайка
Nab kanala Griboedova 14.
Map 6 E1. ☎ *312 4631.*

Le Café Bahlsen
Nevskiy pr 142. **Map** 7 C2.
☎ *271 2811.*

Nevskiy 40
Невский 40
Nevskiy pr 40. **Map** 6 F1.
☎ *312 2457.*

Schwabskiy domik
Швабский домик
Novocherkasskiy pr 28/19.
☎ *528 2211.*

NORTH AMERICAN

Bistro Sadko
Бистро Садко
Mikhaylovskaya ulitsa 1/7.
Map 6 F1. ☎ *329 6000.*

California Grill
Nevskiy pr 176.
Map 8 E3. ☎ *274 2422.*

Daddy's Steak Room
Moskovskiy pr 73.
☎ *252 7744.*

Montreal Steak
Apraksin per 22.
Map 6 E3. ☎ *310 9256.*

MEXICAN AND SPANISH

La Cucaracha
See p197.

**Snack Bar Casa de
Don Quixote**
В гостях у Дон-Кихота
House of Friendship,
Nab reki Fontanki 21.
Map 7 A1. ☎ *210 4517.*

FAST FOOD

Carrol's
Кэрролс
Kamennoostrovskiy pr 31.
Map 2 D1.

Green Crest
Грин крест
Vladimirskiy pr 7.
Map 7 A2. ☎ *113 1380.*

Grill Master
Гриль Мастер
Nevskiy pr 46. **Map** 6 F1.
Sadovaya ul 22. **Map** 6 F2.

Layma
Лайма
Nab kanala Griboedova 16.
Map 6 E1. ☎ *315 5545.*

McDonalds
Kamennoostrovskiy pr 39.
Sennaya pl 4. **Map** 6 E3.

Minutka
Минутка
Nevskiy pr 20. **Map** 6 E1.
☎ *325 8224.*

PASTRIES AND SWEETS

Kafe Sankt-Peterburg
Кафе Санкт-Петербург
Nab kanala Griboedova 5.
Map 6 E1. ☎ *210 7673.*

Nevskiy 27
Невский 27
Nevskiy pr 27. **Map** 6 E1.
☎ *312 1080.*

Sladkoezhka
Сладоежка
Marata ul 11. **Map** 7 B2.
☎ *315 4880.*

Vienna Café
Кафе Вена
Nevskiy pr 57. **Map** 7 B2.
☎ *275 2001.*

PUBS

Korsar
See p197.

Maltiyskiy orden
Мальтийский орден
Nab reki Moyki 6.
Map 2 E5. ☎ *314 8989.*

Mollie's Irish Bar
See p197.

Rose Pub
See p197.

Shamrock
See p197.

Tribunal
See p197.

Wooden Pub
Chaikovskovo ul 36.
Map 3 B4. ☎ *275 7147.*

DAY TRIPS

Aziya
Азия
Shteikova ul 22, Novgorod.
☎ *(81622) 722 27.*

Beresta
See p182.

Detinets
See p182.

Kafe Charodeyka
Кафе Чародейка
Volosova ul 1/1, Novgorod.
☎ *(81622) 751 54.*

Podvorye
Подворье
Filtrovskoye shosse 16,
Pavlovsk. ☎ *465 1399.*

Trapeza
Трапеза
Kalininskaya ul 9, Peterhof.
☎ *427 9393.*

Tsarskoe Selo
Царское Село
Detskoe Selo Railway
Station, Tsarskoe Selo.
☎ *470 1349.*

SHOPS AND MARKETS

A TRIP ROUND St Petersburg's shops, markets and large department stores provides an intriguing insight into local life. In addition to the many traditional stores, the city is dotted with street-sellers trading in an eclectic miscellany of goods.

Shopping in Russia requires a certain amount of spontaneity, flexibility and even a sense of adventure since you never quite know when and where you will find what is

Matryoshka doll

needed. As a rule, shop windows reveal surprisingly little about what might be found within. In recent years, imported goods (sold at inflated prices) have sadly pushed out many local products. Vodka, caviar and time-honoured Russian crafts and toys, however, make wonderful gifts.

Most shops tend to be concentrated around the city's main streets such as Nevskiy, Kamennoostrovskiy and Bolshoy (Petrogradskaya) prospekts.

Clothes in showroom of local designer Tatyana Parfyonova

OPENING HOURS

O PENING HOURS vary, but shops are usually open from around 10am until 7pm or later. Most close for an hour at lunch, food shops generally between 1–2pm and consumer goods stores between 2–3pm. On Sunday, the large department stores are open between 11am–6pm, and each area has food shops and a chemist open all day.

HOW TO PAY

C ASH PAYMENTS can only be made in roubles and nowadays prices are rarely quoted in foreign currency. Paying in non-Russian currency is a criminal offence. The only place where you might be able to pay in foreign currency is at a tourist market. Between 10am and 6pm, there is no shortage of exchange offices *(see p206)*,

some in the shops themselves, where you can get roubles for cash or on credit card. There are relatively few stores, even those selling imported goods, which will accept credit card payments. The larger antique shops are the exception to this rule and nearly all now accept Visa and Mastercard.

In most shops, customers are forced to peer at goods stacked behind the counter. If you would like a closer look, just point to what you want and say "*mozhno*" ("may I?"). To purchase something, pay for it at the cash desk and then return to collect the item from the counter. Shop assistants will usually realise if you do not speak Russian and will write down the prices for you to hand to the cashier. In theory, defective goods can be taken back if you keep the receipt.

Second-hand bookshop sign

BARGAINING ETIQUETTE

I F A SET PRICE is displayed at markets, this indicates no bargaining. In all other cases you can usually get some reduction if you haggle, especially since visitors are often likely to be quoted a higher price than locals. Haggling in Russia, however, is not to be treated as a pleasant pastime. It is a serious matter, so do not bother unless you genuinely intend to buy.

Russian box-camera (1920s)

BUYING ART AND ANTIQUES

B Y LAW, all objects pre-1956, and all precious objects such as gold, silver, jewellery and furs, are subject to strict export controls. Works of art, including contemporary water-colours, also fall under this ruling and likewise books published before 1946. All suitcases are x-rayed at the airport check-in, so it is pointless to try to hide, for instance, an icon with a metal cover. In practice, prints and watercolours without frames are generally ignored, and unless a book is extremely rare you are likely to be able to export it. Permission to export books is processed fairly quickly by the **Russian National Library**. Permission for art objects can be received from a department of the **Ministry of Culture**, but it

DLT department store

is so complicated that the art gallery or artist from whom you are purchasing should undertake this for you. They generally have their own contacts which should make the longwinded process faster.

If you have not obviously tried to cheat customs, any objects not allowed through customs can simply be handed over to someone staying in St Petersburg. Otherwise, the item will be placed in storage at the airport, for which, if you wish to reclaim it later, there will be a charge. Objects unclaimed for a year are confiscated, as are objects which have obviously been hidden to avoid detection. Valuable pieces will be donated to a museum.

DEPARTMENT STORES

KNOWN AS "univermag" or universal shop, Russian department stores generally evolved from the old trading rows, which were literally rows of kiosks owned by different traders. Present-day department stores have in fact altered very little from their original kiosk style and still operate as a complex of sections or boutiques. Every visitor to St Petersburg should explore **Gostinyy dvor** (see p108) and **Passazh** (see p48) as well. Although they now have a large proportion of imported goods, and prices for local goods are relatively high, it is worthwhile observing what the locals are buying.

DLT, also in the city centre, is more Western in layout and is

in itself an interesting piece of Style-Moderne architecture. To empty your pockets of any surplus roubles after a visit to St Petersburg, a good place to stop off en route to the airport is **Moskovskiy univermag**.

MARKETS AND BAZAARS

MANY LOCALS shop for food in one of the numerous markets dotted around the city. The most centrally located market is **Kuznechnyy**, just off Nevskiy prospekt, which sells flowers, fruit, vegetables, delicious home-made cream cheese and wonderful natural honey which you can sample. In front of the main entrance old ladies sell mushrooms in autumn, woollen socks in winter, flowers in summer and a hundred other odds and ends from pickled cucumbers and dried fish to old shoes and the family crystal ware.

These days the yard inside **Apraksin market** (see p95) is best known for wholesale and retail sales of liquor, cigarettes, and clothes, especially Turkish leather jackets.

Flea markets, thought by the local administration to reflect badly on the city's image, are perpetually being moved on. Yet sellers continue to pop up relentlessly at the city's main fruit and vegetable markets.

Slightly different are the metal kiosks which could once be found everywhere but now tend to be concentrated on **Sennaya ploshchad** (see p122). Petersburgers come here from all over the city to buy a variety of cheap food. Souvenir watercolours and prints are sold throughout the

year at the open-air market, **Vernisazh**, which takes place outside St Catherine's Church (see p48). **Rynok suvenirov**, a small tourist market near the Church on Spilled Blood (see p100), sells both the best and cheapest selection of *matryoshka* dolls (see p189). You are also likely to find handmade chess sets, watches, fur hats, old cameras, t-shirts and military paraphernalia.

Women selling a variety of goods outside Kuznechnyy market

MUSEUM SHOPS

SOME OF THE BEST quality souvenirs, whether it be jewellery, *matryoshka* dolls, prints or books, are usually found in the museums. The **Hermitage** (see pp84–93) has an excellent second-hand bookstall, while its main shop offers reproduction prints and objects, and books on the city and its art. A superb selection of souvenirs and jewellery is sold in the **Menshikov Palace** (see p62), while the **Russian Museum** (see pp104–107) produces a good range of souvenirs such as scarves, jewellery, textiles and reproduction posters and cards, to accompany special exhibitions. Their shops also have a large stock of beautiful art books. Other large museum shops are found in the **Peter and Paul Fortress** (see pp66–7) and the palaces at **Pavlovsk, Peterhof** and **Tsarskoe Selo** (see pp146–59).

Souvenirs sold at the tourist market opposite the Church on Spilled Blood

What to Buy in St Petersburg

Decorative box

IT IS EASY to find interesting and beautiful souvenirs in St Petersburg. They range in price from small, enamelled badges, which sell for very little, through to hand-painted Palekh boxes and samovars which can be very expensive. Traditional crafts were encouraged by the state in the old Soviet Union and many items, such as lacquered boxes and bowls, matryoshka dolls, wooden toys and chess sets, are still made by craftsmen and women using age-old methods. Memorabilia from the Soviet era also make good souvenirs and Russia is definitely the best place to buy the national specialities, vodka and caviar.

Samovar
Used to boil water to make tea, samovars come in all shapes and sizes (see p179). A permit is needed to export a pre-1945 samovar.

Vodka and Caviar
An enormous variety of both clear and flavoured vodkas (such as lemon and pepper) is available (see p178). They make excellent accompaniments to black caviar (ikra) and red caviar (keta), which are often served with blini (see p176).

Flavoured vodka

Clear vodka

Red caviar

Black caviar

Malachite egg

Amber ring

Semi-precious Stones
Malachite, amber, jasper and a variety of marbles from the Ural mountains are used to make a wide range of items – everything from jewellery and chess sets to inlaid table tops.

Wooden Toy
These crudely carved wooden toys often have moving parts. They are known as Bogorodskiye toys and make charming gifts.

Matryoshka Dolls
These dolls fit one inside the other and come in a huge variety of styles. The traditional dolls are the prettiest, but the models painted to represent Soviet political leaders are also very popular.

Chess Sets
Chess is an extremely popular pastime in Russia. Chess sets made from all kinds of material, including malachite, are widely available. This wooden chess set is painted in the same style as the matryoshka dolls.

LACQUERED ARTIFACTS

Painted wooden or papier-mâché artifacts make popular souvenirs and are sold all over the city. The exquisite hand-painted, lacquered Palekh boxes can be very costly, but the eggs decorated with icons and the typical red, black and gold bowls are more affordable.

Palekh Box

The art of miniature painting on papier-mâché items originated in the late 18th century. Artists in the four villages of Palekh, Fedoskino, Mstera and Kholui still produce these hand-painted marvels. The images are based on Russian fairytales and legends.

Painted wooden egg

Bowl with Spoon

The brightly painted papier-mâché bowls and spoons made in Khokhloma are coated with a hard lacquer. They are not, however, resistant to boiling liquid.

Russian hand-painted tray

Tuners

Strings

Russian Scarf

These brilliantly coloured traditional woollen shawls are good for keeping out the cold of a Russian winter. Mass-produced polyester versions are also available, mostly in big department stores, but these are not as warm.

Musical Instruments

Russian folk music uses a wide range of musical instruments. This gusli is similar to the Western psaltery and is played by plucking the strings with both hands. Also available are the brightly painted balalaika and the bayan (accordion).

Soviet Memorabilia

An eclectic array of memorabilia from the Soviet era is on sale. Old banknotes, coins, pocket watches and Red Army kits, including belt buckles, badges and other items of uniform, can be found alongside watches with cartoons of KGB agents on their faces.

Gzhel Vase

Ceramics with a distinctive blue and white pattern are produced in Gzhel, an area near Moscow. Ranging from figurines to household crockery, they are popular with Russians and visitors alike.

Pocket watch

Badge with Soviet symbols

Red Army leather belt

Where to Shop in St Petersburg

THE MAIN DEPARTMENT stores in the city centre stock everything from souvenirs to vodka and furs, all of a high quality. Some of the smaller shops on and around Nevskiy prospekt, however, give you more chance to avoid the crowds; they also tend to be cheaper. In a city which prides itself on its native intellectuals, books and art are appropriately St Petersburg's other main exports. Soviet memorabilia have also become very popular.

VODKA AND CAVIAR

BUYING VODKA from anywhere other than a reputable shop is not advisable. Cheaper brands can be fairly potent and a certain amount of illegal vodka still makes its way into the smaller outlets. **Gostinyy dvor** department store and **Yeliseev's** are the most central and reliable places for vodka. Alternatively, the **Liviz** outlets' normally stock a good range. The better local brands of clear vodka are the Russian Smirnov and Sinopskaya *(see p178)*.

For good quality caviar, Yeliseev's fish department and **Ryba** are the best places to go, and on occasions they have fresh caviar, for which you bring your own jar. Other reputable supermarkets in the centre are **Bestrun** and **Prima** which is open 24 hours. **Sennaya ploshchad** and **Apraksin dvor** markets have the cheapest food products in the city, but check the date on caviar tins. In the summer it is best to buy only from shops with refrigerators.

SOUVENIRS AND CRAFTS

DURING THE summer months when traders set up stalls by all the major tourist spots, St Petersburg is flooded with *matryoshka* dolls, shawls and painted lacquerware. In the winter, by contrast, it often seems as if everything has gone into hibernation. **Rynok suvenirov** and **Vernisazh** markets, however, operate all year round. The museum shops also stock souvenirs and crafts, and some (such as in the Hermitage) also sell art books.

Probably the smallest souvenir shop, **Matryoshka** is also one of the best, but places like **Nasledie** and **Khudozhest- vennyye promysly** have a larger variety. The city's porcelain factory makes some fine china, particularly coffee cups, and has its own outlet, **Farfor**. Locally made porcelain, glass and crystal is also sold at **Farfor, Khrustal, Steklo**.

SOVIET MEMORABILIA

ARTIFACTS from the Soviet era are often now produced specially for the tourist market. For original blatant propaganda material, **Sekunda** has one of the best stocks. The **Rynok suvenirov** market also has military paraphernalia. Soviet badges are compact and easily transportable. A small selection at moderate prices can be found in antique shops such as **Antikvariat**. Busts of Lenin abound, and the little shop on the first floor of the military bookshop **Dom voyennoy knigi** usually has a cheap selection. They also sell old cameras of all designs, from the 1920s to the 1970s.

ANTIQUES AND ART

BEARING IN MIND all the restrictions on antiques and art, it is still worth seeing what might fall outside the export rules, whether it be a small watercolour, a modern print or a quaint 1960s tea service from stalls at **Apraksin dvor**. Shops such as **Antik tsentr**, **Tertsiya** and **Rapsodiya** are mainly for the tourist trade, while **Peterburg Antikvariat** caters for all, but is at the top of the price range. Only buy an expensive object subject to customs regulations if you are sure the relevant paperwork and export applications can be obtained *(see p202)*.

Paintings all require export licences, but galleries generally do this themselves, so drop in to **Palitra** or the **Soyuz khudozhnikov** and see what they have. The most original and exciting gallery is **Borey** which has rapidly changing exhibitions and performance art to watch.

BOOKS

ST PETERSBURGERS perceive their city as an intellectual focal point, with a great literary and artistic past. The centre has many new and second-hand bookshops, which also tend to sell prints and often antiques. The best, and most famous, are the magnificent **Dom knigi** *(see p47)* and **Knizhnaya lavka pisateley**. Art books, both new and old, can be found at **Iskusstvo**, **The Art Shop** and **Mir**, while if you are looking for English-language literature, **Planeta** sells new classics and second-hand thrillers. Rummaging around antiquarian shops, such as **Bukinist**, **Staraya kniga**, and **Na Liteynom**, can turn up interesting old prints, literature and travel guides, but foreign language publications tend to be heavily overpriced. **Severnaya lira** sells sheet music, ranging from classical to folk songs, as well as instruments, CDs and books.

FASHION AND ACCESSORIES

CLOTHES, SHOES and other accessories are generally imported nowadays, and the big names in fashion shopping are all foreign. Only one local designer has opened her own showroom, **Tatyana Parfyonova modnyy dom**, and her garments have been purchased by the Russian Museum *(see pp104–7)*.

Locally made jewellery of semi-precious stones from the Urals and amber from the Baltic is sold in outlets such as **Kristall** and souvenir shops such as **Samotsvety** and **Nasledie**. One north-Russian speciality is niello silver jewellery, with its distinctive patterns and pictures etched in black.

For furs, the city offers a wide variety and a range of prices. Traditional Russian hats can be bought all year round in the department stores.

DIRECTORY

DEPARTMENT STORES

DLT
ДЛТ
Bolshaya Konyushennaya
ulitsa 21/23.
Map 6 E1.

Gostinyy dvor
Гостиный двор
Nevskiy prospekt 35.
Map 6 F2.

Moskovskiy univermag
Московский универмаг
Moskovskiy prospekt 205.

Passazh
Пассаж
Nevskiy prospekt 48.
Map 6 F1.

MARKETS AND BAZAARS

Andreevskiy rynok
Андреевский рынок
Bolshoy prospekt,
Vasilevskiy Island.
Map 5 A1.

Apraksin dvor
Апраксин двор
Sadovaya ulitsa.
Map 6 E2.

Kuznechnyy rynok
Кузнечный рынок
Kuznechnyy pereulok 3.
Map 7 A3.

Rynok suvenirov
Рынок сувениров
Kanal Griboedova, by
Church on Spilled Blood.
Map 2 E5.

Sennaya ploshchad
Сенная площадь
Sennaya ploshchad.
Map 6 D3.

Vernisazh
Вернисаж
Nevskiy prospekt 32–34.
Map 6 E1.

SHOPS

Antik tsentr
Антик-центр
(Antiques)
Nalichnaya ulitsa 21.

Antikvariat
Антиквариат
(Antiques)
Ulitsa Marata 10.
Map 7 B3.

The Art Shop
(Art Books)
Nevskiy prospekt 52.
Map 6 F1.

Bestrun
Бестран
(Food)
Bolshaya Morskaya ul 11.
Map 6 D1.

Borey
Борей
(Art)
Liteynyy prospekt 58.
Map 7 A1.

Bukinist
Букинист
(Old Books)
Liteynyy prospekt 59.
Map 7 A1.

Dom knigi
Дом книги
(Books)
Nevskiy prospekt 28.
Map 6 E1.

Dom voyennoy knigi
Дом военной книги
(Military books, cameras
and memorabilia)
Nevskiy prospekt 20.
Map 6 E1.

Farfor
Фарфор
(Porcelain)
Nevskiy prospekt 111.
Map 7 C2.

Farfor, Khrustal, Steklo
Фарфор, Хрусталь,
Стекло
(Porcelain, crystal & glass)
Nevskiy prospekt 64.
Map 7 A2.

Iskusstvo
Искусство
(Art shop)
Nevskiy prospekt 16.
Map 6 D1.

Khudozhestvennyye promysly
Художественные
промыслы
(Souvenirs)
Nevskiy prospekt 51.
Map 7 B2.

Knizhnaya lavka pisateley
Книжная лавка
писателей
(Books)
Nevskiy prospekt 66.
Map 7 A2.

Kristall
Кристалл
(Jewellery)
Nevskiy prospekt 34.
Map 6 E1.

Liviz (vodka outlets)
Ulitsa Plekhanova 2.
Map 6 E2.
Ulitsa Zhukovskovo 27.
Map 7 B1.
Ulitsa Belinskovo 6.
Map 7 A1.

Matryoshka
Матрешка
(Souvenirs)
Nevskiy prospekt 27.
Map 6 E1.

Mir
Мир
(Art books)
Nevskiy prospekt 13.
Map 6 D1.

Na Liteynom
На Литейном
(Antiques)
Liteynyy prospekt 61 (in
the yard).
Map 7 A2.

Nasledie
Наследие
(Souvenirs)
Nevskiy prospekt 116.
Map 7 B2.

Palitra
Палитра
(Art)
Nevskiy prospekt 166.
Map 8 D3.

Peterburg Antikvariat
Петербург Антиквариат
(Antiques)
Nevskiy prospekt 54.
Map 6 F1.

Planeta
Планета
(Books)
Liteynyy prospekt 30.
Map 3 A5.

Prima
Прима
(Food)
Bolshaya Morskaya ul 26.
Map 6 D1.

Rapsodiya
Рапсодия
(Antiques)
Bolshaya Konyushennaya
ulitsa 13.
Map 2 E5.

Ryba
Рыба
(Food)
Nevskiy prospekt 21.
Map 6 E1.

Samotsvety
Самоцветы
(Souvenirs & jewellery)
Mikhaylovskaya ulitsa 4.
Map 6 F1.

Sekunda
Секунда
(Soviet memorabilia)
Liteynyy prospekt 61 (in
the yard).
Map 7 A2.

Severnaya lira
Северная лира
(Sheet music, instruments
and books)
Nevskiy prospekt 26.
Map 6 E1.

Soyuz khudozhnikov
Союз художников
(Art)
Bolshaya Morskaya
ulitsa 38.
Map 6 D2.

Staraya kniga
Старая книга
(Second-hand books,
antiques & prints)
Nevskiy prospekt 18.
Map 6 D1.

Tatyana Parfyonova modnyy dom
Татьяна Парфенова
модный дом
(Clothes)
Nevskiy prospekt 51.
Map 7 B2.

Tertsiya
Терция
(Antiques)
Italyanskaya ulitsa 5.
Map 6 E1.

Yeliseev's
Елисеевский гастроном
(Food)
Nevskiy prospekt 56.
Map 6 F1.

ENTERTAINMENT IN ST PETERSBURG

S T PETERSBURG has an impressive and varied choice of entertainment. Its ballet, opera, classical music and theatre are among the best in the world. In addition to this, a thriving and vibrant nightlife is made up of numerous rock and jazz clubs, bars, discos, nightclubs and casinos.

Increasingly, international artists are adding St Petersburg to their tours, and mainstream now exists harmoniously alongside underground in music, theatre and cinema. The

Folk dancer

St Petersburg Philharmonia and the Mariinskiy (Kirov) ballet dancers *(see p119)* deserve their impressive reputation, though this means they are often away on tour. Along the Nevskiy prospekt, street musicians are usually found, from local accordionists to Peruvian musicians. The White Nights in June have given birth to many festivals *(see p51)* that take over all the city venues. At this time of year St Petersburg sways to the sounds of classical music, rock, pop and jazz.

The magnificent, gilded interior of the Yusupov Theatre

ENTERTAINMENT INFORMATION

S T PETERSBURG can be quite a difficult city to keep up with, as both official and unofficial events are organized at short notice. Even the programmes of major venues, such as the Mariinskiy Theatre, can change.

The best regular listings in English can be found in the Friday edition of *The St Petersburg Times*, a twice-weekly newspaper, and in the monthly magazine *Pulse (see p209)*, both free in hotels, foreign bars and shops. These listings are selective and tend towards youth culture. A much broader range of information, including details about exhibitions, performances and other special events, is provided in a complete programme produced each month, in Russian,

Mariinskiy poster pillar

by the **Institute of Cultural Programme**. Classical concerts and theatre are also advertised at ticket offices and kiosks *(teatralnaya kassa)*.

Most of the theatres and concert halls officially close down for July, August and part of September because their troupes go on tour. Whilst this may deprive visitors of local performers, some theatres bring in guest troupes from Moscow and abroad. Smaller venues, such as the Yusupov Theatre *(see p120)* and the Hermitage Theatre *(see p84)*, which depend heavily on foreign visitors, maintain their programme all summer. Matinees start at midday and evening performances at 7pm (6:30pm at the Mariinskiy Theatre).

BUYING TICKETS

T O DO THINGS the Russian way, tickets must be purchased with cash and in person. Theatre ticket offices and kiosks can be found all over town, offering tickets up to a week in advance. They display a full programme (in Russian) of all theatre and classical music performances for the next ten days and are generally open daily from 10am–1pm and 4–7pm. Offices within theatres tend to work from 11am–3pm and 4–8pm and sell tickets up to a month in advance. The Philharmonia *(see p194)* sells season tickets for a series of concerts.

For non-Russian speakers, the best service for booking tickets is provided either by a hotel concierge or **Ost-West Kontaktservice**, where staff speak English and German.

A few venues, notably the Mariinskiy Theatre *(see p119)* and the Mussorgsky Theatre of Opera and Ballet *(see p98)*, have separate ticket prices for foreigners and Russian citizens. Russian-speaking visitors who try to buy the cheaper, Russian-only tickets may be refused entry if discovered.

Tourists may find they can still obtain tickets for sold-out performances at the Mariinskiy Theatre if they go on the day. As in most cities, touts sell tickets for major events but beware of possible fakes or that prices might be inflated.

Ticket for a theatre performance

Spectacular performance of the famous *Sleeping Beauty* ballet

LATE NIGHT TRANSPORT

THE METRO CLOSES its doors at midnight and buses run until 12:15 (infrequently after 11pm). There is no all-night public transport, so expect to take a taxi late at night. Avoid the private taxis which wait outside foreign hotels and bars as they are far more costly than official yellow cabs (*see p219*).

CHILDREN'S ENTERTAINMENT

THERE ARE relatively few public facilities for children in St Petersburg. Many theatres, notably **TYuZ** and **Zazerkalye**, stage plays in Russian for children, but few give English-language performances. At New Year, however, some theatres stage English shows.

The **Circus** is an obvious choice for children, with a permanent site on the Fontanka, while in the summer a circus tent also goes up at Avtovo metro. Look out for posters and announcements in listings.

Classical concerts for children are held at the **Children's Philharmonia** and the two puppet theatres offer a wide variety of fairytales and short plays. Alternatively, the **Interior Theatre** displays costumes and special effects.

WHITE NIGHTS FESTIVALS

THERE ARE AT LEAST four or five festivals bearing the name White Nights (*see p51*). The original and most internationally respected is the classical music festival, now known as Stars of the White Nights. This incorporates special performances in the Mariinskiy (*see p119*) and other theatres. Ticket prices for concerts and ballet during the White Nights sometimes increase twofold.

Jazz and art festivals are also now associated with the White Nights name, leading to an explosion of events in June.

A group of street musicians entertaining the crowds

THE RUSSIAN CIRCUS

Circuses first appeared in Russia in the early 19th century, but it was not until 1876–7 that Russia's first permanent circus building was erected for Giuseppe Ciniselli's Italian circus. St Petersburg's circus is still based at this historic site, modernized in 1963, and continues to practise the traditional training, skills and animal acts (some animal-lovers may find these distressing) which have made the Russian circus justifiably famous.

Acrobatic performers, St Petersburg's circus

DIRECTORY

USEFUL ADDRESSES

Institute of Cultural Programme
Институт культурных программ
Institut kulturnykh programm
Ul Rubinshteyna 8. **Map** 7 A2.
C **FAX** 312 9572.

Central Theatre Ticket Office
Nevskiy pr 39. **Map** 6 F1.
C 310 4240.

Ticket Kiosks
Hermitage foyer. **Map** 2 D5.
Pl Ostrovskovo. **Map** 6 F2.
Gostinyy dvor (corner of ul Lomonosova). **Map** 6 F2.
Gostinyy Dvor metro. **Map** 6 F1.

Ost-West Kontaktservice
Ul Mayakovskovo 7/27. **Map** 7 B1.
C 279 7045.

CHILDREN'S ENTERTAINMENT

Children's Philharmonia
Детская Филармония
Detskaya Filarmoniya
Dumskaya ulitsa 1/3. **Map** 6 E2.
C 219 4175.

Circus
Цирк
Tsirk
Nab reki Fontanki 3. **Map** 7 A1.
C 314 8478.

Interior Theatre
Интерьерный театр
Interyernyy teatr
Nevskiy pr 104. **Map** 7 B2.
C 273 1454.

Large Puppet Theatre
Большой театр кукол
Bolshoy teatr kukol
Ul Nekrasova 10. **Map** 7 B1.
C 272 8215.

Marionette Puppet Theatre
Театр марионеток
Teatr marionetok
Nevskiy pr 52. **Map** 6 F1.
C 311 1900.

TYuZ
Театр юных зрителей
Teatr yunykh zriteley
Pionerskaya pl 1. **Map** 6 F4.
C 164 0679.

Zazerkalye
Зазеркалье
Ul Rubinshteyna 13. **Map** 7 A2.
C 112 5135.

The Arts

For a city renowned worldwide for its rich tradition in ballet and classical music, it is not surprising that St Petersburg has a wide range of cultural events on offer. An evening at the Mariinskiy is an essential part of any visit to the city, but it is also worth venturing into the many other theatres, music halls and churches to absorb more of the city's cultural diversity. Classical music is vastly popular and local orchestras are much in demand the world over. In addition there are the evocative sounds of church choirs, the lively ambience of folk cabarets, and numerous festivals *(see pp50–53)* held to encourage young musicians, composers, film makers and dancers.

BALLET

Some of the best dancers in the world have come from the **Mariinskiy Theatre** *(see p119)*. Its main company tours for much of the year, but usually gives performances in St Petersburg during the winter months. The greatest highlight of the year is the Christmas performances of *The Nutcracker*, danced largely by children from the Vaganova Ballet School *(see p110)*.

Dancers from the Mariinskiy also perform in the **Hermitage Theatre** and the **Mussorgsky Theatre of Opera and Ballet**. At the **Rimsky-Korsakov Conservatory** *(see p120)* ballet is of varied quality, but often includes dancers from abroad.

Outside the more traditional spheres, Boris Eifmann's modern ballet company is very popular, but the success of recent years has been Valery Mikhaylovskiy's entirely male Mushchkoy Ballet, performing classics such as *Swan Lake*, complete with tutus. They perform at venues like the **Great October Concert Hall**.

OPERA

Tchaikovsky's opera *Eugene Onegin*, Mussorgsky's *Boris Godunov* and Prokofiev's *Love of Three Oranges* remain stalwarts in any repertory. Operas are performed (usually in their original language) at the **Mussorgsky Theatre of Opera and Ballet** and the **Mariinskiy Theatre**. Valery Gergiev's brilliant artistic direction and sensitive conducting at the Mariinskiy have made a huge difference to standards

in recent years. The more intimate 18th-century **Hermitage Theatre** and the tiny **Yusupov Theatre** stage lighter operas.

CLASSICAL MUSIC

The composers Tchaikovsky, Shostakovich, Mussorgsky and Rimsky-Korsakov lived in St Petersburg and their music is performed frequently.

The **Great Philharmonia** *(see p98)*, the **Small Philharmonia** *(see p48)* and **Glinka Capella** *(see p112)*, are all historic venues for classical concerts. The former is where the renowned St Petersburg Philharmonic Orchestra plays when it is not on tour. Russian emigrés such as the violinist Gidon Kremer are frequent visitors, and foreign conductors such as Claudio Abbado and the late Sir Georg Solti have also performed here.

The Hermitage has its own orchestra which has a highly active independent life, with concerts in the **Hermitage Theatre** *(see p84)* and international tours. The **Menshikov Palace** *(see p62)* has some excellent original restored keyboard instruments, including an 18th-century English organ, on which concerts are given.

CHURCH MUSIC

The music of an Orthodox choir resounding over the priest's intoning is perhaps one of the most evocative sounds in Russia. Professional singers from the Capella and elsewhere often sing in church choirs. The best can be heard on Saturday evening and Sunday morning services at the

Holy Trinity Cathedral in Alexander Nevsky Monastery *(see p130)* and at the **Cathedral of the Transfiguration** *(see p127)*. The services in the **Kazan Cathedral** *(see p111)* are also of a high standard. More formal religious music can be heard in the **Smolnyy Cathedral** *(see p128)*.

FOLK MUSIC

The local tourist industry encourages visits to concerts of Russian folk music and dancing. The ensembles can be very good, with balalaikas and *bayans* or accordions, girls with red kerchiefs and whirling Cossack dancers. Some of the best performances are found at the **Beloselskiy-Belozerskiy Palace** and the **Nikolaevskiy Palace**.

Many restaurants include a folk cabaret, though these tend to be kitsch and fairly raucous. For authentic Russian village folk songs, Podvorye restaurant *(see p184)* in Pavlovsk has an excellent small ensemble.

STREET MUSIC

Democracy had the unexpected effect of allowing many informal activities such as busking, which brought some highly talented musicians on to the streets. As skilled players stake their pitches, the sounds of music fill the city's streets. The two underpasses beneath Nevskiy prospekt by Gostinny Dvor are busy busking spots, while other metro stations are popular sites for old ladies singing Russian romances, rather like ballads.

THEATRE

For many years, the Soviet Union's leading light in the drama world was the **Bolshoy Dramatic Theatre** (BDT), which remains the city's main traditional theatre. The **Alexandriinskiy Theatre** *(see p110)*, whose company is the oldest in Russia, offers a wider repertoire than the BDT.

In recent years, Lev Dodin's direction of the **Malyy Drama Theatre** has brought it international fame, even though all performances are in Russian.

Productions of well-known plays, such as the *Cherry Orchard*, may be interesting to experience, but other theatres, staging modern plays, are likely to be less accessible to non-Russian speakers. The **Kommissarzhevskaya**, **Liteynyy** and **Akimov** theatres also have good reputations.

CINEMA

Most cinemas now show Hollywood blockbusters but the majority of foreign films are dubbed rather than subtitled. The **Spartak Cinema** shows dubbed European classics, while the **Leningrad Cinema** has popular films in English twice weekly. The hi-tech **Crystal Palace** also has regular showings in English.

A large number of film festivals are held every year, often including films in the original language. *The St Petersburg Times* gives full coverage of all festivals including the main Festival of Festivals *(see p51)*.

DIRECTORY

TICKETS

Tickets are sold in city kiosks and individual theatres unless otherwise stated.

BALLET AND OPERA

Hermitage Theatre
Эрмитажный театр
Ermitazhnyy teatr
Dvortsovaya nab 34.
Map 2 E5. 311 9025.
(Tickets from city kiosks and hotels only.)

Mussorgsky Theatre of Opera and Ballet
Театр оперы и балета имени Мусоргского
Teatr opery i baleta imeni Musorgskovo
Pl Iskusstv 1. **Map** 6 E1.
219 1949.
late Jul–Aug.
(Tickets for foreigners from the theatre and hotels only.)

Mariinskiy Theatre
Мариинский театр
Mariinskiy teatr
Teatralnaya pl 1. **Map** 5 B3.
114 5264.
late Jul–Aug.
(Tickets for foreigners from the theatre and hotels only.)

Great October Concert Hall
Большой концертный зал Октябрьский
Bolshoy kontsertnyy zal Oktyabrskiy
Ligovskiy pr 6. **Map** 7 C1.
277 6960.

Rimsky-Korsakov Conservatory
Консерватория имени Римского-Корсакова
Konservatoriya imeni Rimskovo-Korsakova
Teatralnaya pl 3. **Map** 5 C3.
312 2519.

Yusupov Theatre
Юсуповский театр
Yusupovskiy teatr
Yusupovskiy dvorets, nab reki Moyki 94. **Map** 5 B3.
314 9883.

CLASSICAL MUSIC

Glinka Capella
Капелла имени Глинки
Kapella imeni Glinki
Nab reki Moyki 20.
Map 2 E5. 314 1058.

Menshikov Palace
Меньшиковский дворец
Menshikovskiy dvorets
Universitetskaya nab 15.
Map 1 B5. 213 1112.

Great Philharmonia (Shostakovich Hall)
Большой зал филармонии имени Шостаковича
Bolshoy zal Filarmonii imeni Shostakovicha
Mikhaylovskaya ulitsa 2.
Map 6 F1 110 4257.

Small Philharmonia (Glinka Hall)
Малый зал филармонии имени Глинки
Malyy zal Filarmonii imeni Glinki
Nevskiy pr 30. **Map** 6 F1.
311 8333.

CHURCH MUSIC

Church of the Transfiguration
Спасо-Преображенский собор
Spaso-Preobrazhenskiy sobor
Preobrazhenskaya pl 1.
Map 3 B5. 272 3662.
10am & 6pm daily.

Holy Trinity Cathedral
Свято-Троицкий собор

Svyato-Troitskiy sobor
Alexander Nevsky Monastery, pl Aleksandra-Nevskovo. **Map** 8 E4.
274 3606.
10am & 6pm daily.

Kazan Cathedral
Казанский собор
Kazanskiy sobor
Kazanskaya ploshchad 2.
Map 6 E1. 311 4826.
9am & 6pm daily.

Smolnyy Cathedral
Смольный собор
Smolnyy sobor
Ploshchad Rastrelli 3.
Map 4 F4.
311 3560.

FOLK MUSIC

Beloselskiy-Belozerskiy Palace
Дворец Белосельских-Белозерских
Dvorets Beloselskikh-Belozerskikh
Nevskiy pr 41. **Map** 7 A2.
315 5236.

Nikolaevskiy Palace
Николаевский дворец
Nikolaevskiy dvorets
Pl Truda 4. **Map** 5 B2.
311 9304.

THEATRE

Akimov Comedy Theatre
Театр комедии имени Акимова
Teatr komedii imeni Akimova
Nevskiy pr 56. **Map** 6 F1.
312 4555.

Alexandriinskiy Theatre
Александринский театр
Aleksandriinskiy teatr
Ploshchad Ostrovskovo 2.
Map 6 F2.
312 1545.

Bolshoy Drama Theatre (BDT)
Большой драматический театр
Bolshoy dramaticheskiy teatr
Nab reki Fontanki 65.
Map 6 F2. 310 0401.

Komissarzhevskaya Drama Theatre
Театр им. Комиссаржевской
Teatr im Komissarzhevskoy.
Italyanskaya ulitsa 19.
Map 6 F1. 311 3102.

Liteyniy Theatre
Театр на Литейном
Teatr na Liteynom
Liteynyy pr 51. **Map** 7 A1.
273 44 58.

Malyy Drama Theatre
Малый драматический театр
Malyy dramaticheskiy teatr
Ulitsa Rubinshteyna 18.
Map 7 A2. 113 2078.

Molodyozhnyy Theatre
Молодёжный театр
Molodyozhnyy teatr
Nab reki Fontanki 114.
Map 3 A5. 316 6564.

CINEMA

Crystal Palace
Кристаль–Палас
Kristal-Palace
Nevskiy pr 72. **Map** 7 A2.
272 2382.

Leningrad Cinema
Кинотеатр Ленинград
Kinoteatr Leningrad
Potemkinskaya ulitsa 4.
Map 3 C4. 273 3116.

Spartak Cinema
Кинотеатр Спартак
Kinoteatr Spartak
Ul Saltykova-Shchedrina 8.
Map 3 C5.
272 7897.

Live Music and Nightlife

ST PETERSBURG was at the heart of the underground Soviet rock scene and some of the best new Russian sounds still originate here. Rock, rockabilly and jazz clubs have sprung up in abandoned bomb shelters and cinemas all over the city, and most feature an eclectic mix, with live music one night and alternative fashion shows or avant-garde films the next. The nightclub scene, offering mostly rave and techno music, is moving out of the bunkers and into vast halls with strobe lights that attract the nouveaux riches. The newly moneyed classes are also the main clients at the city's casinos.

ROCK VENUES

UNDER THE Soviet regime, Leningrad rock was rebellious without being overtly political. Though there is now less emphasis on the lyrics, Russian rock still owes much to the past, while also managing to incorporate the latest in Western music trends.

There is a wide variety of styles on offer, from pop to hard rock. **Moloko** is a cheap venue offering live rock and a good atmosphere. **Polygon** is popular with fans of hard rock.

Rockabilly gave birth to **Money Honey Saloon**, which in turn led to an explosion of rockabilly groups in the city. **Cosmonaut** and **Vatrushka** only hold special events but maintain a high standard with the latest in St Petersburg rock.

Mass rock and pop concerts are held in the **Oktyabrskiy kontsertnyy zal**, **Yubileynyy dvorets sporta** and **SKK**.

JAZZ VENUES

FOR MANY YEARS the jazz scene was dominated by David Goloshchokin who set up the **Jazz Philharmonic Hall** where, as its name suggests, dancing or talking are often prohibited. As young musicians emerged, the resulting competition on the jazz scene led Goloshchokin to open the **Ellington Hall** which is more like a relaxed Western jazz club. For improvisation and innovative jazz, **JFC Jazz Club** leads the way, with a variety of acid-jazz and blues. The musicians who make the club such a success also perform on a guest basis elsewhere. **Kvadrat Jazz Club** is where

many young musicians meet for jam sessions. In summer, the city's best swing band can be seen free of charge on the corner of Nevskiy prospekt and Mikhaylovskaya ulitsa.

BARS

A NUMBER OF BARS, such as **Shamrock**, the Mexican **La Cucaracha**, **Mollie's Irish Bar** or the **Rose Pub**, have live music. **Bistro Sadko**, in the Grand Hotel Europe, was one of the few official bars where new bands used to play. It has recently been left behind by the appearance of numerous rock clubs, but maintains the tradition by putting on occasional live music.

Liverpool is an all-round Beatles experience, hosting live bands playing nothing but Beatles cover versions.

Two venues occupy a special place on the city's entertainment scene, neither of them exactly bars or art clubs. **Fish Fabrique**, hidden away in the depths of the artists' colony dubbed "Pushkinskaya desyat", is a drinking club, occasional concert venue, film club and favourite hang-out for punks, rock 'n' rollers and youth in general. The **Idiot**, named after Dostoevsky's novel (*see p123*), has rapidly become one of the city's most popular bars for young intellectuals and artistic foreigners. The scatter cushions and stacks of books make it an ideal place to relax in the daytime, or to attend a poetry reading in the evening.

Korsar and **Chayka** both have regular jazz evenings, while the noisy **Tribunal**, always filled with a young crowd, has occasional discos.

NIGHTCLUBS AND DISCOS

SMALLER, MORE DIVERSE clubs, such as the underground **Griboedov**, are still very much of the alternative culture trend, playing a variety of the latest hits from Europe, and hosting fashion shows and other cultural events. **Port Club** goes one step further, providing video halls and an art gallery.

Nevsky Melody is a vast entertainment complex, with casinos, restaurants and nightclubs. **Candyman**, the place for the pop and TV elite, is a huge disco and dance hall located on the outskirts of town in the high-rise heartland. **Domenico's** introduces a touch of humour with its occasional live Russian pop and erotica. One of the most respectable clubs, **Hollywood Nites**, invites more serious acts and has one of the city's best casinos. **Metro**, mainly for the young and upwardly mobile, plays house, techno and Russian dance music. **Piramid**, with its Egyptian theme, is always fun. **Harley Davidson Club** is another example of a good theme club. The "erotic" **Monroe Club** has video screens and peepshows, as well as Russian and European pop music and dancing.

On the gay scene, **69 Club** is where things are happening while other gay clubs tend to come and go. Since gay culture in St Petersburg is very much involved in the art world, events are often advertised at Saturday exhibitions in the New Academy of Fine Arts at Pushkinskaya ulitsa 10.

CASINOS

FREQUENT CHANGES to local legislation have had a negative effect on the city's handful of casinos. Since they are visited mainly by the highest wealth band, casinos tend to attract many members from the semi-criminal classes. **Premier**, in the Titan Cinema, has roulette and cards and is a trouble-free option along with **Venice**, **Astoria Club** and **Hollywood Nites**. All are top of the list for quality and style. **Nevsky Melody** is more lively but a little impersonal.

DIRECTORY

ROCK VENUES

Cosmonaut
Космонавт
Kosmonavt
Bronnitskaya ulitsa 24.
Map 6 E5.
[316 2040.
○ 7–11pm Fri & Sat.

Moloko
Молоко
Perekupnoy pereulok 12.
Map 8 D3.
[274 9467.
○ 7–11:30pm Thu–Sat.

Money Honey Saloon
Apraksin dvor 14.
Map 6 E2.
[310 0147.
○ 7:30pm–midnight daily.

Oktyabrskiy kontsertnyy zal
Октябрьский
концертный зал
Ligovskiy prospekt 6.
Map 7 C1.
[275 1273.

Polygon
Полигон
Poligon
Lesnoy prospekt 65.
(Check listings for events.)

SKK
СКК
Prospekt Yuriya Gagarina 8.
[298 1211.

Vatrushka
Ватрушка
Ul Pravdy 10. **Map** 7 A3.
[164 3236.
(Check listings for special events only.)

Yubileynyy dvorets sporta
Юбилейный дворец
спорта
Prospekt Dobrolyubova 18.
Map 1 B3.
[119 5601/5604.

JAZZ VENUES

Ellington Hall
Эллингтоновский зал
Ellingtonovskiy zal
Zagorodnyy prospekt 27.
Map 6 F3.
[164 8565.
○ 7–11pm Wed–Sun.

Jazz Philharmonic Hall
Джаз-Филармоник холл
Dzhaz-filarmonik kholl
Zagorodnyy prospekt 27.
Map 6 F3.
[164 8565.
○ 7–11pm Wed–Sun.

JFC Jazz Club
Shpalernaya ulitsa 33.
Map 3 C4.
[272 9850.
○ 7–11pm daily.

Kvadrat Jazz Club
Джаз клуб квадрат
Dzhaz klub kvadrat
Ul Pravdy 10. **Map** 7 A3.
[315 9046.
○ 8–11pm Tue.

BARS

Bistro Sadko
Grand Hotel Europe,
Mikhaylovskaya ulitsa 1/7.
Map 6 F1. [329 6000.
○ noon–1am daily.

Chayka
Чайка
Naberezhnaya kanala
Griboedova 14. **Map** 6 E1.
[312 4631.
○ 11am–3am daily.

La Cucaracha
Nab reki Fontanki 39.
Map 7 A2.
[110 4006.
○ noon–1am Sun–Thu,
noon–5am Fri & Sat.

Fish Fabrique
Pushkinskaya ulitsa 10,
5th floor. **Map** 7 B2.
○ 7pm–midnight Wed,
9pm–5:30am Fri & Sat.

Idiot
Nab reki Moyki 82.
Map 5 C2. [315 1675.
○ noon–11pm daily.

Korsar
Корсар
Bolshaya Morskaya
ulitsa 14. **Map** 6 D1.
[219 4184.
○ 1pm–1am Mon–Fri,
1pm–4am Sat & Sun.

Liverpool
Ливерпуль
Liverpul
Ulitsa Mayakovskovo 16.
Map 7 B1.
[279 2054.
○ 11am–2am daily.

Mollie's Irish Bar
Ulitsa Rubinshteyna 30.
Map 7 A3.
[319 9768.
○ 11am–2am daily.
(Live music Tue–Thu & Sun).

Rose Pub
Роуз паб
Furshtadtskaya ulitsa 1/14.
Map 3 A4.
[275 3554.
○ noon–2am daily.

Shamrock
Ulitsa Dekabristov 27.
Map 5 B3.
[219 4625.
○ noon–2am daily.
(Live music Mon, Thu, Sat.)

Tribunal
Corner of Angliyskaya nab
& proezd Dekabristov.
Map 5 C1.
[311 1690.
○ 11am–4am daily.

NIGHTCLUBS AND DISCOS

69 Club
Клуб 69
Klub 69
2-ya Krasnoarmeyskaya
ulitsa 6.
Map 6 D5.
[259 5163.
○ 1pm–6am Tue–Sun.

Candyman
Кэндимен
Kendimen
Prospekt Kosygina 17.
[521 1410.
○ 10pm–7am Wed–Sun.

Domenico's
Доменикос
Nevskiy prospekt 70.
Map 7 A2.
[272 5717.
○ noon–6am daily.

Griboedov
Грибоедов
Voronezhskaya ulitsa 2A.
Map 7 B4.
[164 4355.
○ 11pm–5:30am
Thu–Sat.

Harley Davidson Club
Ulitsa Kurchatova 1/39.
[247 6500.
○ noon–late daily.

Hollywood Nites
Nevskiy prospekt 46.
Map 6 F1.
[311 6077.
○ 8pm–6am daily.

Metro
Метро
Ligovskiy prospekt 174.
[166 0204.
○ 10pm–6am daily.

Monroe Club
Клуб Монро
Klub Monro
Nab kanala Griboedova 8.
Map 6 E1.
[312 1331.
○ noon–11pm Tue–Sun,
5–11pm Mon.

Nevsky Melody
Невские Мелодии
Nevskie Melodii
Sverdlovskaya nab 62.
[227 1596.
○ 10pm–6am daily.

Piramid
Пирамид
Ulitsa Lomonosova 1.
Map 6 F2.
[312 3600.
○ 10pm–6am Thu–Sun.

Port Club
Клуб Порт
Klub Port
Pereulok Antonenko 2
(in yard).
Map 6 D2.
[314 2609.
○ 3pm–6am daily.

CASINOS

Astoria Club
Клуб Астория
Klub Astoriya
Malaya Morskaya ul 20.
Map 6 D1.
[210 5020.
○ 6pm–6am daily.

Premier
Премьер
Nevskiy prospekt 47.
Map 7 A2.
[315 7893.
○ noon–9am.

Venice
Венеция
Venetsiya
Ulitsa Korablestroiteley 21.
[356 4661.
○ 7pm–6am daily.

SURVIVAL
GUIDE

PRACTICAL INFORMATION

THE STREET SIGNS and maps of St Petersburg are not as difficult to negotiate as it may first appear when confronted with daunting Cyrillic letters. Not only do hotels, restaurants and all service sectors attempt to compensate by being helpful to foreigners, but in recent times the city has started putting up English signs pointing out major sights and shops.

Conventional tourist offices do not exist in the city and information points, along with other services such as foreign exchange offices, are often concentrated in hotels and other areas frequented by foreigners. Once out on the street, things will seem unfamiliar, but with a modicum of patience and determination everything is eventually possible, from making international telephone calls and exchanging money to finding emergency medical treatment.

Telecommunications are rapidly gaining ground but, as quality improves, prices come closer to, and occasionally outstrip, Western equivalents.

Sign advertising Ost-West Kontaktservice

Grand Hotel Europe concierge

TOURIST INFORMATION

THE CITY'S HOTELS provide the main source of guidance for tourists in St Petersburg. In the Europe, Nevskij Palace and Hotelship Peterhof the concierge will provide travel and booking services and general assistance. Other, Russian-run, hotels have a Service Bureau offering similar services, although advice is often indifferent. **Ost-West Kontaktservice** runs a reliable, free tourist information service as well as selling maps and booking accommodation and entertainment.

English-language newspapers *(see p209)* give details on events and up-to-the-minute opening hours for museums.

EXCURSIONS

HOTELS CAN BOOK guided group tours and day trips in several languages. In addition to city tours and canal cruises, there are day trips to the suburban palaces and Novgorod *(see pp144–63)*.

Ost-West Kontaktservice offers several excellent tours, in English and German. City-run excursions, which gather tourists on Palace Square by the Admiralty *(see p83)* and the Portik Rusca on Nevskiy prospekt *(see p48)*, tend to be in Russian only, as do ordinary river cruises *(see p218)*.

On summer weekends there are helicopter tours operating on a turn-up basis from the Peter and Paul Fortress *(see pp66–7)*. Groups of 20 can book through **Baltic Airlines**.

ADMISSION CHARGES

MANY MUSEUMS and theatres, notably the Hermitage *(see pp84–93)*, the Russian Museum *(see pp104–107)* and the Mariinskiy *(see p119)* charge foreigners considerably more than Russians, although prices are still within European and American norms. Students and schoolchildren are entitled to discounts. Credit cards are not accepted at any sights.

Ticket office sign

The ticket office or *kassa* is often far from the entrance, so look for the KACCA sign.

Tour helicopter picking up tourists by the Peter and Paul Fortress

OPENING HOURS

MOST SIGHTS open standard hours, 10 or 10:30am to 6pm, with no break for lunch, and close one day a week. They also close one day at the end of each month for major cleaning; this date varies so phone to check. Parks, including those around the palaces, are usually open from 8am to 8pm, later during White Nights.

ОТКРЫТО

Sign for open (otkryto)

ЗАКРЫТО

Sign for closed (zakryto)

VISITING CHURCHES

ATTENDING an Orthodox service is a fascinating experience. Since services tend to run for several hours, it is polite to make a donation and certain dress codes must be observed: no shorts; men should remove hats; ladies should cover their shoulders and chest and preferably wear a hat or headscarf. Women in trousers are accepted in town churches, but all monasteries will strictly enforce the no trousers rule. The most important services are on Saturday evening, Sunday morning and on church holidays.

Most major faiths are represented in the city. Churches tend to be open all day from early morning till late. Church service times are published in Friday's *St Petersburg Times (see p209).*

Friends greeting with a handshake

LANGUAGE

C YRILLIC, the alphabet used in the Russian language, is named after the 9th-century monk Cyril who invented it. The apparent similarity between Cyrillic and roman letters can be misleading. Some letters are common to both alphabets, others look similar but represent totally different sounds. Various systems of transliteration are in usage, but they do not differ enough to cause serious confusion.

Most people who come into contact with tourists speak some English and passers-by on the street will do their best if asked directions. Knowledge of a few Russian words *(see pp252–6)* will be appreciated and taken as a sign of respect.

ETIQUETTE

D ESPITE AN ever increasing Westernization of manners and language, the use is still strictly in force of the formal you (*vy*) and the informal (*ty*).

On public transport, it is accepted that young men should relinquish their seats to children or the elderly.

Smoking is prohibited in cinemas, museums, theatres and on public transport. Special areas are usually allocated for smoking in these places.

Drinking and smoking are two activities in which the Russians take great pleasure and frequent toasts are required to justify the filling and draining of glasses. At a private home you should always offer a toast to the hostess (*za khozyayku*) or to the host (*za khozyayina*). Introductions, and greetings amongst friends, take place with a handshake.

House number and Cyrillic street name

PAYING AND TIPPING

R OUBLES ARE the sole valid currency in Russia (*see p207*). Some large shops and hotels give prices in American dollars or Deutschmarks, but all cash payments must be in roubles only. Credit cards are accepted in some restaurants and most hotels, but rarely in shops, other than those selling imported goods at a much higher price than abroad.

Tipping is a matter of choice, but baggage handlers at the airport and the train station may ask or expect exorbitant sums. Simply pay as you think fit; a few roubles are sufficient.

ADDRESSES

R USSIAN ADDRESSES are given in reverse order: index/zip code, city, street name, house number, apartment number and finally name of person.

After 1917, many streets and sights were renamed to avoid imperial connotations or in order to commemorate new Soviet heroes. Since the city itself resumed its original name after a referendum in 1991, most streets in the centre have officially reverted to their pre-1917 names, while others are still being discussed. The area surrounding the city, however, is still the Leningrad Region. Many people happily use both the original and Soviet names; no offence is caused when one is used in preference to another.

Index/zip code   **City**   **Street name**

193015 Санкт-Петербург
улица Восстания
д. 34, кв. 52
Милане Прекрасной

House number   **Apartment number**   **Name of recipient**

Dvortsovyy most (leading to Vasilevskiy Island), raised to allow ships access along the Neva

BRIDGE OPENING TIMES

From early April until mid-November, when navigation is possible on the Neva river, all its bridges are raised between approximately 2am and 5am except for one short break. Make sure you are on the right side of the river before the bridges go up.

Dvortsovyy most: 1:55–3:05am & 3:15–4:45am.
Troitskiy most: 2–4:40am.
Most Leytenanta Shmidta: 1:55–4:50am.
Liteynyy most: 2:10–4:40am.
Birzhevoy most: 2:25–3:20am & 3:40–4:40am.
Tuchkov most: 2:20–3:10am & 3:40–4:40am.
Most Petra Velikovo: 2:45–4:55am.
Most Aleksandra Nevskovo: 2:35–4:50am.
Volodarskiy most: 2–3:45am & 4:25–5:45am.

Ost-West Kontaktservice, offering free advice and literature to visitors

VISAS

V ISAS ARE REQUIRED by all visitors to Russia. Package tour companies will organize visas for you, but independent travellers need to arrange their own. This can be a complex, time-consuming process and by far the easiest option is to pay a small fee for your travel agency to obtain a visa for you. The alternative is to go in person to the Russian Embassy where visas are issued. Document requirements change regularly and it is essential to check these in advance. You will need to show proof of either pre-booked accommodation or an invitation (visa support) from a tour company, business or private individual in Russia. **Ost-West Kontaktservice** can fax express invitations directly. Private invitations cannot be faxed and the process of issuing them takes at least one month through **OVIR** (Visa Registration Department).

The cost of a visa ranges from around £10 for a short-term, single entry visa to about £100 for multiple entry business visas. A visa usually takes ten days, but for an extra fee can be arranged in one day.

Inside Russia, visa extensions can only be granted by the organization which issued the initial invitation. If you over-

Official Russian visa

stay, expect to be stopped at the airport and turned back until you have either obtained the necessary extension visa or paid a considerable fine.

CUSTOMS AND IMMIGRATION

P ASSPORTS AND VISAS are checked thoroughly at immigration. All visitors must fill out a customs declaration form, available in several languages. These completed forms are returned to customs, together with a new form on departure. Essentially there are no limitations on the amount of money allowed into Russia but visitors should have less hard currency on departure and Russian money cannot be exported. Items of considerable value, such as diamond jewellery and computers, should be noted on the customs form on entry. All such valuables must be re-exported, or import duty will be charged. On arrival and departure, all items of luggage go through X-ray machines.

Departure customs are strict, particularly with works of art and antiques (*see p186*) but there should be no problem at all with modest quantities of consumer goods.

REGISTRATION

A LL FOREIGNERS must register with **OVIR** within three days of arrival, and obtain a stamp of registration on their visa. Hotels automatically do this for their guests, but those staying in private accommodation must register at the branch of **OVIR** where their invitation was issued. For an extended visa an application must be made at the same local branch. Visitors who forget to register become liable for a fine and can be prevented from leaving Russia until all the necessary paperwork is in order.

EMBASSIES AND CONSULATES

A NYONE INTENDING to reside in Russia for longer than three months is advised to register with their consulate or embassy. If visitors are hospitalized, robbed, imprisoned or otherwise rendered helpless, consular officials will help make arrangements, find an interpreter, or at least offer advice. They can re-issue passports and in some emergency cases provide money to get visitors home.

Great Britain, USA, Canada and South Africa have consulates in St Petersburg. Visitors from New Zealand, Australia or Ireland, however, have to contact their embassies in Moscow.

DISABLED TRAVELLERS

S T PETERSBURG has almost no facilities for the disabled. Transport is inaccessible, entrances have steps and narrow doors and there are rarely public lifts. It takes real determination for disabled travellers to get around.

STUDENT TRAVELLERS

I NTERNATIONAL student cards of all kinds are accepted for discounts in museums and on rail and air travel booked through the **International Youth Hostel** (*see p168*) or its affiliated agent, **Sindbad Travel**.

Sign for St Petersburg's International Youth Hostel

TRAVELLING WITH CHILDREN

RUSSIANS adore children, and travellers in the company of under-tens are likely to attract a good deal of attention and many compliments. Russian *babushki* (grannies) also think nothing of telling parents of their failings.

Men's toilet sign

Women's toilet sign

The city has many play parks and during school holidays temporary playgrounds are sometimes set up around town.

Museums and public transport are free for under-fives. Schoolchildren pay the full price on transport but pay a reduced price at museums.

Children playing on temporary bouncy castle in Palace Square

PUBLIC TOILETS

MANY CAFÉS and bars have no toilet facilities and in general the rather unhygienic public toilets are best avoided. It is much better to go to the nearest hotel or, if lacking an alternative, to use the pay toilets in department stores, for example. The person who takes the money hands out toilet paper rations.

PHOTOGRAPHY

PHOTOGRAPHIC restrictions have more or less disappeared. In museums expect to purchase a ticket for the right to photograph or use a video camera – tripods and flashes are prohibited.

ELECTRICAL APPLIANCES

THE ELECTRICAL CURRENT IS 220 V. Two-pin plugs are required, but some of the old Soviet two-pin sockets do not take modern European plugs which have slightly thicker pins. American appliances require a 220:110 current adaptor. Adaptors are widely available in St Petersburg.

TIME DIFFERENCE

ST PETERSBURG, throughout the year, follows Moscow time which is three hours ahead of Greenwich Mean Time (GMT). Russia has recently come into line with the rest of Europe and now puts its clocks forward one hour at the end of March and back at the end of October.

CONVERSION TABLE

Imperial to Metric
1 inch = 2.54 centimetres
1 foot = 30 centimetres
1 mile = 1.6 kilometres
1 ounce = 28 grams
1 pound = 454 grams
1 pint = 0.6 litres
1 gallon = 4.6 litres

Metric to Imperial
1 centimetre = 0.4 inches
1 metre = 3 feet, 3 inches
1 kilometre = 0.6 miles
1 gram = 0.04 ounces
1 kilogram = 2.2 pounds
1 litre = 1.8 pints

Standard Russian two-pin plug

DIRECTORY

TOURIST INFORMATION AND GUIDED TOURS

Ost-West Kontaktservice
Ul Mayakovskovo 7.
Map 4 B1. **(** 279 7045.
FAX 327 3417.

Baltic Airlines
Baltiyskie avialinii
Nevskiy pr. 7/9, Office 12.
Map 5 D1.
(FAX 311 0084.

VISA FORMALITIES IN UK

Progressive Tours
12 Porchester Pl, Connaught Sq, London W2 2BS.
(0171 262 1676.
FAX 0171 724 6941.

Scott's Tours
141 Whitfield St,
London W1P 5RY.
(0171 383 5353.
FAX 0171 383 3709.

VISA FORMALITIES IN RUSSIA

OVIR
Овир
(Tsentralnyy district)
Foreign department,
Pereulok Krylova 5.
Map 6 F2.
(310 4117.
⏰ 10am–6pm Mon–Fri.

EMBASSIES AND CONSULATES

Australia
Moscow, Kropotkinskiy
pereulok 13.
((095) 956 6070.
FAX (095) 956 6170.

Canada
Malodetskoselskiy pr 32.
Map 5 E3. **(** 325 8448.
FAX 325 8393.

Ireland
Moscow, Grokholskiy per 5.
((095) 742 0901;
(095) 2806500.
FAX (095) 742 0920.

New Zealand
Moscow, Povorskaya ul 7.
((095) 956 3579.
FAX (095) 956 3589.

South Africa
Nab reki Moyki 11.
Map 1 E5. **(** 325 6363.

UK
Pl Proletarskoy Diktatury 5.
Map 4 E4. **(** 325 6036.
FAX 325 6073.

USA
Furstadskaya ulitsa 15.
Map 3 B4. **(** 275 1701.
FAX 110 7022.

DISABLED TRAVEL

RADAR
Unit 12, City Forum,
250 City Road, London
EC1V 8AF, UK.
(0171 250 3222.
FAX 0171 250 1212.

STUDENT TRAVEL

International Youth Hostel
3-ya Sovetskaya ul 28.
Map 7 C2.
(329 8018.
FAX 329 8019.
@ ryh@ryh.spb.su

Sindbad Travel
3-ya Sovetskaya ul 28.
Map 7 C2.
(327 8384.
FAX 329 8019.
@ sindbad@ryh.spb.su

Personal Security and Health

DESPITE LURID media reports worldwide about the mafia, St Petersburg is still a relatively safe city. Petty crime should be the only concern for tourists, and even this is generally avoided if the usual precautions are taken. Make copies of your passport and visa, note traveller's cheque and credit card numbers and, for language reasons, keep a card with your Russian address on it.

Medical insurance is essential, as local healthcare compares poorly with Western standards, and English-speaking services or medical evacuation via Finland are very expensive. Many medicines are readily available, but it is best to bring specific medicines needed.

PROTECTING YOUR PROPERTY

EVERY VISITOR to Russia is seriously advised to take out travel insurance. Once in St Petersburg, simple rules should be observed, such as not displaying large sums of money; carrying cash in a concealed money belt, and keeping passports, tickets and all valuables in the hotel safe whenever possible. Security in Western-run hotels is very high, but in all hotels it is advisable to place valuables in the safe. Traveller's cheques *(see p206)* may have an insurance policy but are expensive to use and are easily laundered in Russia.

Avoid the gypsies who occasionally group on Nevskiy prospekt, apparently begging. If they do approach, do not stop for them and keep a firm hold of your possessions.

If you have property stolen, report it to the local police station for insurance purposes. They are unlikely to have an interpreter, so you should ask your hotel for assistance.

Beat-cops or *gorodovoy*, identifiable by their red caps

PERSONAL SAFETY

THE GREATEST danger faced by foreigners is that posed by pickpockets and petty thieves who might use violence if they meet with resistance. As in any country, it is advisable to hand over belongings that are demanded with menace.

The mafia, an organization largely overrated by the media nowadays, has almost no contact with tourists, who are generally much less wealthy than Russian businessmen.

Women on their own are unlikely to encounter sexual harrassment, though they should ignore kerb-crawlers and avoid taking a cab alone at night. The main threats to people on the

GAI policemen checking documents

streets come from local drivers, who see all pedestrians as a nuisance, and from manhole covers, which tend to rock or even collapse under your feet.

POLICE

SEVERAL KINDS of police operate on St Petersburg's streets. Their uniforms change according to the weather, with the addition of fur hats and big coats in the winter.

Nevskiy prospekt now has the *gorodovoy* or beat-cop, an institution revived in 1997 to

Free, state-run ambulance service

New-look police fleet as Volvos (top) replace Ladas (below)

Fire engine in central St Petersburg

create the reassuring presence of educated, young policemen who should be capable of giving directions in a foreign language. The red uniform caps they wear in the summer months inspired their nickname "Red Riding Hood".

The other street officers or militia *(militsya)* wear dark blue-grey combat-style uniforms and many carry guns.

Militsya **policeman** Their uniform is similar to that worn by the riot police or OMON, the only noticeable difference being their badges.

Totally separate are the GAI (ГАИ) or traffic police, whose uniforms have a badge on the chest and shoulder. They have the authority to stop any vehicle to check documents.

Both the militia and traffic police supplement their low income by fining people for minor infringements, notably for crossing Nevskiy between signals. It is best to pay the moderate "fine" imposed – no more than 50 roubles.

PHARMACIES

THE BEST PHARMACIES *(apteka)*, are located along Nevskiy prospekt. These sell many imported medicines, some with Russian instructions, others in their original language. Strong medications can be bought over the counter, so prescriptions are not necessary. Every assistant is a trained pharmacist and can advise alternative drugs. If you have very specific requirements, particularly insulin, you should bring a sufficient supply for your stay.

MEDICAL TREATMENT

IF YOU FALL ILL, seek advice in your hotel, which should have its own doctor. Several companies, notably **Emergency Medical Consulting** and

American Medical Center, specialize in dealing with foreigners. They cover everything from dental care, X-rays and pre-natal care to medical evacuation. Their charges are fairly high, but they are used to dealing with foreign insurance policies. Slightly cheaper is the **Clinic Complex** which has English-speaking Russian doctors and can deal competently with minor emergencies.

For those in need of immediate attention, the casualty department of the **Trauma Clinic of the Central District** is just off Nevskiy prospekt. English is not spoken here, but basic care involving stitches or injections can be administered.

If you are taken to a local hospital and require further treatment, it is advisable to contact either your consulate or one of the above medical centres. They can arrange to have you moved or alternatively they can oversee your treatment in the hospital.

Pharmacy in a Nevskiy underpass

HEALTH PRECAUTIONS

VISITORS AND residents should not drink tap water, which contains heavy metals and *giardia*, a parasite causing stomach problems. To be safe drink bottled water only.

Foreign food often unsettles the stomach, but Russian food is unlikely to do any serious harm. Avoid fruit and raw vegetables that may have been washed in tap water, and the meat pies sold on the streets.

In past years diphtheria has become more prevalent, and inoculation is advisable. Of growing concern is the rise in syphilis, HIV and other sexually transmitted diseases.

АПТЕКА

Sign for pharmacy or *apteka*

MOSQUITOES

MOSQUITOES *(komari)* are rife between June and late September. Repellents are available locally but not all are very effective and it is best to come well equipped. Burning oils, sprays or plugs which heat chemical tablets are recommended at night time, particularly out on the Gulf of Finland or in the woods.

DIRECTORY

EMERGENCY SERVICES

Fire *(pozhar)*
[01.

Police *(militsiya)*
[02.

Ambulance *(skoraya pomoshch)*
[03.

MEDICAL SERVICES

American Medical Center
Serpukhovskaya ul 10. **Map** 6 E5.
[326 1730. ○ 24 hours.

Clinic Complex
Ao Poliklinicheskiy kompleks
Moskovskiy pr 22. **Map** 6 D5.
[316 6272. ○ 24 hours.

Dental Palace
Millionnaya ul 10. **Map** 2 E5.
[314 1459.

Emergency Medical Consulting
Izmailovskiy pr 14, entrance
fr Sovetskiy per.
[112 6510 (24-hour call service).

Trauma Clinic of the Central District
Travmpunkt pripoliklinike n. 35
Malaya Konyushennaya ul 2.
Map 6 E1.
[311 4396. ○ 24 hours.

PHARMACIES

Nevskiy pr 5.
[312 7078.

Nevskiy pr 66.
[315 5881.

Nevskiy pr 83.
[277 6065.

24-Hour Pharmacy
Nevskiy pr 22.
[314 0859.

Banking and Local Currency

S T PETERSBURG IS MOVING into the credit card age and major European debit and credit cards can now be used in hotels and some restaurants and shops. Everywhere else, however, cash is the norm, and roubles are the only legal currency. The city is well provided with exchange points where you can turn your currency (US dollars still being the most popular), travellers' cheques or credit cards into roubles, at varying rates of commission. Since bank rates are so good, money should never be changed on the streets. What appear to be higher offers from individuals will lead to visitors being cheated.

CHANGING MONEY

R OUBLES CANNOT be obtained outside Russia, but there are numerous exchange offices throughout St Petersburg, including at the airport. Some offices open 24 hours a day. A passport has to be shown when changing money. Any visible defect on foreign bank notes, especially vertical tears or ink or water stains, makes them invalid in Russia and they will be refused at the exchange. Make sure that all notes brought into Russia are in good condition, and that any US dollars were issued after 1990.

On completion of an exchange transaction, a receipt slip is issued. Keep these slips safe as they will need to be attached to the customs declaration form filled in on arrival in Russia (*see p202*), and returned to customs on departure.

CURRENCY EXCHANGE
ОБМЕН ВАЛЮТЫ
Принимаем старые и ветхие купюры $US, DM

Sign for Russian exchange office
(*obmen valyuty*)

BANKS AND EXCHANGE OFFICES

N ONE OF THE foreign banks in Russia offers over-the-counter services and the most reliable Russian banks are **Inkombank** and **Promstroybank**. Exchange offices are plentiful in St Petersburg. They are often branches of banks, offering both cash currency exchange and cash advances on credit or debit cards. Larger branches also cash travellers' cheques. Exchange offices often work long hours: the branches of Inkombank at the Europe and Nevskij Palace hotels are open 24 hours, with short breaks in the small hours. Inkombank and **Most-bank** consistently offer the best exchange rates.

A fast and safe, but expensive, way of transferring cash to Russia is by Western Union, available at Promstroybank, Inkombank, Most-bank and the **American Express** office.

Official currency exchange slip

CREDIT CARDS

I T IS NOW POSSIBLE to obtain cash, both roubles and US dollars, with a credit card through the larger banks and from automatic cash dispensers which are springing up all over town. The local commission is between 2 and 5 per cent, plus whatever the card company

Automatic cash dispenser

DIRECTORY

BANKS

American Express
Grand Hotel Europe,
Ground Floor Concourse,
Mikhaylovskaya ulitsa 1/7.
Map 6 F1. [329 6060.
[] 9am–5pm daily.

Inkombank
Инкомбанк
Grand Hotel Europe,
Ground Floor Concourse,
Mikhaylovskaya ulitsa 1/7.
Map 6 F1. [] 24 hours daily.

Inkombank
Инкомбанк
Nevskij Palace Hotel Concourse,
Nevskiy prospekt 57. **Map** 7 B2.
[] 24 hours daily.

Most-bank
Мост-банк
Nevskiy prospekt 27. **Map** 6 E1.
[] 9:30am–1pm & 2pm–
7:30pm daily.

Promstroybank
Промстройбанк
Mikhaylovskaya ulitsa 4.
Map 6 F1. [] 9:30am–1pm &
3pm–7pm daily (Sun until 6pm).

CASH DISPENSERS

Hotel Astoria
Гостиница Астория
Bolshaya Morskaya ulitsa 39.
Map 6 D2. [] VISA, Eurocard.

Grand Hotel Europe
Гранд Отель Европа
Ground Floor Concourse,
Mikhaylovskaya ulitsa 1/7.
Map 6 F1. [] VISA.

Most-bank
Мост-банк
Nevskiy prospekt 27. **Map** 6 E1.
[] VISA, Eurocard, MasterCard.

charges. The most commonly accepted card is VISA, with MasterCard, Eurocard, Diners Club and American Express much less widely recognized. The cash dispensers at **Most-bank** take MasterCard, VISA and Eurocard. It is best to take out cash in roubles; less commission is charged this way.

Lost or stolen credit cards should be reported immediately to the credit card company back home as no local security service is offered.

TRAVELLERS' CHEQUES

BANKS CHARGE at least 3 per cent to cash travellers' cheques. Only the large banks, such as **Promstroybank**, **Most-bank** and **Inkombank**, offer this service. The cheapest alternative is American Express cheques. The commission on these is only 2 per cent if they are cashed at the **American Express** office. Travellers' cheques can only be used as payment for goods or services in the largest hotels, and are acceptable only in US dollars, Deutschmarks, British pounds and French francs. In all cases dollar cheques are preferred.

LOCAL CURRENCY

THE RUSSIAN currency is the rouble (or ruble), written рубль or abbreviated to p. or руб. The higher denominations of roubles are available in bank notes, which all bear images of Russian cities; the lower denominations in coins. The kopek, of which there are 100 in a rouble, is coin only.

The designs of banknotes have changed several times in the 90s. In 1998 the rouble was revalued owing to its stronger value and lower inflation, and new notes were issued. Values were divided by 1,000 (1,000 roubles became 1 rouble). Visitors exchanging money will be given new notes, but the old ones are valid until 1999 and prices may be shown in both.

Banknotes

New notes come in denominations of 10, 50, 100 and 500 roubles. Pre-1998 notes have the same designs as their new equivalents. Divide the old face value by 1,000 to get their new worth. From 31st December 1998, only major banks will exchange them.

10 roubles

50 roubles

100 roubles

500 roubles

Coins

The revaluation of the Russian rouble in 1998 led to the revival of the long-redundant but much-loved kopek. Traditionally, the rouble had always consisted of 100 kopeks. As well as coins for 1, 2 and 5 roubles, there are now coins for 1, 5, 10 and 50 kopeks. Any coins which were issued before 1997, prior to revaluation, are essentially valueless and you are perfectly within your rights to refuse to accept them.

1 rouble　　**2 roubles**　　**5 roubles**

1 kopek　　**10 kopeks**　　**50 kopeks**

Communications

International telephone sign

Telecommunications is one of the biggest growth areas in northwest Russia. A once-antiquated phone system has rapidly been brought up to date, with satellite and digital lines, and direct dialling worldwide. The same period has seen an explosion of magazines, newspapers and TV channels. Unfortunately, ordinary home phone lines and everyday post are not improving at the same rate, but St Petersburg offers many inexpensive and efficient alternatives.

Reaching The Right Number

- St Petersburg directory enquiries, dial 09.
- There is no international directory enquiries.
- Inter-city call booking, dial 07.
- International call booking, dial 315 0012.
- To phone the **UK**, dial 8 (tone) 1044 followed by the number, omitting first 0 from area code.
- To phone **Canada** or the **US**, dial 8 (tone) 101 followed by the number.
- To phone the **Irish Republic**, dial 8 (tone) 10353 followed by the number.
- To phone **Australia**, dial 8 (tone) 1061 followed by the number.
- To phone **New Zealand**, dial 8 (tone) 1064 followed by the number.
- To phone **South Africa**, dial 8 (tone) 1027 followed by the number.

Telephone Services

Blue BCL satellite call boxes are installed at the airport, business centres, hotel foyers and some restaurants. They operate on credit cards and BCL phonecards widely available.

The local system, Petersburg Telephone Network (PTS or, in italic Cyrillics, *"cnm"*) is, however, perfectly adequate and much cheaper. PTS phone boxes are green and located on the streets and in some metro stations. The **Central Telegraph Office** also has dozens of international and local PTS phones. Calls abroad can be made directly from a card-operated PTS phone. PTS phonecards come in units and are available from kiosks and post offices. International calls require at least 100 units. Inter-city and international calls are cheaper between 10pm and 8am and at weekends.

Non-card PTS phones can only be used for local calls. These operate on metro tokens, which can be bought in metro stations *(see p215)*. All call boxes, both PTS and BCL, display instructions in English. Local calls made from private phones are free of charge.

BCL satellite phone

Using a PTS Card-Operated Phone

2 Wait until the display tells you to insert your card.

3 Insert your card in the slot, where it should remain for the duration of the call.

4 When your card has been cleared, dial the number. PTS phones require you to press the star button when there is an answer.

1 When using a PTS card phone, begin by lifting the handset.

5 When you have finished your call, hang up, and only remove your card when instructed to by the display.

A PTS phonecard

Using a PTS Token Phone
Lift the handset and check that you have a dialling tone before you dial the number. When you are connected, drop the metro token into the slot at the top of the phone box.

Metro token

Post office sign

Postal Services

The state-run, international postal system is generally slow and unreliable, and it is best to avoid it, except when sending postcards. Efficient and cheap services are run by **Westpost** and **Post International** who offer ordinary, express, courier and poste restante services. American Express *(see p206)* also operates a poste restante service for cardmembers. The Europe and Nevskij Palace hotels *(see p173)* run cheap and remarkably quick postal services, taking three days to the UK via Finland, which costs about $2 per letter.

Distinctive pale blue postbox

Ordinary post offices, such as the **Main Post Office** (*see p122*) and those in hotels, sell normal and commemorative Russian stamps, postcards, envelopes and local phonecards. Russian postboxes are marked Почта *(Pochta)* and are most plentiful in the city centre. Tourists should use the small pale blue boxes. The yellow ones are used for special local services only.

Westpost on Nevskiy prospekt

FAX, TELEX, TELEGRAM AND E-MAIL SERVICES

M OST OF THE CITY hotels and the **Main Post Office** offer fax, telex and telegram services. Telegrams in foreign languages can also be sent from the **Central Telegraph Office**. **Post International** offers fax and e-mail services.

COURIER SERVICES

S T PETERSBURG is well supplied with courier services. **DHL**, **Federal Express** and **TNT** take about two days to Europe and three to Australasia and USA. A slower but cheaper service is provided by local companies **Westpost** and **Post International**. Anything other than papers, especially computer discs, must go through customs, which can add an extra day.

TELEVISION AND RADIO

R USSIAN-LANGUAGE television is dominated by imported soap operas, which are dubbed rather than subtitled. Channel 6 shows NBC News in English every morning at 8:30am, while the best news in Russian is on NTV, or on Channel 5 for local news.

Most hotels have satellite television offering Eurosport, CNN, BBC World Service TV, NBC and many other Western programmes. The best English-language radio broadcasts on shortwave are still BBC World Service and Voice of America. A few local radio stations, such as Radio Modern (104 FM) and Radio Maximum (102.8 FM), do English music programmes.

Commemorative Russian stamps

NEWSPAPERS AND MAGAZINES

T HERE ARE THREE English-language newspapers and magazines available in the city, which are distributed free to all hotels, major restaurants and most fast-food chains. *The St Petersburg Times* appears twice weekly with international and sporting news and coverage of local events. The Friday edition provides detailed listings and reviews. The monthly *Pulse* is leisure oriented, and its listings section is worth perusal. *Neva News* runs occasional local history articles which are of interest, and each edition has a useful pull-out map of the city and its major sights.

Foreign papers can be picked up at highly inflated prices from the major hotels.

St Petersburg local newspapers

DIRECTORY

TELEPHONE SERVICES

Central Telegraph Office
Международная телефонная станция
Mezhdunarodnaya telefonnaya stantsiya
Bolshaya Morskaya ulitsa 3–5.
Map 6 D1. **C** 274 9383.
O 9am–9pm daily.

POSTAL SERVICES

Main Post Office
Главпочтамт
Glavpochtamt
Pochtamtskaya ul 9. **Map** 5 C2.
C 312 8302. **O** 8am–8pm
Mon–Sat, 8am–6pm Sun.

Post International
Nevskiy prospekt 20. **Map** 6 E1.
C 219 4472. **FAX** 219 4473.
O 10am–7pm Mon–Fri,
11am–4pm Sat.

Post Office No. 11
Почтовое отделение 11
Pochtovoe otdelenie 11
Nevskiy pr 40–42. **Map** 6 F1.
C 311 1462. **O** 8am–12:30pm
& 1–8pm Mon–Fri, 8am–12:30pm
& 1–5pm Sat.

Westpost
Nevskiy prospekt 86. **Map** 7 B2.
C 275 0784. **FAX** 275 0806.
O 10am–8pm Mon–Fri,
noon–6pm Sat & Sun.

COURIER SERVICES

DHL Express Center
Nevskij Palace Hotel,
Nevskiy prospekt 57. **Map** 7 B2.
C 325 6100. **FAX** 325 6116.
O 9am–6pm Mon–Fri.

DHL Worldwide Express
Izmaylovskiy pr 4. **Map** 5 C5.
C 326 6400. **FAX** 326 6410.
O 9am–7pm Mon–Fri,
10am–4pm Sat.

Federal Express
Ul Mayakovskovo 2. **Map** 7 B2.
C 279 1287. **FAX** 273 2139.
O 9am–6pm Mon–Fri,
9am–2pm Sat.

TNT Express Worldwide
Grand Hotel Europe,
Mikhaylovskaya ul 1/7. **Map** 6 F1.
C 329 6467. **FAX** 118 1904.
O 10am–2pm & 3–7pm Mon–Fri.

GETTING TO ST PETERSBURG

ST PETERSBURG IS SLOWLY regaining its popularity as a tourist destination, after the severe drop in numbers during the early 1990s. Now, as the number of businessmen regularly travelling in and out is also rising, the number of flights and alternative means of transport is on the increase. Flying remains the most popular way of travelling to St Petersburg, both for individuals and groups, with the train from Moscow or Helsinki a close second.

Aeroflot plane landing in St Petersburg

Independent travel in Russia is difficult as well as costly and for this reason it is worth considering a package tour. British companies run a variety of tours with specialist guides, which often incorporate St Petersburg and Moscow. Since overall tourist numbers are still fairly limited, package tours are not among the cheapest. Shopping around can uncover some good deals, particularly on flights with stopovers in Europe or low-season packages.

Stalinist architecture at Pulkovo 2, St Petersburg's international airport

ARRIVING BY AIR

DIRECT FLIGHTS from the UK to St Petersburg run five days a week on British Airways and three days on Aeroflot. There are connecting flights on other airlines every day and these are often much cheaper. **Progressive Tours** and **Scott's Tours** in London are particularly good for budget fares. A plane journey from London takes around three-and-a-half hours, or about six hours with a stopover in a European city.

Direct flights to St Petersburg from Ireland, US, Canada, South Africa and Australasia are either extremely limited or simply do not exist. The usual route from these destinations is to fly via a European city or via Moscow from where you can transfer to another flight or continue by road or rail.

The only direct flight to St Petersburg from Ireland is a weekly Aeroflot service from Shannon on the west coast. From the US, Aeroflot operates a direct flight from New York to St Petersburg three times a week. From Canada and South Africa, direct flights, also on Aeroflot, only go to Moscow. Travelling from Australasia can be fairly complicated. The most usual route is to pick up a European carrier in Singapore, with a stopover in Europe.

On landing, passengers are sometimes required to confirm onward flights. You can do this through the airline you are travelling with or the **Central Air Communication Agency** on Nevskiy prospekt.

ST PETERSBURG AIRPORTS

INTERNATIONAL FLIGHTS arrive at **Pulkovo 2** which, although recently modernized, is still small and relatively primitive. Its separate arrival and departure buildings each have a small duty-free shop. Arrivals also has a foreign exchange office. On arrival, the longest wait is likely to be for baggage, while departures on the weekend can be hectic and it is best to arrive at least 90 minutes before a flight in high season.

Pulkovo 1 is for domestic flights only. The 1970s building is cramped and dark, but foreigners and those using commercial flights to and from Moscow have a separate arrivals and departure lounge. Located on the first floor, this has its own entrance which cannot be reached from inside the main terminal building.

GETTING INTO THE CITY

BOTH AIRPORTS are located 17 km (11 miles) south of the city centre. The major hotels operate cars to pick up individual tourists for a cost of around $45. The service, which can be charged to

Limousine transfer service from the Grand Hotel Europe (see p181)

Ordinary yellow taxi waiting outside the domestic airport, Pulkovo 1

No. 13 bus from Pulkovo 2 to Moskovskaya metro station

Minibus or *marshrutnoye taksi*

the hotel bill, should always be requested when making a hotel booking. The luxury taxis waiting at the airport only tend to undercut hotel cars by about $5 while ordinary yellow cabs, rarely found at the international airport, are a great deal cheaper, charging around $10–15 in roubles. Official yellow cabs are usually plentiful at the domestic airport.

Anyone on a more limited budget, and who has already changed money at the airport, can take the No. 13 bus (from Pulkovo 2) and No. 39 (from Pulkovo 1) to Moskovskaya

metro station. Minibuses, known as *marshrutnoye taksi* or route taxi, travel the same route and charge a minimally higher fare *(see p219)*.

TRAVELLING BY TRAIN

RAIL IS a relatively cheap way to travel from Finland, Moscow and within Russia in general, although European student discount passes provide little or no reduction in fares.

Ten trains a day run in each direction between Moscow and **Moscow Station** and two between Helsinki and **Finland Station** *(see p126)*. For those with time and some sense of adventure, it is possible to

Ticket office or *kassa* at Central Train Ticket Office

Exterior of Finland Station, the point of arrival for daily trains from Helsinki in Finland

travel by train between London and St Petersburg via Central Europe (Warsaw, Prague, Berlin). It takes about three days and is generally more costly than flying. The trains are comfortable and usually run on time, but carriages can be overcrowded and thefts are common. Transit visas may also be necessary for countries such as Ukraine. The simplest and most reliable route is via Belarus (Belorussia) which accepts a Russian visa for transit passengers. (All visitors to Russia need a visa and obtaining one can be a complicated procedure. For information on visa acquisition see page 202.)

Trains travelling from Eastern Europe arrive and depart from **Vitebsk** or **Warsaw Station**. Tickets for train journeys from St Petersburg should be bought from the upstairs booking hall at the **Central Train Ticket Office**.

Taxis from stations can be overpriced, but all train stations have efficient transport connections.

TRAVELLING BETWEEN MOSCOW AND ST PETERSBURG

Many visitors fly in to Moscow and out of St Petersburg, or vice versa. The most popular form of transport between the two cities is the train, of which there are ten a day. Daytime trains take about ten hours, while faster night-time trains take eight and a half hours. Prices vary according to the class of the train – the Red Arrow being most expensive – and the choice of seat. All trains have a choice of *SV* (two-person compartment), *coupé* (four-person), *platzkarte* (open seating), or *sidyashchyy* (open seating). All except *sidyashchyy* are sleepers.

St Petersburg – Moscow sign in train carriage

For daytime travelling *sidyashchyy* is more comfortable and cheaper than *platzkarte*. One-way prices range from the equivalent in roubles of around $80 for *SV* to $12 for *sidyashchyy*. Prices do not include bed linen, for which there is an additional charge when you purchase your ticket. On cheaper trains, the *provodnik*, or carriage attendant, will issue and charge for bed linen. Food may be available but it is best to travel with your own supplies.

Regular commercial flights connecting the two cities take about 50 minutes. These are run by Aeroflot and independent companies such as Pulkovo and Transaero. A one-way foreigner ticket costs $180 in roubles on Pulkovo Airlines, and an economy return around $240. Tickets are sold at the airport, or at the **Central Air Communication Agency**. Travelling by boat to and from Moscow is also possible *(see p212)*.

SV compartment on the luxurious Red Arrow train from Moscow

One of Finnord's coaches

Travelling by Coach

COMFORTABLE coaches run to and from Helsinki in Finland, offering a cheaper alternative to the train. **Finnord** runs one daytime coach and one overnight in each direction; the journey takes around seven hours. Coach companies do not always use the city's inconvenient coach stations but will drop off instead at various locations in St Petersburg. Finnord's final stop is at their office on Italyanskaya ulitsa. Advance booking is advised with this company as many Russians take advantage of these coaches to go shopping in Lappeenranta, just over the border, or in Helsinki itself.

Travelling by Boat

A RRIVING by boat can be one of the most exciting and novel ways to approach St Petersburg. However, ferries and cruises operate irregularly and it is best to check with a travel agent for details.

Ferries from Scandinavia usually dock at the **Maritime Passenger Terminal**, on the west side of Vasilevskiy Island. Trolleybus No. 10 and bus No. 7 run from here to the centre or, heading in the other direction, to Primorskaya metro station.

In summer, river cruises between Moscow and St Petersburg are run along the Volga and across Lake Ladoga. The trips, lasting about two weeks, take in many sights en route, making this a very pleasurable way to see more of Russia. The cruises are bookable

in the UK through **Noble Caledonia** or **Voyages Jules Verne**. The ships dock at St Petersburg's **River Terminal**, ten minutes' walk from Proletarskaya metro station. Cruise companies run buses to and from the city centre.

Luxury cruise ships from London and elsewhere arrive at the city's cargo port, 5 km (3 miles) southwest of the centre. Access to the port is restricted, so the ships have their own coaches to carry tourists into town and back.

Ferry moored at Maritime Passenger Terminal on western edge of Vasilevskiy Island

---

DIRECTORY

Tour Companies in Britain

Progressive Tours
12 Porchester Place,
London W2 2BS.
☎ 0171 262 1676.
FAX 0171 724 6941.

Scott's Tours
141 Whitfield Street,
London W1P 5RY.
☎ 0171 383 5353.
FAX 0171 383 3709.

Voyages Jules Verne
21 Dorset Square,
London NW1 6QG.
☎ 0171 616 1000.
FAX 0171 723 8629.

Noble Caledonia
11 Charles Street,
London W1X 8LE.
☎ 0171 409 0376.
FAX 0171 409 0834.

Airport Information

Pulkovo 1
Пулково 1
☎ 104 3822.

Pulkovo 2
Пулково 2
☎ 104 3444.

Airline Offices

Austrian Airlines
Nevskiy pr 57. **Map** 7 B2.
☎ 325 3260.
☎ 104 3443 (Pulkovo 2).

British Airways
Malaya konyushennaya
ulitsa 1/3. **Map** 6 E1.
☎ 325 2565.
☎ 104 3749 (Pulkovo 2).

Central Air Communication Agency
Nevskiy pr 7/9. **Map** 6 D1.
☎ 315 0072 (inter).
☎ 311 8093 (dom & CIS).

Finnair
Malaya Morskaya ulitsa 19.
Map 6 D1.
☎ 315 9736.
☎ 104 3739 (Pulkovo 2).

KLM
Zagorodnyy prospekt 5.
Map 7 A3.
☎ 325 8989.

Lufthansa
☎ 314 4979.

☎ 104 3432 (Pulkovo 2).

Malev Hungarian Airlines
☎ 315 5455.
☎ 104 3435 (Pulkovo 2).

SAS
☎ 325 3255.
☎ 104 3443 (Pulkovo 2).

Transaero
Liteynyy pr 48. **Map** 7 A1.
☎ 279 6463/1974.

Trains

All Train Enquiries
☎ 168 0111.

Central Train Ticket Office
Центральные железно
Tsentralniye zhelezno
Nab kanala Griboedova 24
(upstairs for foreigners).
Map 6 E2. ☎ 162 3344.

Finland Station
Финляндский вокзал
Finlyandskiy vokzal
Pl Lenina 6. **Map** 3 B3.

Moscow Station
Московский вокзал
Moskovskiy vokzal
Pl Vosstaniya. **Map** 7 C2.

Vitebsk Station
Витебский вокзал
Vitebskiy vokzal
Zagorodnyy prospekt 52.
Map 6 E4.

Warsaw Station
Варшавский вокзал
Varshavskiy vokzal
Nab Obvodnovo
kanala 118.

Coaches

Finnord
Italyanskaya ulitsa 37.
Map 6 F1. ☎ 314 8951.

Boats

Maritime Passenger Terminal
Морской пассажирский вокзал
Morskoy passazhirskiy vokzal
Pl Morskoy Slavy.
☎ 355 1310.

River Terminal
Речной вокзал
Rechnoy vokzal
Prospekt Obukhovskoy
Oborony 195.
☎ 262 0239/8994.

GETTING AROUND ST PETERSBURG

ALTHOUGH PUBLIC transport in the city is abundant, efficient and very cheap, the most enjoyable way to get around and fully appreciate St Petersburg is on foot. A glance at a map reveals that some attempt was made to bestow the city with a rational, organized layout, which makes it considerably easier to negotiate. When exhaustion sets in, however, a boat cruise along the waterways can be a wonderful way to become acquainted with the city.

Sign indicating pedestrian crossing

Nevskiy prospekt is where many of the city's transport routes and main roads meet. Metro lines, tram, bus and trolleybus routes radiate out from here, criss-crossing the city with a network of rail tracks and overhead wires. It is possible to travel without too much difficulty to almost anywhere in town from this main avenue.

Driving is not recommended due to the combination of poor road conditions, aggressive Russian driving and over-efficient traffic police.

WALKING

IN SOME AREAS, particularly around Palace Embankment, sights are situated so close together that using public transport from place to place is pointless. A few of the more scattered sights are at some distance (20 mins on foot) from the nearest transport and walking the last stretch is often the most practical option. Apart from the ease, getting around on foot can be a most rewarding way to explore the city, allowing you to soak up the atmosphere and appreciate the fascinating architectural and sculptural detail on many of St Petersburg's buildings.

As soon as the sun appears, in winter as well as in summer, people of all ages emerge onto the streets and into the

Street sign for Nevskiy prospekt

parks. Locals are very fond of walking, whether it be promenading up and down Nevskiy prospekt, or ambling around the Neva at 2am during the White Nights *(see p51)*. The Summer Gardens *(see p95)* and Mikhaylovskiy Gardens have long been popular with Petersburgers. For longer walks mixed with some architectural interest, two good areas to try are Kamenniy and Yelagin islands *(see pp136–7)*, with their official residences and *dachas*, many dating from the early years of the 20th century.

For a romantic stroll around the city away from the traffic, walk along the Moyka or Griboedov canals *(see pp134–5)*. To the south of Nevskiy prospekt, majestic buildings gradually give way to smaller, 19th-century residential blocks, complete with rows of trees by the waterside and leafy squares and courtyards.

Drivers have little respect for pedestrians and traffic is the main hindrance to walking. Cars drive on the right-hand side, so look left first when crossing the road. If there is an underpass, use it and, if not, look for a light-controlled crossing with red and green figures indicating pedestrian right of way. Crossings without lights are marked by a blue sign showing a pedestrian, but

Mikhaylovskiy Gardens, behind the Russian Museum *(see pp104–107)*

Street signs indicating street directions and major shops

these are simply recommended crossing sites and drivers are not obliged to stop. Be warned that if you are caught crossing a road where there are no marked crossings, you are liable to be fined by a traffic policeman *(see p205)*.

There are few bicycles on the roads, but cyclists tend to ignore traffic lights and signs of all descriptions, causing an additional hazard for the unwary pedestrian.

On the main city streets, sponsored dark blue nameplates give the street names in both Russian and English. Elsewhere, black-on-white street names are in Russian (ie Cyrillic) only. Many maps, like the free pull-out in *Neva News (see p209)*, give the main street names in Cyrillic and in transliteration. If you get lost, a dual-language map can be helpful when asking Russian passers-by for assistance.

Sign showing a pedestrian underpass

Excellent walking tours in English, both general and on specialized topics, can be booked through **Ost-West Kontaktservice** *(see p200)*.

Travelling by Metro

Blue neon metro sign

Since overland transport is the most efficient means of getting around the city centre, the metro is used mainly to get to and from the outskirts of the city. As a tourist attraction, however, the metro's stunning stations, intended by Stalin to be "palaces for the people", should be high on your itinerary.

The metro is extremely safe and runs a full service until after midnight. Travelling in the late evening will avoid most of the two million people estimated to use the metro each day. The main setback is that signs are only in Cyrillic but, with just four lines, negotiating the network is still fairly straightforward.

Steep escalators to platforms

is no rush hour as such but the metro tends to be full at most times of day which makes it very safe. Platforms are not staffed, but there is an attendant in a booth at the bottom of each escalator who can call for assistance.

Because of the many waterways in the city, stations are buried deep underground and long escalators lead down to the platforms. Stand on the right, leaving the left side free for those walking.

New stations are still being added, the latest ones being Krestovskiy Ostrov and Staraya Derevnya on the yellow line. Structural problems on the red line have resulted in its closure between Lesnaya and Ploshchad Muzhestva. A courtesy bus service runs between these stations.

Exterior of Ploshchad Vosstaniya metro station

The metro now has 58 stations, ranging in style and ambience from the dim lighting and memorial atmosphere of Ploshchad Muzhestva (Courage Square, 1975) near Piskarovskoe Memorial Cemetery *(see p126)*, to the 1980s vulgarity of Udelnaya and the crisp, clean coldness of Sadovaya (1992).

THE METRO AS A TOURIST ATTRACTION

The soviet union's best architects were employed to design St Petersburg's metro stations. Thousands of tonnes of marble, granite and limestone were used to face the walls, and sculptures, mosaics and chandeliers were commissioned from leading artists. The first line opened in 1955, its eight stations connecting ploshchad Vosstaniya with the new Stalinist blocks of flats in the southwest and the city's largest factory, the Kirov Factory. This line is one of the most fascinating, being the supreme embodiment of Stalinist style and ideals. The station at Kirovskiy Zavod is a fine example, a vast basilica, a temple to the factory workers. The line's crowning glory has to be Avtovo, incorporating a wealth of style and detail, even down to the moulded glass columns.

THE NETWORK

The metro is vital for getting to and from the further afield hotels and the airport. The four lines run from the outskirts through the centre, where they intersect at one of six main stations. Trains run every few minutes during the day and every five minutes late at night and, although doors into stations close at midnight, the last trains leave the centre ten minutes after this. There

Directional sign listing all stops on this line in Cyrillic

Mosaics and unusual glass columns at richly decorated Avtovo metro station

Interchange sign listing all stations on the other line

FINDING YOUR WAY

Before setting foot in St Petersburg's metro, ensure you have a network map with the Cyrillic and transliterated names to hand. All signs inside the metro are in Cyrillic only and wall maps have become rare in station ticket halls and on the trains. Inside a station, the name is only written on the far wall of the platform which means that, if the train is in the station, or if you are on the train itself, it is not possible to see the sign.

**Metro platform sign showing
stations and interchanges**

Busy stations in the city centre
have a central concourse with
safety doors between this and
the trains. When the train
stops, these doors open, and
only then do the train doors
open. At these stations, a map
of the line you are on is to be
found on the concourse. Other
stations have platforms and the
map of the line is on the wall
on the far side of the tracks.

Before the train doors close,
the driver will announce,
*"Ostorozhno. Dveri zakryva-
yutsya"* (Be careful. The doors
are closing). As the train
approaches a stop, he will
say the name of the station
and mention if you need to
change here for another line,
followed by the name of the
next station. It is always best
to keep count of the stops,
in case you do not catch
the announcements.

To change to another line,
follow the interchange signs
for переход (*perekhod* –
crossing). The exception is at
Tekhnologicheskiy Institut,
where the two southbound
lines are on parallel platforms,
as are the two northbound
lines: thus to continue
in the same direction
on another line you
simply cross the
central concourse.

Exits are marked
выход (*vykhod*). Some
stations, such as of the
Moskovskaya (for the
airport) and Gostinyy Dvor,
have two or more exits,
sometimes at a distance from
each other at ground level.

TICKETS AND
TRAVEL CARDS

THE MOST COMMON means of
paying for the metro is the
token *(zheton)*, purchasable
only from metro stations, but
also usable on public phones
(see p208). Magnetic cards,
valid for ten trips, are also
available. When travelling on
the red line, due to the line

ST PETERSBURG'S METRO

KEY

– – Line closed

Пр Просвещения / Pr Prosveshcheniya	Девяткино / Devyatkino
Озерки / Ozerki	Гражданский пр / Grazhdanskiy Pr
Старая деревня / Staraya derevnya	Удельная / Udelnaya	Академическая / Akademicheskaya
Крестовский остров / Krestovskiy ostrov	Пионерская / Pionerskaya	Политехническая / Politekhnicheskaya
Чкаловская / Chkalovskaya	Черная речка / Chernaya Rechka	Пл Мужества / Pl Muzhestva
Приморская / Primorskaya	Петроградская / Petrogradskaya	Лесная / Lesnaya
Спортивная / Sportivnaya		
Василеостровская / Vasileostrovskaya	Горковская / Gorkovskaya	Выборгская / Vyborgskaya
Гостиный двор / Gostinyy Dvor		Пл Ленина / Pl Lenina
	Пл Восстания / Pl Vosstaniya	Чернышевская / Chernyshevskaya
Невский пр / Nevskiy Pr		Маяковская / Mayakovskaya
Сенная пл / Sennaya Pl	Садовая / Sadovaya	Владимирская / Vladimirskaya
Пушкинская / Pushkinskaya		Достоевская / Dostoevskaya
Технологический инст / Tekhnologicheskiy Inst	Технологический инст / Tekhnologicheskiy Inst	Лиговский пр / Ligovskiy Pr
	Пл Александра Невского / Pl Aleksandra Nevskovo	
Балтийская / Baltiyskaya	Фрунзенская / Frunzenskaya	
Нарвская / Narvskaya	Моск ворота / Mosk vorota	Елизаровская / Elizarovskaya	Пл Александра Невского / Pl Aleksandra Nevskovo
Кировский завод / Kirovskiy Zavod	Электросила / Elektrosila	Ломоносовская / Lomonosovskaya	Новочеркасская / Novocherkasskaya
Автово / Avtovo	Парк Победы / Park Pobedy	Пролетарская / Proletarskaya	Ладожская / Ladozhskaya
Ленинский пр / Leninskiy Pr	Московская / Moskovskaya	Обухово / Obukhovo	Пр болшевиков / Pr Bolshevikov
Пр Ветеранов / Pr Veteranov	Звездная / Zvezdnaya	Рыбацкое / Rybatskoe	Ул Дыбенко / Ul Dybenko
	Купчино / Kupchino		

Metro token

closure between Les-
naya and Ploshchad
Muzhestva, you will
have to take the
courtesy bus part of
the way so, for con-
venience, purchase a
single-journey magnetic
transit *(tranzitnyy)*
card. This ticket can be reused
when returning to the metro
to continue your journey.

Machines are installed at
the top of the escalators; the
larger ones are clearly marked
for the use of magnetic cards
only, while the others are for
tokens. Cards must be inserted
with the magnetic strip facing
up. If you try to go through a
machine without paying, an
automatic barrier closes in
front of you. At the far right an
attendant checks passes and
allows you to put your token
in a machine which does not

have automatic barriers. Those
with magnetic cards cannot
pass through this machine.

Monthly magnetic passes
for the metro or for all forms
of public transport are valid for
an infinite number of journeys
during a calendar month. They
can only be purchased at the
beginning of the month (or
on the 16th for half-monthly
passes). There are no ticket
checks once you are past the
barriers inside the station.

**Monthly travel cards, valid on all
forms of city transport**

Travelling by Tram, Bus and Trolleybus

Tram-stop sign, seen hanging over the rails

OVERGROUND TRANSPORT is crowded during the day, particularly at rush hour, but it is still the best way to make short trips around the city or simply to sightsee. In the centre of town, an array of tramline tracks and overhead tram and trolleybus cables crisscross many roads. Each form of transport has its advantages and disadvantages. Trolleybuses are frequent and conveniently routed but overcrowded; trams run on a less main-line route across town and are less busy but noisy; buses are usually sporadic. The newer outlying areas, however, are often accessible only by bus. On all forms of public transport you are unlikely to get a seat during the day; more frequent and comfortable, but more expensive, are the commercial bus and minibus routes.

People getting on a tram

TRAMS

TRAMS OFFER a marvellous way to see St Petersburg and discover some of the less well-known areas. Trams are less crowded than trolleybuses, so there is more chance of finding a seat. Tram stops are marked by red and white signs suspended on wires above the tram rails. Separate islands for people to embark are found only on wide roads outside the centre; elsewhere passengers wait on the pavement. When the tram doors open, the oncoming traffic is obliged to wait and let passengers cross to and from the pavement. In practice, there is always one car which cannot wait, so take care before stepping out.

At various crossroads along the route, the driver may need to change points on the rails. He will open his door or the front passenger door to do this. Do not attempt to board or exit a tram when it has stopped for this purpose.

Tram at a stop in front of the Mariinskiy Theatre

GENERAL INFORMATION

TRAMS, BUSES and trolleybuses start at around 5:30am, and a little later along the middle of the routes. The services operate with rather arbitrary frequency during the day and very infrequently after 11pm, grinding more or less to a halt around midnight. Only a few of the city bus routes display timetables. Each form of overground transport has its own separate stops, and distances between them can be great.

Queueing is not standard practice, so be prepared for an unruly rush to get on first. Trams, buses and trolleybuses can be boarded at the front, middle or back. The front eight seats are reserved for the disabled, the elderly and people with children, all of whom have precedence getting on and off at the front. On board, a conductor collects the fares.

As a stop approaches, people near an exit may be asked *Vy vykhodite?* ("are you getting out?"), which really means "could you move aside?". At busy times, head for the exit well before your stop, or prepare to do some pushing.

Good for sightseeing is the No. 10 trolleybus, which runs from ploshchad Aleksandra Nevskovo through the centre and across Vasilevskiy Island (*see pp56–63*) to Primorskaya metro station. Other scenic routes are the No. 12 tram from the Field of Mars (*see p94*) to the east of the city, the No. 22 bus from the Smolnyy Institute (*see p128*) via St Isaac's Square (*see p79*) and the Mariinskiy Theatre (*see p119*) towards the Stalinist architecture in the southwest, and the No. 46 bus from the Field of Mars up Kamennoostrovskiy prospekt (*see p70*) and onto Kamenniy Island (*see pp136–7*).

Sign for a bus stop, showing name of stop and bus numbers

BUSES AND MINIBUSES

BUSES OPERATE mostly on the outskirts of the city. All services run about every 20 minutes, sometimes less often. Bus stops in the city centre are marked by white signs with a red letter "A" for *avtobus*, placed by the side of the road or attached to building walls. These are slowly replacing the old-style yellow signs.

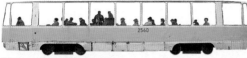

Side view of a single section tram

City trolleybus on Nevskiy prospekt

A commercial bus on Vasilevskiy Island

Many routes are now dupli-
cated by commercial buses or
minibuses, marked with a "T"
before the route number or
with an "Э" for express. Fares
on these buses are two to three
times those on non-commercial
equivalents, and are paid to
the driver when getting on or
off – just follow what other
passengers do. These buses
can be hailed or requested to
stop anywhere along the route.

TROLLEYBUSES

TROLLEYBUSES ARE the most
frequent form of transport
along the city's main artery,
Nevskiy prospekt. They offer
convenient routes and stops
around the city but are nearly
always overcrowded. Ticket
inspectors are most often on
patrol on trolleybuses.

Trolleybus stops are marked
by small blue and white signs
suspended from wires, indicating the trolleybus numbers.
On main roads, stops are also
marked by other signs on
building walls.
These show what
seems to be a flat-
topped blue "M",
but is in fact an
italic "T" for *trolley-
bus*, placed on a
white background.
    The power rods
on the roofs of the
trolleybuses are known famil-
iarly as "horns" *(roga)* or "little
whiskers" *(usiki)*. Occasionally
these become detached from
the overhead cables and the
trolleybus lurches to a halt. It
is the driver's responsibility to
reattach them, causing a slight
but generally negligible delay.

**Trolleybus-stop sign on
building wall**

TICKETS AND TRAVEL CARDS

A FLAT FARE is payable on all
forms of transport, what-
ever the length of the journey.
Tickets are purchased from the
conductor (who wears a red
armband saying "Кондуктор"
but is not in uniform) or, on
commercial transport, from
the driver. The ticket must be
bought before the next stop
after you got on, and large
items of baggage must be paid
for separately. Fines for non-
payment can be imposed on
the spot by plain-clothes inspectors. If you are accused of
evasion, check that the inspect-
or has an identity document.
Fines are payable in roubles
only, and should not come to
more than a few dollars' worth.
    The cheapest way to travel
in St Petersburg, if you are
staying a few weeks or more,
is to buy a monthly or half-
monthly card for all forms of
transport, including the metro
(see pp214–15). The magnetic
monthly card, or
yedinyy bilet, is
valid from the first
to the last day of
a calendar month
and cannot be
bought any time
in between. Half-
monthly *yedinyy
bilety* run from the
16th to the end of the month
(they are not available for the
first half of the month). Separate monthly cards are also
sold for each form of transport.
Travel cards are valid for trips
to Tsarskoe Selo and Pavlovsk,
but not Peterhof, Gatchina or
Oranienbaum *(see pp220–21)*.

Waiting at a trolleybus stop on Nevskiy prospekt, near ploshchad Vosstaniya

Canal and River Cruises

Sign for water taxi

ST PETERSBURG'S NUMEROUS natural waterways were adapted and added to, to make it resemble Peter the Great's beloved Amsterdam *(see pp20–21)*. Indeed, it would be true to say the city vies with Amsterdam for the title "Venice of the North".

A wide selection of cruises, for small and large groups, in open and closed boats, depart from bridges along Nevskiy prospekt. They offer marvellous opportunities to see more of the city, especially for those unable to walk long distances. Forming part of any cruise are the broad Fontanka river with its Neo-Classical palaces, the leafy Moyka river with its ironwork bridges, and the Griboedov canal which twists and turns its way through southwest St Petersburg. Bring a bottle of champagne, a picnic and a warm jumper and just relax.

Canal cruise on the Moyka

GENERAL INFORMATION

THE WEATHER plays a vital role in determining the exact time of year canal cruises start and finish. Most boats operate daily from mid-May to late September. Their routes also vary because regular construction work, reinforcing the granite embankments, sometimes prevents movement along small parts of the canals.

The Gulf of Finland is tidal and this affects the Neva and inland waterways. Stong winds can cause the water level to rise significantly and all boat trips may then be cancelled.

GUIDED CANAL TRIPS

LARGE, COVERED cruise boats depart every 30 minutes, between 11:30am and 8pm, from the Anichkov Bridge on Nevskiy prospekt *(see p49)*.

Tickets for the next available boat should be purchased from the kiosk on the embankment, although, if the queues are long, tickets may be sold in advance for later cruises on the same day. The trip lasts 70 minutes and takes in the Moyka, Griboedov and Fontanka. Weather permitting, the boats usually go out onto the Neva, from where there are superb views of the whole city.

Foreigners pay around $5 in roubles for these trips, slightly more than the Russians. The guided tour is in Russian only. Large groups are advised to book in advance, through the kiosk or by phone, especially during school holidays. Boat trips providing guided tours in English can be booked through any of the major hotels.

During hot weather, it can get very stuffy and confined inside the boats. The visibility through the scratched perspex windows can also be less than perfect at times. If you wish to stand outside to see more, there is a platform at the back of the boat for which there may be an extra charge. Take your own soft drinks and sandwiches, as these are rarely available on board these cruises.

Cruise boat on the Neva with the Hermitage and Palace Embankment in the background

Ticket kiosk for canal trip, Anichkov Bridge

DIRECTORY

City Excursion Bureau of St Petersburg
Angliyskaya nab 56. **Map** 5 B1.
📞 311 2445.

Nord-Soyuz
Bol Posadskaya ul 9A. **Map** 2 E2.
📞 238 8261.

Luxury Catered Cruises
📞 232 7605.

Taxi Reservations
📞 312 0022.

NEVA CRUISES

A VARIETY OF BOATS cruise up and down the Neva between the Gulf of Finland and the River Station *(Rechnoy vokzal)* to the southeast. The trips, operating hourly between 10am and 10pm, last an hour. Foreigners pay more than the locals, but the tickets are not expensive and can be bought on the landing stage or on the boat. The boats leave from the landing stage opposite the Bronze Horseman on Decembrists' Square, and from the one near the main entrance of the Hermitage *(see p75)*.

These boat trips are a pleasant way of passing the time rather than a serious sightseeing opportunity. Food and drink are usually served and, in the evenings, alcohol is available on some of the boats.

Luxury catered cruises for up to ten people can be booked in advance for trips along the Neva. These cost about $50 per hour, with an extra $15 or more per person for catering.

Water taxis moored on Griboedov canal near Kazanskiy most by Nevskiy prospekt

WATER TAXIS

WATER TAXIS are similar to private motorboats, carrying anything from 4 to 20 people. During White Nights, boats run late into the night.

For a small boat, wait at the landing stage on the north side of Politseyskiy most where Nevskiy prospekt *(see pp46–9)* crosses the Moyka, or alongside the Gostinyy Dvor metro station on the Griboedov canal close to Kazanskiy most. Larger boats may need to be negotiated at least a couple of hours in advance to ensure their availability.

Prices are negotiable, but generally range from about $30 to $50 an hour, depending on the size of the boat and the route you decide to follow. One hour takes you along the inland waterways, but an extra half hour includes the Neva, crossing over to go round the Peter and Paul Fortress *(see pp66–7)* and giving a good view of all the

Water taxis on the Moyka by Politseyskiy most

waterfronts. Most drivers can at least point out major sights in English, others can give you a basic guided tour. If you ask in advance, it may be possible to find an English-speaking guide. Boats can be booked in advance on payment of a small deposit, but are generally plentiful and are best picked up spontaneously.

Since the boats are open and it can be cold on the waterways, particularly at night, warm clothing is necessary, even during the summer months. There is usually at least one blanket on board for anyone who is unequipped. Pilots allow you to do more or less as you like on board the boat as long as it is safe, and tend to be undisturbed by the noise of popping champagne corks or other sounds of merrymaking.

Taxis

ST PETERSBURG'S official yellow taxis are gradually being superseded by unmetered private cabs. Most locals, however, use the cheaper alternative of catching a *chastnik*, effectively hitching a ride in any passing vehicle.

St Petersburg's bright yellow taxi

OFFICIAL TAXIS

THE CITY'S DISTINCTIVE yellow official taxi fleet has in recent years faced tough competition from expensive private taxi firms which run imported modern cars. The private taxis, which usually charge a flat fare agreed in advance, tend to monopolize certain areas near many major hotels, restaurants, bars and the airport. In order to save money, try hailing a yellow cab a short distance away from such places.

Whatever type of taxi you choose to take, always name your destination before getting in. Taxis are not obliged to take you, and they may well refuse, or simply drive away if they do not wish to go in the same direction as you. Taxi fares are relatively cheap. Newer yellow cabs are fitted with modern meters, which indicate the sum to be paid, but meters in the older taxis are unreliable or simply switched off. For this reason it is wise to agree on a price before starting out on the journey to avoid unnecessary confusion. If you feel you have been over-charged however, it is worth disputing the matter.

In some areas, official taxis are not readily available, and you must either book one by phone or hope for a *chastnik*.

CHASTNIKI

FOR MANY YEARS Russians have been used to flagging down private drivers, who are easier to locate and often cheaper to use than official taxis. A 1997 local ruling seeks to ban *chastniki*, or make them purchase a taxi licence. Unless this takes serious effect, and Russians are notorious for ignoring such rulings, you may find that an ordinary car stops when you stick out your hand to hail a taxi. Do not get into any car with more than the driver already in it. Neither private cars or taxis are particularly recommended if travelling alone at night.

As with ordinary taxis, name your destination and, if the driver agrees, settle a price before setting off. Private cars are usually cheaper than taxis and the drivers are also more likely to help with baggage.

St Petersburgers flagging down a *chastnik*, or private car

Travelling out of St Petersburg

E VERY WEEKEND DURING THE SUMMER, and even in winter, a large proportion of locals leave the city. They head for their *dacha* or for the woods, to gather seasonal fruits and vegetables, go cross-country skiing or visit one of the former imperial summer residences. Buses and suburban trains operate frequently throughout the year and are the usual means of transport to access sites out of town. Peterhof is a unique exception in being accessible by hydrofoil across the Gulf of Finland. Foreigners tend to take coach excursions out of town but, with a bit of planning, travelling independently can be part of the fun.

Passengers boarding suburban train at Vitebsk Station

Interior view of one of St Petersburg's suburban trains

SUBURBAN TRAINS

T HESE ARE THE most conven-ient way to visit most of the outlying sights. Tickets can be bought from the local cash desks *(prigorodnyye kassy)* at each station, where a timetable is displayed. Return tickets are no cheaper than two singles. Note that smoking is prohibited and that, between the hours of 10am and midday, there is often a break in the timetable.

Style-Moderne architecture in Vitebsk station restaurant

GETTING TO TSARSKOE SELO AND PAVLOVSK

T RAINS for Tsarskoe Selo *(see pp150–53)* and Pavlovsk *(see pp156–9)* depart every 20 minutes from **Vitebsk Station**. The line was originally built for the royal family to reach their summer residences and the station is a marvellous example of Style-Moderne architecture. The ticket office is on the right of the main building. All local trains take about 25 minutes, stopping first at Tsarskoe Selo (Detskoe Selo), then Pavlovsk.

At Detskoe Selo station, the 382 and 371 buses go to Tsarskoe Selo, stopping near the palace. At Pavlovsk, the train station is opposite the entrance to the park, through which it is a pleasant half-hour walk to the palace, or catch bus No. 370, 370a, 383 or 383a.

The 370 and 383 buses also run between Pavlovsk palace and Detskoe Selo station. City bus tickets and monthly passes continue to be valid.

The No. 287 bus is a conve-nient way to get to Tsarskoe Selo from ploshchad Pobedy, south of Moskovskaya metro.

GETTING TO PETERHOF AND ORANIENBAUM

T HERE ARE SUBURBAN trains for Peterhof *(see pp146–9)* and Oranienbaum *(see pp144–5)* departing every 20 minutes from **Baltic Station**. The trains that reach Oranienbaum are those destined for Kalishche, or Oranienbaum itself.

For Peterhof, get off the train at Novyy Petergof (40 minutes from town), from where it is ten minutes to the palace on bus No. 351, 352, 354 or 355.

By far the easiest and most pleasant way to get to Peterhof during the summer months is by hydrofoil, which costs about $5 in roubles each way.

Oranienbaum is the first stop after the Gulf of Finland comes into view an hour into the journey. Turn right out of the station and walk about 200 m (650 ft) to the main road. Almost directly opposite is the entrance to the park, and from here it is only a five minute walk to the Great Palace or into the heart of the park.

GETTING TO GATCHINA

T RAINS RUN approximately every half hour from **Baltic Station** to Gatchina *(see p145)* and the journey takes an hour. Opposite Gatchina train station is a short road leading directly to the square in front of the palace. Trains also run from **Warsaw Station**, arriving at a different station in the town, further from the palace.

Alternatively, there is a bus No. 431, which departs from ploshchad Pobedy, south of Moskovskaya metro station. On this particular suburban route, city bus tickets and monthly passes are not valid.

GETTING TO REPINO AND THE GULF OF FINLAND

For Repino *(see p144)* and the Gulf of Finland, trains depart every 20 minutes or so from **Finland Station**. Tickets should be bought at cash desks within the main building. Avoid any train marked Beloostrov or Krugovoy.

At Repino, cross the main road, head down the hill towards the Gulf of Finland and turn left onto the asphalt road until you reach Penaty.

Bus No. 411 also runs to Repino and stops right outside Penaty. The bus leaves from Chernaya Rechka metro.

Coach No. 948 to Novgorod

GETTING TO NOVGOROD

Coach no. 948 leaves for Novgorod *(see pp160–63)* every two hours from **Coach Station 2**. A quicker alternative to the four-hour coach journey is to travel on the weekend by train. The weekend train sets off from **Moscow Station** just before 7am and takes two-and-a-half hours. It returns to St Petersburg around 6pm.

DRIVING IN ST PETERSBURG

Car hire is still not widely available in Russia and, at present, cars and minibuses in St Petersburg can only be hired with company drivers. This can be organized through hotels and firms like **Hertz** who have a pick-up point at the airport.

For the few who do find themselves at the wheel, there are a number of things to bear in mind. An international licence is obligatory, as well as international insurance and documents proving you have the right to be driving the car, eg registration documents or a hire agreement bearing your name, failing that a witnessed power of attorney in Russian from the registered owner. Traffic policemen *(see p205)* have the right to stop you and check your documents. They can also fine you on the spot for minor infringements, such as having a dirty number plate, not having a first-aid kit, or more serious offences such as drink-driving. Drivers are not allowed to drink any alcohol whatsoever. The traffic police are highly active as they regard fining drivers as a means to increasing their income and it is a matter of luck whether or not you are stopped and fined.

Local drivers tend to ignore rules of the road and do more or less as they like, so be on your guard. Drive on the right and make no left turns on any main roads unless a road sign indicates that it is permitted.

In winter conditions, driving requires studded tyres as chains can be damaged on tram lines and vice versa. It is also advisable not to use your handbrake in cold weather as it has a tendency to freeze.

Unleaded petrol is rarely available and you should use nothing lower than grade 98 petrol. There is a charge for parking in most parts of the city centre. The Nevskij Palace and Europe hotels *(see p173)* have 24-hour security parking which is recommended since car theft is a fairly popular business in St Petersburg.

Road sign in Russian indicating driver must stop

THE HYDROFOIL TO PETERHOF

Hydrofoil arriving at the Hermitage landing stage

The most enjoyable and by far the most scenic way to reach the imperial summer palace of Peterhof is the 45-minute trip across the Gulf of Finland by hydrofoil. The service runs from early June until early October and sets off from the second landing stage outside the Hermitage *(see p75)* where a weekly timetable is posted. Generally hydrofoils operate every hour from 9:30am with the last boat returning at 6pm. Buy your return ticket on arrival at Peterhof. A fee is charged to enter the lower park and this ticket is needed to get back into the park to return by hydrofoil.

ST PETERSBURG STREET FINDER

THE KEY MAP below shows the areas of St Petersburg covered by the *Street Finder*. The map references given throughout the guide for sights, restaurants, hotels, shops or entertainment venues refer to the maps in this section. All the major sights have been clearly marked so they are easy to locate. The key below shows other features marked on the

Pausing on the steps of Kazan Cathedral

maps, such as post offices, metro stations, ferry stops and churches. The *Street Finder* index lists street names in transliteration, followed by Cyrillics (on the maps, Cyrillics are only given for major roads). This guide uses the now reinstated old Russian street names, rather than the Soviet versions *(see p201)*. Places of interest are listed by their English name.

```
0 kilometre    1
0 mile         1
```

KEY TO STREET FINDER

▨ Major sight	⛴ River boat pier	⊠ Post office
▨ Place of interest	🚖 Taxi rank	═ Railway line
▨ Other building	✚ Hospital	⇢ One-way street
🚆 Train station	🏛 Police station	«45 House number (main street)
Ⓜ Metro station	✛ Orthodox church	
🚋 Tram stop	✝ Church	**SCALE OF MAP PAGES**
🚎 Trolleybus terminus	✡ Synagogue	
🚌 Bus terminus	☪ Mosque	0 metres 300
		0 yards 300

Street Finder Index

ABBREVIATIONS & USEFUL WORDS

ul	ulitsa	street
pl	ploshchad	square
pr	prospekt	avenue
per	pereulok	lane
	most	bridge
	sad	garden
	shosse	road

General Index

Acknowledgments

DORLING KINDERSLEY would like to thank the following people whose contributions and assistance have made the preparation of this book possible.

MAIN CONTRIBUTORS
CHRISTOPHER RICE holds a PhD in Russian history from the University of Birmingham. He and his wife Melanie, also a writer, first visited Russia in 1978 and have been returning regularly ever since. Together they have written numerous travel guides to the city, and to a variety of other destinations, including Prague, Berlin and Istanbul, as well as the *Eyewitness Travel Guide to Moscow.*

CATHERINE PHILLIPS is an art historian who arrived in Russia in 1985 and has lived there ever since, moving to St Petersburg in 1989. She covered major events for British and American TV and radio during the early years of *perestroika* and authored and contributed to some of the first guides to the new Russia. Today she concentrates on translating and editing scholarly texts and writing for works of reference.

ADDITIONAL CONTRIBUTOR
ROSE BARING began to study Russian at the age of 12. She has an MA in Modern History and divided her time between London, Moscow and St Petersburg for much of the early 1990s. She has written guides to St Petersburg, Moscow and other destinations, including the *Eyewitness Travel Guide to Istanbul.*

SPECIAL ASSISTANCE
DORLING KINDERSLEY would like to thank Ian Wizniewski (food and drink consultant), Valera Katsuba (photo permissions), Marina Maydanyuk (researcher), Oleksiy Nesnov (language consultant), Victoria Rachevskaya (language consultant), Yuliya Motovilova of the St Petersburg Tourist Company and the staff of Peter TiPS, and Sylvain Borsi at Nikita's restaurant, London, for preparing the food for *What to Eat in St Peterburg.*

PROOFREADER
Stewart J Wild.

INDEXER
Hilary Bird.

DESIGN AND EDITORIAL ASSISTANCE
Liz Atherton, Laurence Broers, Dawn Davies-Cook, Claire Folkard, Freddy Hamilton, Paul Hines, Leanne Hogbin, Adam Moore, Fiona Morgan, Jane Oliver, Marianne Petrou, Luke Rozkowski, Alison Stace, Ingrid Vienings, Veronica Wood.

ADDITIONAL ILLUSTRATIONS
Claire Littlejohn, John Woodcock.

ADDITIONAL PHOTOGRAPHY
Victoria Buyvid, Andy Crawford, Erich Crichton, Neil Fletcher, Steve Gorton, Paul Miller, Ian O'Leary, Clive Streeter.

PHOTOGRAPHY PERMISSIONS
THE PUBLISHER would like to thank all those who gave permission to photograph at their establishments, including museums, palaces, cathedrals, churches, restaurants, hotels, shops and other sights, too numerous to thank individually.

PICTURE CREDITS
t = top; tl = top left; tlc = top left centre; tc = top centre; trc = top right centre; tr = top right; cla = centre left above; ca = centre above; cra = centre right above; cl = centre left; c = centre; cr = centre right; clb = centre right below; cb = centre below; crb = centre right below; bl = bottom left; b = bottom; bc = bottom centre; bcl = bottom centre left; br = bottom right; d = detail.

The publisher would like to thank the following individuals, companies and picture libraries for their kind permission to reproduce their photographs:

AISA, Barcelona: 18t, 44t, 55 (insert), 106tr; AKG, London: 16, 17t, 20bl/cl, 20–21c, 25tl, 26cl, 27c, 28br, Erich Lessing 28bl, 29c, 37b, 42cl/bl/br, 43br; ANCIENT ART & ARCHITECTURE COLLECTION: 45cr; APA: Jim Holmes 93tl; AXIOM: Jim Holmes 151b.

VALENTIN BARANOVSKY: 84bl, 85tl, 193t; IAN BAVINGTON-JONES: 130t; YURI BELINSKY: 31t; BRIDGEMAN ART LIBRARY, London/New York: 151c; Forbes Magazine Collection 28–9c; State Hermitage, St Petersburg 21cb, 24–5c, 25cl, 86t/b, 87t/b, 88b, 89tr/b, 90t/b, 91t/c, *La Danse,* Henri Matisse (1910) @ Succession Henri Matisse/DACS 1998 87c; Private Collection *20th Century Propaganda Poster 1920,* D Moor @ DACS 1998 29tr; State Russian Museum, St Petersburg *The Cyclist,* Natalya Goncharova (1913) @ ADAGP, Paris and DACS, London 1998 40b; Tretyakov Gallery, Moscow 19t, *The Circus,* Marc Chagall, 1919 @ ADAGP, Paris and DACS, London 1998 45tl.

CAMERA PRESS: Roxana Artacho 85bl; DEMETRIO CARRASCO: 2–3, 6b, 15b, 36t, 53bl, 76ca, 80bl, 93cr/br, 102–103; CENTRAL STATE ARCHIVE OF PHOTOGRAPHS AND FILM DOCUMENTS, ST PETERSBURG: 42t, 72c, 110c, 118bl; JEAN-LOUP CHARMET: 23t; CHRISTIE'S IMAGES: 82b; CORBIS: Dean Conger 52tr; E. O Hoppe/Bettmann 118cr; Bob Krist 193b; Library of Congress 28tl; Michael Nicholson 150t; Gianni Dagli Orti 8–9, 119bl; Steve Raymer 31crb, 118br; State Hermitage, St Petersburg 24bl; State Russian Museum 25bl.

E T ARCHIVE: Bibliotheque Nationale, Paris 17cl; Hermitage, St Petersburg 88t, 89tl; MARY EVANS PICTURE LIBRARY: 9 (insert), 19b, 21br, 22c, 23c, 24cl/br, 25br, 26t, 29br, 62b, 139 (insert), 159bl, 199 (insert).

GIRAUDON: State Russian Museum 43cr, 105cr; Tretyakov Gallery, Moscow 163cr. ROBERT HARDING PICTURE LIBRARY: 84br;

MICHAEL HOLFORD: 18c, 19c, 21bl; HULTON GETTY: 43tr, 118cl, 121c, 178tr;

INTERIOR ARCHIVE: Fritz von der Schulenburg 159c.

KATZ PICTURES: 165 (insert); KEA PUBLISHING SERVICES: Francesco Venturi 92 (all three); DAVID KING COLLECTION: 29tl, 30t, 45b, 69b, 129c.

PAUL MILLER: 51cr.

NOVOSTI (London): 20br, 21tl, 26b, 27t, 30cl, 31c, 43tl, 50c, 51b, 78b, 163t/l.

ORONOZ, Madrid: 22t, 43bl.

PICTOR INTERNATIONAL: 81t; PLODIMEX AUSSENHANDELS GMBH, Hamburg: 178cr/bl.

NATASHA RAZINA: 150b, 151t; REX FEATURES: V. Sichov/SIPA Press 30cr; ELLEN ROONEY: 53t, 79t, 83b, 138–9.

GREGOR M SCHMID: 50br; SCIENCE PHOTO LIBRARY: CNES, 1989 Distribution Spot Image 11cr; STATE RUSSIAN MUSEUM: 7cr; *Blue Crest,* Wassily Kandinsky (1917) @ ADAGP, Paris and DACS, London 1998 39br; 93tr, 104cl /bl/br, 105tl/br, 106tl/b, 107 (all 3), 110b.

TRAVEL LIBRARY: Stuart Black 85br.

VISUAL ARTS LIBRARY: 44b; State Hermitage, St Petersburg *L'Homme aux bras croisés,* Pablo Picasso (1905) @ Succession Picasso/DACS 1998 91b; 123c.

Jacket: all special photography except GREGOR M SCHMID: front cover centre.

Phrase Book

IN THIS GUIDE THE RUSSIAN LANGUAGE has been transliterated into Roman script following a consistent system used by the US Board on Geographic Names. All street and place names, and the names of most people, are transliterated according to this system. For some names, where a well-known English form exists, this has been used – hence, Leo (not Lev) Tolstoy.

In particular, the names of Russian rulers, such as Peter the Great, are given in their anglicized forms. Throughout the book, transliterated names can be taken as an accurate guide to pronunciation. The Phrase Book also gives a phonetic guide to the pronunciation of words and phrases used in everyday situations, such as when eating out or shopping.

GUIDELINES FOR PRONUNCIATION

The Cyrillic alphabet has 33 letters, of which only five (a, к, м, о, т) correspond exactly to their counterparts in English. Russian has two pronunciations (hard and soft) of each of its vowels, and several consonants without an equivalent.

The right-hand column of the alphabet, below, demonstrates how Cyrillic letters are pronounced by comparing them to sounds in English words. However, some letters vary in how they are pronounced according to their position in a word. Important exceptions are also noted below.

On the following pages, the English is given in the left-hand column, with the Russian and its transliteration in the middle column. The right-hand column provides a literal system of pronunciation and indicates the stressed syllable in bold. The exception is in the *Menu Decoder* section, where the Russian is given in the left-hand column and the English translation in the right-hand column, for ease of use. Because of the existence of genders in Russian, in a few cases both masculine and feminine forms of a phrase are given.

THE CYRILLIC ALPHABET

А а	a	**a**limony
Б б	b	**b**ed
В в	v	**v**et
Г г	g	**g**et (see note 1)
Д д	d	**d**ebt
Е е	e	**ye**t (see note 2)
Ё ё	e	**yo**nder
Ж ж	zh	lei**s**ure (but a little harder)
З з	z	**z**ither
И и	i	s**ee**
Й й	y	bo**y** (see note 3)
К к	k	**k**ing
Л л	l	**l**oot
М м	m	**m**atch
Н н	n	**n**ever
О о	o	r**o**b (see note 4)
П п	p	**p**ea
Р р	r	**r**at (rolling, as in Italian)
С с	s	**s**top
Т т	t	**t**offee
У у	u	b**oo**t
Ф ф	f	**f**ellow
Х х	kh	**kh** (like loch)
Ц ц	ts	le**ts**
Ч ч	ch	**ch**air
Ш ш	sh	**sh**ove
Щ щ	shch	fre**sh sh**eet (as above but with a slight roll)
ъ		hard sign (no sound, but see note 5)
Ы ы	y	l**i**d
ь		soft sign (no sound, but see note 5)
Э э	e	**e**gg
Ю ю	yu	**you**th
Я я	ya	**ya**k

Notes

1) Г   Pronounced as *v* in endings -oro and -ero.
2) Е   Always pronounced *ye* at the beginning of a word, but in the middle of a word sometimes less distinctly (more like *e*).
3) Й   This letter has no distinct sound of its own. It usually lengthens the preceeding vowel.
4) О   When not stressed it is pronounced like *a* in a**c**ross.
5) ъ, ь The hard sign (ъ) is rare and indicates a very brief pause before the next letter. The soft sign (ь, marked in the pronunciation guide as ') softens the preceeding consonant and adds a slight *y* sound: for instance, *n'* would sound like *ny* in 'ca**ny**on'.

IN AN EMERGENCY

Help!	Помогите! *Pomogite!*	pama**gee**t-ye!
Stop!	Стоп! *Stop!*	stop!
Leave me alone!	Оставьте меня в покое! *Ostavte menya v pokoe!*	as**ta**vt'-ye mye**nya** v pa**ko**ye!
Call a doctor!	Позовите врача! *Pozovite vracha!*	paza**vee**t-ye vra**cha**!
Call an ambulance!	Вызовите скорую помощь! *Vyzovite skoruyu pomoshch!*	**vee**za**vee**t-ye **sko**ru-yu **po**mash'!
Fire!	Пожар! *Pozhar!*	pa**zhar**!
Call the fire brigade!	Вызовите пожарных! *Vyzovite pozharnykh!*	**vee**za**vee**t-ye pa**zhar**nikh!
Police!	Милиция! *Militsiya!*	mee**lee**tsee-ya!
Where is the nearest...	Где ближайший... *Gde blizhayshiy...*	gdye blee**zhay**shee-y...
...telephone?	...телефон? *...telefon?*	...tye-lye**fon**?
...hospital?	...больница? *...bolnitsa?*	...bal'**neet**sa?
...police station?	...отделение милиции? *...otdelenie militsii?*	...atdye**lye**nye mee**lee**tsee-ee?

COMMUNICATION ESSENTIALS

Yes	Да *Da*	da
No	Нет *Net*	nyet
Please	Пожалуйста *Pozhaluysta*	pa**zhal**sta
Thank you	Спасибо *Spasibo*	spa**see**ba
You are welcome	Пожалуйста *Pozhaluysta*	pa**zhal**sta
Excuse me	Извините *Izvinite*	eezvee**neet**-ye
Hello	Здравствуйте *Zdravstvuyte*	zdra**stvooy**t-ye
Goodbye	До свидания *Do svidaniya*	da svee**dan**ya
Good morning	Доброе утро *Dobroe utro*	**do**bra-ye **oo**tra
Good afternoon/day	Добрый день *Dobryy den*	**do**bree dyen'
Good evening	Добрый вечер *Dobryy vecher*	**do**bree **vye**chyer
Good night	Спокойной ночи *Spokoynoy nochi*	spa**koy**nay **no**chee
Morning	утро *utro*	**oo**tra
Afternoon	день *den*	dyen'
Evening	вечер *vecher*	**vye**chyer
Yesterday	вчера *vchera*	fchye**ra**
Today	сегодня *sevodnya*	sye**vo**dnya
Tomorrow	завтра *zavtra*	**za**ftra
Here	здесь *zdes*	zdyes'

There	там	tam
	tam	
What?	Что?	shto?
	Chto?	
Where?	Где?	gdye?
	Gde?	
Why?	Почему?	pachyemoo?
	Pochemu?	
When?	Когда?	kagda?
	Kogda?	
Now	сейчас	seychas
	seychas	
Later	позже	pozhe
	pozzhe	
Can I...?	можно?	mozhna...?
	mozhno?	
It is possible/allowed	можно	mozhna
	mozhno	
It is not possible/allowed	нельзя	nyelzya
	nelzya	

USEFUL PHRASES

How are you?	Как дела?	kak dyela?
	Kak dela?	
Very well, thank you	Хорошо, спасибо	kharasho, spaseeba
	Khorosho, spasibo	
Pleased to meet you	Очень приятно	ochen' pree-yatna
	Ochen priyatno	
How do I get to...?	Как добраться до...?	kak dabrat'sya da...?
	Kak dobratsya do...?	
Would you tell me when we get to...?	Скажите, пожалуйста, когда мы приедем в...?	skazheet-ye, pazhalsta, kagda mi pree-yedyem v...?
	Skazhite, pozhaluysta, kogda my priedem v...?	
Is it very far?	Это далеко?	eta dalyeko?
	Eto daleko?	
Do you speak English?	Вы говорите по-английски?	vi gavareet-ye po-angleeskee?
	Vy govorite po-angliyski?	
I don't understand	Я не понимаю	ya nye paneema-yoo
	Ya ne ponimayu	
Could you speak more slowly?	Говорите медленнее	gavareet-ye myedlyenye-ye
	Govorite medlennee	
Could you say it again please?	Повторите, пожалуйста	paftareet-ye, pazhalsta
	Povtorite, pozhaluysta	
I am lost	Я заблудился (заблудилась)	ya zabloodeelsya (zabloodeelas')
	Ya zabludilsya (zabludilas)	
How do you say... in Russian?	Как по-русски...?	kak pa-rooskee...?
	Kak po-russki...?	

USEFUL WORDS

big	большой	bal'shoy
	bolshoy	
small	маленький	malyen'kee
	malenkiy	
hot (water, food)	горячий	garyachee
	goryachiy	
hot (weather)	жарко	zharka
	zharko	
cold	холодный	khalodnee
	kholodnyy	
good	хорошо	kharasho
	khorosho	
bad	плохо	plokha
	plokho	
okay/fine	нормально	narmal'na
	normalno	
near	близко	bleezka
	blizko	
far	далеко	dalyeko
	daleko	
up	наверху	navyerkhoo
	naverkhu	

down	внизу	fneezoo
	vnizu	
early	рано	rana
	rano	
late	поздно	pozdna
	pozdno	
vacant (unoccupied)	свободно	svabodna
	svobodno	
free (no charge)	бесплатно	byesplatna
	besplatno	
cashier/ticket office	касса	kasa
	kassa	
avenue	проспект	praspyekt
	prospekt	
bridge	мост	most
	most	
embankment	набережная	nabyeryezhnaya
	naberezhnaya	
highway/motorway	шоссе	shasse
	shosse	
lane/passage	переулок	pyeryeoolak
	pereulok	
square	площадь	ploshat'
	ploshchad	
street	улица	ooleetsa
	ulitsa	
flat/apartment	квартира	kvarteera
	kvartira	
floor	этаж	etash
	etazh	
house/block	дом	dom
	dom	
entrance	вход	fkhot
	vkhod	
exit	выход	vikhot
	vykhod	
river	река	ryeka
	reka	
summer country house	дача	dacha
	dacha	
swimming pool	бассейн	basyeyn
	basseyn	
town	город	gorat
	gorod	
toilet	туалет	tooalyet
	tualet	

MAKING A TELEPHONE CALL

Can I call abroad from here?	Можно отсюда позвонить за границу?	mozhna atsyooda pazvaneet' za graneetsoo?
	Mozhno otsyuda pozvonit za granitsu?	
I would like to speak to...	Позовите, пожалуйста...	pazaveet-ye, pazhalsta...
	Pozovite, pozhaluysta	
Could you leave him/her a message?	Вы можете передать ему/ей?	vi mozhet-ye pyeryedat' yemoo/yay?
	Vy mozhete peredat emu/ey?	
My number is...	Мой номер...	moy nomyer...
	Moy nomer...	
I'll ring back later	Я позвоню позже	ya pazvanyoo pozhe
	Ya pozvonyu pozzhe	

SIGHTSEEING

castle	замок	zamak
	zamok	
cathedral	собор	sabor
	sobor	
church	церковь	tserkaf'
	tserkov	
circus	цирк	tseerk
	tsirk	
closed for cleaning "cleaning day"	санитарный день	saneetarnee dyen'
	sanitarnyy den	
undergoing restoration	ремонт	remont
	remont	
exhibition	выставка	vistafka
	vystavka	
fortress	крепость	kryepost'
	krepost	
gallery	галерея	galeryeya
	galereya	

garden	сад	sad
	sad	
island	остров	**o**straf
	ostrov	
kremlin/fortified stronghold	кремль	kryeml'
	kreml	
library	библиотека	beeblee-at**ye**ka
	biblioteka	
monument	памятник	p**a**myatneek
	pamyatnik	
mosque	мечеть	myech**ye**t'
	mechet	
museum	музей	mooz**ye**y
	muzey	
palace	дворец	dvar**ye**ts
	dvorets	
park	парк	park
	park	
parliament	дума	d**oo**ma
	duma	
synagogue	синагога	seenag**o**ga
	sinagoga	
tourist information	пункт информации для туристов	poonkt eenfarm**a**tsee-ee dlya toor**ee**staf
	punkt informatsii dlya turistov	
zoo	зоопарк	zap**a**rk
	zoopark	

SHOPPING

open	открыто	atkr**i**ta
	otkryto	
closed	закрыто	zakr**i**ta
	zakryto	
How much does this cost?	Сколько это стоит?	sk**o**l'ka **e**ta st**o**eet?
	Skolko eto stoit?	
I would like to buy.....	Я хотел (хотела) бы купить...	ya khat**ye**l (khat**ye**la) bi koop**ee**t'...
	Ya khotel (khotela) by kupit...	
Do you have.....?	У вас есть...?	oo vas yest'...?
	U vas yest...?	
Do you take credit cards?	Кредитные карточки вы принимаете?	kryed**ee**tnye kart**a**chkee vy preeneem**a**yetye?
	Kreditnye kartochki vy prinimaete?	
What time do you open/close?	Во сколько вы открываетесь/ закрываетесь?	Va sk**o**l'ka vy atkriv**a**yetyes'/ zakriv**a**yetyes?
	Vo skolko vy otkryvaetes/ zakryvaetes?	
This one	этот	**e**tat
	etot	
expensive	дорого	d**o**raga
	dorogo	
cheap	дёшево	dyosh**ye**va
	deshevo	
size	размер	razm**ye**r
	razmer	
white	белый	b**ye**lee
	belyy	
black	чёрный	ch**yo**rnee
	chernyy	
red	красный	kr**a**snee
	krasnyy	
yellow	жёлтый	zh**o**ltee
	zheltyy	
green	зелёный	zyel**yo**nee
	zelenyy	
dark blue	синий	s**ee**nee
	siniy	
light blue	голубой	gal**oo**b**oy**
	goluboy	
brown	коричневый	kar**ee**chnyevee
	korichnevyy	

TYPES OF SHOP

bakery	булочная	b**oo**lachna-ya
	bulochnaya	
bookshop	книжный магазин	kn**ee**zhnee magaz**ee**n
	knizhnyy magazin	
butcher	мясной магазин	myasn**oy** magaz**ee**n
	myasnoy magazin	

camera shop	фото-товары	foto-tav**a**ri
	foto-tovary	
chemist	аптека	apt**ye**ka
	apteka	
delicatessen	гастроном	gastran**o**m
	gastronom	
department store	универмаг	ooneevyerm**a**g
	univermag	
florist	цветы	tsvyet**i**
	tsvety	
grocer	бакалея	bakal**ye**-ya
	bakaleya	
hairdresser	парикмахерская	pareekm**a**khyerskaya
	parikmakherskaya	
market	рынок	r**i**nak
	rynok	
newspaper stand	газетный киоск	gaz**ye**tnee kee-**o**sk
	gazetniy kiosk	
post office	почта	p**o**chta
	pochta	
record shop	грампластинки	gramplast**ee**nkee
	gramplastinki	
shoe shop	обувь	**o**boof'
	obuv	
travel agent	бюро путешествий	by**oo**r**o** pootyesh**e**stvee
	byuro puteshestviy	
bank	банк	bank
	bank	

STAYING IN A HOTEL

Do you have a vacant room?	У вас есть свободный номер?	oo vas yest' svab**o**dnee n**o**myer?
	U vas yest svobodnyy nomer?	
double room with double bed	номер с двуспальной кроватью	n**o**myer s dvoosp**a**l'noy krav**a**t'-yoo
	nomer s dvuspalnoy krovatyu	
twin room	двухместный номер	dvookhm**ye**stnee n**o**myer
	dvukhmestnyy nomer	
single room	одноместный номер	adnam**ye**stnee n**o**myer
	odnomestnyy nomer	
bath	ванная	v**a**na-ya
	vannaya	
shower	душ	doosh
	dush	
porter	носильщик	nas**ee**l'sheek
	nosilshchik	
key	ключ	kly**oo**ch
	klyuch	

EATING OUT

A table for two, please	Стол на двоих, пожалуйста	stol na dva-**ee**kh, pazh**a**lsta
	Stol na dvoikh, pazhalsta	
I would like to book a table	Я хочу заказать стол	ya khach**oo** zakaz**a**t' stol
	Ya khochu zakazat stol	
The bill, please	Счёт, пожалуйста	shyot, pazh**a**lsta
	Schet, pozhaluysta	
I am a vegetarian	Я вегетерианец (вегетерианка)	ya vyegyetaree**a**nyets (vyegyetaree**a**nka)
	Ya vegeterianets (vegeterianka)	
breakfast	завтрак	z**a**ftrak
	zavtrak	
lunch	обед	ab**ye**t
	obed	
dinner	ужин	**oo**zheen
	uzhin	
waiter!	официант!	afeetsee-**a**nt!
	ofitsiant!	
waitress!	официантка!	afeetsee-**a**ntka!
	ofitsiantka!	
dish of the day	фирменное блюдо	f**ee**rmenoye bly**oo**da
	firmennoe blyudo	
appetizers/starters	закуски	zak**oo**skee
	zakuski	

main course	второе блюдо *vtoroe blyudo*	ftaroye blyooda
meat and poultry dishes	мясные блюда *myasnye blyuda*	myasniye blyooda
fish and seafood dishes	рыбные блюда *rybnye blyuda*	ribniye blyooda
vegetable dishes	овощные блюда *ovoshchnye blyuda*	avashshniye blyooda
dessert	десерт *desert*	dyesyert
drinks	напитки *napitki*	napeetkee
vegetables	овощи *ovoshchi*	ovashshee
bread	хлеб *khleb*	khlyeb
wine list	карта вин *karta vin*	karta veen
rare (steak)	недожаренный *nedozharennyy*	nyedazharenee
well done (steak)	прожаренный *prozharennyy*	prozharenee
glass	стакан *stakan*	stakan
bottle	бутылка *butylka*	bootilka
knife	нож *nozh*	nosh
fork	вилка *vilka*	veelka
spoon	ложка *lozhka*	loshka
plate	тарелка *tarelka*	taryelka
napkin	салфетка *salfetka*	salfyetka
salt	соль *sol*	sol'
pepper	перец *perets*	pyeryets
butter/oil	масло *maslo*	masla
sugar	сахар *sakhar*	sakhar

MENU DECODER

абрикос *abrikos*	abreekos	apricot
апельсин *apelsin*	apyel'seen	orange
апельсиновый сок *apelsinovyy sok*	apyel'seenavee sok	orange juice
арбуз *arbuz*	arbooz	water melon
белое вино *beloe vino*	byelaye veeno	white wine
бифштекс *bifshteks*	beefshtyeks	steak
блины *bliny*	bleeni	pancakes
борщ *borshch*	borshsh	borsch (beetroot soup)
варенье *varene*	varyen'ye	Russian syrup-jam
варёный *varenyy*	varyonee	boiled
ветчина *vetchina*	vyetcheena	ham
вода *voda*	vada	water
говядина *govyadina*	gavyadeena	beef
грибы *griby*	greebi	mushrooms
груша *grusha*	groosha	pear
гусь *gus*	goos	goose
джем *dzhem*	dzhem	jam
жареный *zharenyy*	zharyenee	roasted/grilled/fried
икра *ikra*	eekra	black caviar
икра красная/кета *ikra krasnaya/keta*	eekra krasna-ya/kyeta	red caviar

капуста *kapusta*	kapoosta	cabbage
картофель *kartofel*	kartofyel'	potato
квас *kvas*	kvas	kvas (sweet, mildly alcoholic drink)
клубника *klubnika*	kloobneeka	strawberries
колбаса *kolbasa*	kalbasa	salami sausage
кофе *kofe*	kofye	coffee
красное вино *krasnoe vino*	krasnoye veeno	red wine
креветки *krevetki*	kryevyetkee	prawns
курица *kuritsa*	kooreetsa	chicken
лук *luk*	look	onion
малина *malina*	maleena	raspberries
минеральная вода *mineralnaya voda*	mineral'naya vada	mineral water
мороженое *morozhenoe*	marozhena-ye	ice-cream
мясо *myaso*	myasa	meat
огурец *ogurets*	agooryets	cucumber
осетрина *osetrina*	asyetreena	sturgeon
пельмени *pelmeni*	pyel'myenee	meat or fish dumplings
персик *persik*	pyerseek	peach
печенье *pechene*	pyechyen'ye	biscuit
печёнка *pechenka*	pyechyonka	liver
печёный *pechenyy*	pyechyonee	baked
пиво *pivo*	peeva	beer
пирог *pirog*	peerok	pie
пирожки *pirozhki*	peerashkee	small parcels with savoury fillings
помидор *pomidor*	pameedor	tomato
продукты моря *produkty morya*	pradookti marya	seafood
рыба *ryba*	riba	fish
салат *salat*	salat	salad
свинина *svinina*	sveeneena	pork
сельдь *seld*	sye'ld'	herring
сосиски *sosiski*	saseeskee	sausages
сыр *syr*	sir	cheese
сырой *syroy*	siroy	raw
утка *utka*	ootka	duck
фасоль *fasol*	fasol'	beans
форель *forel*	faryel'	trout
чай *chay*	chai	tea
чеснок *chesnok*	chyesnok	garlic
шашлык *shashlyk*	shashlik	kebab
яйцо *yaytso*	yaytso	egg
слива *sliva*	sleeva	plum
фрукты *frukty*	frookti	fruit
яблоко *yabloko*	yablaka	apple

TRANSPORT

north	север *sever*	**sy**ever
south	юг *yug*	yook
east	восток *vostok*	vast**ok**
west	запад *zapad*	za**pat**
airport	аэропорт *aeroport*	aera**port**
aeroplane	самолёт *samolet*	samal**yot**
traffic police	ГАИ *GAI*	Ga-**ee**
bus	автобус *avtobus*	aft**oboos**
bus station	автобусная станция *avtobusnaya stantsiya*	aft**oboosna-ya** stant**see-ya**
bus stop	остановка автобуса *ostanovka avtobusa*	astan**ofka** aft**oboosa**
car	машина *mashina*	mash**eena**
flight	рейс *reys*	ryeys
metro (station)	(станция) метро *(stantsiya) metro*	(stant**see-ya**) myet**ro**
no entry	нет входа *net vkhoda*	nyet fkh**oda**
no exit	нет выхода *net vykhoda*	nyet v**ikhada**
parking	автостоянка *avtostoyanka*	aftosto**yanka**
petrol	бензин *benzin*	byenz**een**
railway	железная дорога *zheleznaya doroga*	zhel**yezna-ya** dar**oga**
railway station	вокзал *vokzal*	vagz**al**
return ticket	обратный билет *obratniy bilet*	ob**ratnee** beel**yet**
seat	место *mesto*	m**yesta**
suburban train	пригородный поезд *prigorodniy poezd*	pree**garadnee** po-**yezd**
straight on	прямо *pryamo*	**pry**ama
taxi	такси *taksi*	tak**see**
ticket	билет *bilet*	beel**yet**
token (for a single metro journey)	жетон *zheton*	zhet**on**
to the left	налево *nalevo*	nal**yeva**
to the right	направо *napravo*	nap**rava**
train	поезд *poezd*	po-**yezd**
tram	трамвай *tramvay*	tramv**ay**
trolleybus	троллейбус *trolleybus*	tral**yeyboos**

NUMBERS

1	один/одна/одно *odin/odna/odno*	a**deen**/ad**na**/ad**no**
2	два/две *dva/dve*	dva/dvye
3	три *tri*	tree
4	четыре *chetyre*	chyet**ir**-ye
5	пять *pyat*	pyat'
6	шесть *shest*	shest'
7	семь *sem*	syem'
8	восемь *vosem*	**vo**syem'
9	девять *devyat*	d**ye**vyat'
10	десять *desyat*	d**ye**syat'

11	одиннадцать *odinnadtsat*	a**dee**natsat'
12	двенадцать *dvenadtsat*	dvyen**atsat'**
13	тринадцать *trinadtsat*	treen**atsat'**
14	четырнадцать *chetyrnadtsat*	chyet**irnatsat'**
15	пятнадцать *pyatnadtsat*	pyatn**atsat'**
16	шестнадцать *shestnadtsat*	shestn**atsat'**
17	семнадцать *semnadtsat*	syemn**atsat'**
18	восемнадцать *vosemnadtsat*	vasyemn**atsat'**
19	девятнадцать *devyatnadtsat*	dyevyatn**atsat'**
20	двадцать *dvadtsat*	dv**atsat'**
21	двадцать один *dvadtsat odin*	dv**atsat'** a**deen**
22	двадцать два *dvadtsat dva*	dv**atsat'** dva
23	двадцать три *dvadtsat tri*	dv**atsat'** tree
24	двадцать четыре *dvadtsat chetyre*	dv**atsat'** chyet**ir**-ye
25	двадцать пять *dvadtsat pyat*	dv**atsat'** pyat'
30	тридцать *tridtsat*	tr**eetsat'**
40	сорок *sorok*	s**orak**
50	пятьдесят *pyatdesyat*	pyad**yesyat'**
60	шестьдесят *shestdesyat*	shes'd**yesyat**
70	семьдесят *semdesyat*	s**yem'dyesyat**
80	восемьдесят *vosemdesyat*	v**osyem'dyesyat**
90	девяносто *devyanosto*	dyevyan**osta**
100	сто *sto*	sto
200	двести *dvesti*	dv**yestee**
300	триста *trista*	treest**a**
400	четыреста *chetyresta*	chyet**iryesta**
500	пятьсот *pyatsot*	pyat'**sot**
1,000	тысяча *tysyacha*	t**isyacha**
2,000	две тысяч *dve tysyach*	dvye t**isyach**
5,000	пять тысяч *pyat tysyach*	pyat' t**isyach**
1,000,000	миллион *million*	meelee-**on**

TIME, DAYS AND DATES

one minute	одна минута *odna minuta*	ad**na** meen**oota**
one hour	час *chas*	chas
half an hour	полчаса *polchasa*	polchas**a**
day	день *den*	dyen'
week	неделя *nedelya*	nyed**yel**-ya
Monday	понедельник *ponedelnik*	panyed**yel'**neek
Tuesday	вторник *vtornik*	ft**orneek**
Wednesday	среда *sreda*	sryed**a**
Thursday	четверг *chetverg*	chyetv**yerk**
Friday	пятница *pyatnitsa*	**pya**tneetsa
Saturday	суббота *subbota*	soob**ota**
Sunday	воскресенье *voskresene*	vaskryes**yen'**ye